Social Security and Private Pensions

Social Security and Private Pensions

Providing for Retirement in the Twenty-first Century

Edited by
Susan M. Wachter

Lexington Books
D.C. Heath and Company/Lexington, Massachusetts/Toronto

Library of Congress Cataloging-in-Publication Data

Social security and private pensions.

   Papers originally presented at the National Press
Club in Washington, D.C., April 24, 1987 at a conference
sponsored by the Institute for Law and Economics of
the University of Pennsylvania.
   Includes index.
   1.   Old age pensions—United States—Congresses.
   2.   Retirement income—United States—Congresses.
   3.   Social security—United States—Congresses.
   4.   Economics forecasting—United States—Congresses.
   5.   United States—Economic conditions—1981-   —
Congresses.   I.   Wachter, Susan M.   II.   University of
Pennsylvania. Institute for Law and Economics.
HD7105.35.U6S615   1988   331.25'2'0973   87-45220
ISBN 0-669-16195-0 (alk. paper)

Published simultaneously in Canada
Printed in the United States of America
International Standard Book Number: 0-669-16195-0
Library of Congress Catalog Card Number 87-45220

The paper used in this publication meets the minimum requirements of
American National Standard for Information Sciences—Permanence of
Paper for Printed Library Materials, ANSI Z39.48-1984. ∞

88 89 90 91 92 8 7 6 5 4 3 2 1

Contents

Preface and Acknowledgments

The chapters in this book are papers presented at the National Press Club in Washington, D.C., on April 24, 1987, at a conference titled "Social Security and Private Pensions: Providing for Retirement in the Twenty-first Century," sponsored by the Institute for Law and Economics of the University of Pennsylvania. The conference was attended by approximately one hundred invited government, academic, and business leaders. Funding for the conference and this book was provided by a grant from Metropolitan Life Insurance Company.

The conference and this book represent the work of many individuals. We wish to express gratitude to John J. Creedon, President and Chief Executive Officer, and Harry P. Kamen, Senior Vice President and General Counsel, of Metropolitan Life Insurance Company; Robert H. Mundheim, Dean and University Professor of Law and Finance of the University of Pennsylvania Law School; Michael L. Wachter, Professor of Economics, Law, and Management, Director, and Martha Keon and Nancy Zurich, Program Directors, of the Institute for Law and Economics of the University of Pennsylvania. Finally, many thanks are owed to the participants and to those, too many to name, without whose help the conference and the book would not have become realities.

The opinions expressed in this book are those of the respective authors and do not necessarily reflect the views of the Institute for Law and Economics or Metropolitan Life Insurance Company.

Introduction:
Private and Public Provision
of Retirement Insurance

A major public concern is adequacy of income in retirement and old age. This concern has been a rationale for public pension policy including the development and enhancement in past decades of Social Security and Medicare (Old Age, Survivors, Disability and Hospital Insurance, or OASDHI) benefits. Although the importance of these benefits has grown over time, income in old age can be and is derived from a variety of sources besides publicly provided insurance. These include employee pensions, individual retirement accounts (IRAs), other private savings, wages from continued employment, and income-in-kind from owner-occupied housing.

Public policies directly and indirectly affect individual households' financial capacities and incentives to provide for their own old age income security from alternative sources. The distribution, taxability, and eligibility criteria for receipt of OASDHI benefits, as well as tax and regulatory policy affecting private pensions and savings, influence individual decision making.

There are public policy and market failure rationales that justify an optimal partial provision of retirement and old age income through social insurance. These include concerns over income distribution for individuals who are retired and optimal portfolio diversification. The existence of such factors suggests that social insurance be only one component of retirement income. A critical issue is the mix between social and private insurance. To the extent that social insurance has become too large a component of the retirement income portfolio, a shift in mix toward private alternatives is called for.

Although Social Security has achieved recognition as one of the more successful policies coming out of the 1930s, its structure was dictated by the economic environment existing at that time. Most importantly, the pay-as-you-go feature enabled the government to pay benefits to older individuals who had themselves contributed little or nothing to the fund. This aspect of the plan, although desirable in the 1930s, may be the basis for subsequent problems. For example, economic research has found theoretical and empirical evidence of negative impacts on labor supply and savings (for a given retirement age).

Many of the original defects in the plan will bear fruit after the turn of the century as a consequence of the demographic changes related to the retirement of the baby boom cohort, the relatively small size of the baby bust cohort, and health advances that have extended the years of retirement. U.S. Social Security projections indicate that these shifts will combine to increase the ratio of Social Security beneficiaries to workers by 60 percent by 2030. As the baby boom starts to retire in 2020, the ratio of workers to beneficiaries, which is now somewhat more than 3 to 1, will begin to decline and reach somewhat more than 2 to 1. To deal with the projected short- and long-run Social Security funding crises, a bipartisan National Commission on Social Security Reform, chaired by Alan Greenspan, was appointed in December 1981. Many of this commission's recommendations became embodied in the Social Security Amendments of 1983.

This legislation will result in benefit reductions for those who retire at age sixty-five and tax increases in the decades to come. The amendments include a permanent six-month delay in the effective date of cost-of-living adjustments (COLA) from July to January, inclusion of up to half of Social Security benefits in taxable income for federal income tax purposes, and, on the positive side, a change in the $1 for $2 reduction in benefits for earnings, after sixty-five, to $1 for $3, beginning in 2009, along with an extension of coverage. In addition, there will be a phase-in to a higher normal retirement age of sixty-seven rather than sixty-five, beginning in 2003. The early retirement age was left at sixty-two, but there is a phased-in decline in the percentage of full benefits payable at that age from 80 percent to 70 percent. In addition, the increase in benefits for delaying retirement will rise from 3 percent to 8 percent per year, beginning in 2009.

Planned tax increases of combined employer and employee payroll taxes to 16 percent by 2035 are expected to enable the funds to pay the projected benefits despite the demographic shift, based upon intermediate assumptions regarding economic growth and other factors. On these assumptions the tax income will exceed the benefit payment each year through 2020, after which there will be an annual deficit. These projections indicate that the trust funds will increase until they amount to approximately sixty-five months of future benefits, a sum equal to about $1.3 trillion. This accumulation of financial resources will enable the Social Security fund to avoid large negative trust fund balances as the baby boom generation retires. Under pessimistic assumptions the combined payroll tax will more than double.

The 1983 changes to protect the solvency of the Social Security trust fund do not deal with the projected Medicare funding crisis. The Medicare trust fund is projected to run out of money in 1990, with a necessary 32 percent decrease in program outlays or a 48 percent payroll tax increase to maintain solvency over the next twenty-five years. As a consequence of the under-financed status of the Medicare portion of OASDHI, there will be pressure to raise wage taxes beyond already planned increases.

Problems with the OASDHI program are not widely known, yet corrective steps to mitigate their costs must be taken quickly to allow individuals to adjust to any programmatic changes before the baby boom retires. The formulation of the appropriate public policy calls for a reexamination of the fundamental rationales for public and private provision of retirement and old age insurance and the optimal mix of each.

This book analyzes the rationales for an optimal mix of the public and private provision of old age and retirement benefits. Part I includes conceptual chapters that analyze the nature of the market failures which, at least implicitly, may motivate Social Security policy.

The first chapter in this section is by Jerry R. Green and focuses on the role of Social Security in the mitigation of risk due to fluctuations in the rate of population growth. This is the type of risk for which no private insurance is feasible because the contracting parties are, in effect, the current generations and the as yet unborn. Green explains the role for public policy through risk diversification. The larger the future generations are, the higher will be the rate of return to accumulated capital and the lower will be the wage rates of workers. Thus, future generations of retirees and workers face risks that are negatively correlated. This negative correlation creates a prima facie case for mutually advantageous insurance. Green's chapter investigates the feasibility of such an insurance arrangement and offers philosophical and practical guidance in the quantification of the benefits of social insurance.

The second conceptual chapter, by Alan S. Blinder, provides an overview of the economic rationales for having a mandatory public pension program like Social Security. He argues that intellectually coherent motives based on market failure—such as overcoming adverse selection and improving risk diversification—exist, but they might be of dubious practical importance. He maintains that redistributive goals might take us farther in explaining important features of Social Security, including why it is mandatory, and that paternalism must play a big role in rationalizing Social Security. Rational people who fear they lack the self-control to save each year might opt for a compulsory saving program. Social Security also can be viewed as a rational response to the free-rider problem that arises when people know that the taxpayers stand ready to support them in old age if necessary. Intergenerational redistribution goals in particular must be used to explain the pay-as-you-go feature of Social Security.

Part II of the book focuses on the current and future financial status of the elderly. The chapter by Michael D. Hurd attempts to estimate the future consumption and wealth of the elderly. Hurd forecasts the consumption path of a single person based on a utility model that accounts for bequeathable wealth, mortality, a bequest motive in saving, and annuities including Social Security and Medicare/Medicaid. He estimates the parameters of this model based on data from the 1969–1979 Retirement History Surveys. He finds that even at the oldest ages, by the turn of the century couples will be reasonably well off: The fraction in poverty as measured by consumption will be 8 percent; as measured by income, it will be 10 percent. The economic status of widows, however, will be much worse: By the turn of the century, about 40 percent in the oldest cohort are forecast to be in poverty. In general, few of the young elderly will be in poverty, while substantial numbers of the old elderly will.

Andrews and Chollet report on the improved economic status of today's elderly, relative to the preceding generation and to the nonelderly, with fewer elderly living in poverty today than ever before. They do note, however, that today's elderly are still more likely than the nonelderly to be poor or nearly poor. They go on to analyze the retirement income prospects of the baby boom generation. Using the Pension and Retirement Income Simulation Model (PRISM) and based on generally conservative assumptions about real wage and pension coverage growth, they arrive at optimistic projections of retirement income among the baby boom cohort. They project that the average real Social Security income will rise, largely as a result of rising real wage growth and significantly greater rates of labor force participation among women. They expect pension recipiency among baby boom retirees to be much greater than among today's retirees, making pension income an increasingly important source of retirement income, with the five-year vesting rule (enacted in the 1986 Tax Reform Act) an important impetus to higher rates of pension recipiency, particularly among women.

Nonetheless, they project the average rate of preretirement earnings replacement from Social Security and pensions to be lower for the baby boom cohort than for workers retiring today. In part, this lower replacement rate reflects scheduled reductions in Social Security payments; it also reflects Social Security's generally lower wage replacement at higher earnings levels. Their PRISM model also projects that an important source of noncash retirement income will be health insurance benefits continued from an employer plan, although the intensity of employer incentives to modify or terminate retiree health insurance benefits for future retirees might cause the loss of this real income among baby boom retirees, which would certainly reduce their real retirement income and their real wage replacement. Thus, the continued provision of health insurance is an important assumption behind their optimistic conclusions. In general, the findings of Andrews and Chollet support Hurd's projections of a lower poverty rate among baby boom retirees than among workers retiring now, with poverty becoming even more distinctly a problem of single women than it is today.

Part III of the book presents views on alternatives to the current mix of private and public income sources for retirement income. Michael J. Boskin's chapter focuses on the macroeconomic implications of the projected surplus in the Old Age, Survivors and Disability Insurance (OASDI) fund, which will peak at a substantial fraction of the current ratio of the privately held national debt to the gross national product (GNP). He uses a sample forecasting model to project, under alternative assumptions, the effect of the Social Security surplus (and subsequent long-run deficit) on national saving in the United States. He concludes that unless these surpluses are offset by changes in private saving or non–Social Security budget deficits, they will cause large systematic swings in the net national saving rate. In turn, this will have a major impact on the level of domestic investment that can be financed internally and/or the patterns of net foreign investment. Unless spent on the projected Medicare deficit, the surplus OASDI will allow the baby boom cohort to retire without increasing currently projected tax rates.

In the following chapter, Mark V. Pauly examines the role of public and private health insurance for the elderly. The main point of departure is that insurance, public or private, plays a different role in acute illness than in chronic illness. For acute illnesses, Pauly suggests that coverage for the elderly (whether public or private) ought to look like the modern comprehensive policies now being purchased by the nonelderly, with nontrivial deductibles and copayments, upper limits on out-of-pocket expenses, and coverage of all medical care. He argues that proposals to update Medicare by adding catastrophic coverage are fully consistent with this view, but the attempts to limit up-front cost sharing (or even to reduce it) are not. Second, he maintains that tax-financed subsidies to the elderly for health care ought to be better related to the income and wealth of the elderly household. In the case of chronic care insurance, Pauly finds no obvious reason for public subsidy of the well-to-do. Private insurance should provide adequate alternatives. He suggests that the most promising response is the provision of retirement health insurance for chronic care as a fringe benefit earned during the working years. Conversion of existing pensions or life insurance into chronic care benefits as individuals retire, or before chronic illness strikes, might be a way of providing such coverage for today's elderly.

The chapter by Boskin, Kotlikoff, and Shoven presents their Personal Security Accounts (PSAs) proposal to reform Social Security. PSAs are structured (1) to provide, on a progressive basis, PSA credits in exchange for Social Security taxes; (2) to share credits equally between spouses; (3) to spend (in an accounting sense) each spouse's PSA credits on up to four indexed and guaranteed insurance policies—an old age annuity, spousal survivor insurance, child survivor insurance, and disability insurance—with Social Security determining the mix of credits spent on each policy based on the composition of the household; (4) to use actuarial formulas to determine the amount of insurance purchased with each spouse's PSA credits; (5) to adjust annually the discount rate used in the actuarial formulas in accord with long-term Social Security financial projections; and (6) to provide annual PSA reports detailing Social Security taxes paid, PSA credits received, and PSA insurance benefits purchased. They posit that PSAs are superior to the current Social Security system for a number of reasons, including a greater equity of full earnings sharing between spouses and reduced work disincentives of Social Security taxation, by clarifying what one gets back at the margin for one's tax contributions.

The final chapter by Lawrence H. Thompson focuses on how changes in the public/private mix of retirement incomes might affect the future cost of the retirement income system and what some consequences might be for the structure of both public and private programs. Thompson notes that the current debate assumes that, at least for the majority of our citizens, retirement incomes are now adequate. The debate is, therefore, motivated by some combination of four different concerns: (1) the future cost of the system, (2) the impact of the system on the rate of investment, (3) the distribution of the costs and benefits of the system, and (4) the effect of the system on retirement behavior.

Thompson points out that according to pessimistic projections, OASDI costs as a percentage of the GNP will rise by 4.5 percent between 1987 and 2060, making the dollar amount of the problem in Social Security over the next seventy-five years about the same size as the current federal deficit problem (leaving aside the Medicare underfunding). He goes on to indicate that the cost growth problem in the next century will be primarily the result of a permanent shift in the projected age distribution of the population and not a temporary phenomenon associated with the retirement of the baby boom generation. He argues that, in principle, our society could use the international capital markets to fund the temporary extra cost of supporting the baby boom generation in retirement. But if costs must be reduced, the most effective approach, he believes, would be to make the retirement income system less generous, either by reducing the future monthly benefits of those people for whom the system is currently most generous or by encouraging workers to delay retirement without giving them an offsetting increase in their monthly benefits.

None of the contributors offers easy solutions to the problems ahead. But if the solutions offered are undertaken on a timely basis with a sufficient period for current workers to adjust, they could ensure, without major economic dislocation, continued provision of retirement income security through combined public and private sources.

Part I
The Optimal Roles for Private and Public Retirement Insurance: Market Failure Rationales

1
Demographics, Market Failure, and Social Security

Jerry R. Green

This chapter is an analysis of the argument for Social Security on the grounds that it can provide a form of insurance that is otherwise unavailable. Individuals in our society face many risks. Some of these are insurable; others, though not completely insurable in a contractual sense, can be mitigated by the cooperative behavior of families and benevolent organizations; still others can be offset by the guarantees implicitly or explicitly provided by government policy.

It is the last category that concerns us here. Within this is a certain class of risk that cannot be diversified over the members of a single generation. To mitigate against this type of risk, a mutual insurance arrangement or an implicit contract involving members of different generations is required. One function of the Social Security system might be to provide a framework in which this type of implicit contract can operate. The contracting parties are, in effect, the current generations and the as yet unborn.

Risks requiring this type of intergenerational insurance are of two types. First are the real economic risks associated with productivity fluctuations, technical progress, wars, and, in an international context, trading relations with the rest of the world. Second is a risk associated with demographic fluctuations, which are a risk to present generations because they affect the future of capital markets and hence the rates of return that can be earned on savings invested for retirement income. These fluctuations are a risk to future generations because, by their very nature, they affect the conditions of the labor markets in which people will operate.

Risks due to fluctuations in population growth require careful cost-benefit analyses. The set of people affected by economic policies is itself a variable. Policies that depend on the realized rates of growth will affect different sets of individuals in different circumstances. Therefore, the benefits of the policy cannot be properly measured by summing up the net willingness to pay over the population. Some of the population will be present only in some circumstances. Hence, we must develop a method for assessing the risk-reducing benefits of policies that affect individuals who are members of the population less than 100 percent of the time.

In the next section, I discuss the principal economic risks being considered. Pay-as-you-go policies, such as the social security system, will be modeled as intergenerational transfers, possibly contingent on the rate of population growth. The sum of all transfers must be zero at all points in time. Direct capital accumulation or decumulation by the government will not be considered. The transfers can be executed in a lump-sum fashion, without distorting market prices.

Following this, I present a set of ballpark estimates of the benefits from risk reduction that might be expected from such intergenerational transfer policies that are made contingent on the realized rate of population growth. I then consider the role of social insurance in this regard, using a two-period model of the individuals' lifetimes. By employing a set of models based on a more than two-period lifetime, I extend this model to include a more complex view of the individuals' saving decisions and a more detailed view of the possibilities for intergenerational transfers. I then give the mathematical details of the above results and provide a summary of these ideas.

Risks: Insurable and Uninsurable

In this section, I enumerate some of the risks that might properly be considered the targets of social insurance. Many economic risks that individuals and families face are not the proper subject of pay-as-you-go social insurance schemes. That is not to say that they are not the proper target for public policy more generally. Nevertheless, I omit them from further consideration.

We can categorize the risks that can be addressed by social insurance into three groups. First, we have risks that are common to all members of a given cohort; second, we have those that are common to all individuals living at the same time but are not necessarily confined to individuals of roughly the same age; finally, we have those that are of a permanent nature, affecting all individuals from some time forward.

The most important source of risk to each cohort is its own size. The larger a cohort is, the lower will be the wages that a typical member of the cohort will receive. As the cohort ages and begins to garner investment income on its accumulated savings, the level of the aggregate stock will increase and the gross return to additional capital accumulation will decrease. Savings behavior is itself determined by the interaction of individuals' motives for saving and their expectations about their needs and about current and future returns. The variability of the size of each generation is the principal source of risk studied in this chapter. This risk is of the first type mentioned above. All individuals of a similar age will be similarly affected. They cannot, therefore, insure themselves. They must pool their common risk with others whose risks are different, and that means pooling with those of different age groups.

The second category, risks common to all individuals contemporaneously alive, include short-run risks of productivity fluctuations, which might affect both the real wage and the return to capital, and other exogenous sources of risk. The need for the government sector to use resources for collective purposes such as defense are in this category. Similarly, risks of an international nature, such as exchange rates or other countries' commercial policies, are a source of economic fluctuation common to all citizens of our country, regardless of age. That is not to say that all individuals are affected by these risks in exactly the same way. There will always be a varying impact, and we should separate the total risk into intracohort and intercohort components.

The final category of risks includes those that tend to be permanent changes in the situation. They affect all current cohorts and are expected to continue to affect all individuals in the future. Examples of particular importance to social insurance are the lengthening of expected lifetimes; the changing health status of older citizens, which affects their need for income in their retirement years; and longer term social trends, such as the reduced frequency of elderly parents living with their children. In a certain sense, these can be viewed as changes in taste, but they are the type of changes that society is likely to validate by using the social insurance system to help spread the burden of the transition over more than one generation.

Another category of risks includes those of a personal nature: whether or not one will marry, have children, become a widow or widower, and so on. As important as these are at the individual level, they are not the proper subject of social insurance policy as considered in this chapter. It is essential, however, to remember that any social security system might wish to take an individual's personal status into account in determining benefits. And as Boskin and Puffert (1987) have shown, this can introduce substantial risks into the system because of the variability of benefit levels.

Rough Estimates of the Benefit of Social Insurance Policies to Mitigate Risks of Demographic Fluctuations

In this section, I give, in very approximate terms, the likely benefits of a policy that can reduce the risks of population fluctuations both for current workers, who will be retired later, and future workers. To begin this calculation, we must have some feel for the range in which the working population could vary. For concreteness, let's focus on a particular date in the future, say 2025.

Fertility rates in the United States have ranged from a high of 3.77 births (estimated total number of births per woman, throughout her childbearing years) to a low of 1.75 births. The high end of this range is surely a phenomenon related to World War II and the large immigration waves of the early twentieth century. For these reasons, it is quite unlikely that this fertility level will be repeated again, and surely not before the year 2025.

A more plausible range is between 2.7 and 1.7 births. In table 1–1, I present the projections for the U.S. population under three alternative assumptions: 2.1 births which is approximately the rate necessary to maintain a constant population (in the absence of immigration), 2.7 births, and 1.7 births per woman.

Next we have to compute how the capital-labor ratio will vary as a result of these variations in population size. If the amount of saving is invariant to the realization of population growth rates, the capital-labor ratio will vary over a range that is 33 percent of its average value. Using a Cobb-Douglas production function with capital's share set at 25 percent, the ratio of the marginal products of capital would vary by about 33 percent.

This seemingly modest variation in the rental price of capital would produce very large swings in the total return to savings, accumulated over a holding period of say twenty years. Depending on our assumptions about the rate at which capital income is taxed, the real net rate of return (annualized) could be as low as 1 percent per year if population growth is slow, or as high as 2 percent per year if population growth is rapid. This translates into a 22 percent fluctuation in the real wealth accumulated for retirement due solely to the variation in the interest rates induced by alternative assumptions about the rate of population growth.

This range is further magnified when we look at the implications for retirement consumption. When accumulation has been rapid due to high real interest rates, retirement consumption will be high for the same reason. Although changes in fertility trends might partially offset these effects during the retirement years themselves, there will definitely be a positive correlation between accumulated savings and the retirement consumption they can finance. In some simulations I have done, which are not reported here, I have found that the average level of consumption feasibly could vary over the retirement interval 2025 to 2045 by as much as 34 percent, with similar fluctuations for other periods.

It is reasonable to believe that future retirees would be willing to take a 5 percent lower average consumption level to offset this risk to a significant extent, if possible, by means of social insurance. Thus, 5 percent of the retirement income of the generation that will be retired in the 2025 to 2045 interval (today's thirty-year-olds) is a very rough approximation of the benefit they would receive from the risk-reducing aspects of a social insurance policy that is contingent on the future rates of population growth.

To translate this into a present value, again very roughly, we can take the retirement income of this twenty-year cohort out of their accumulated savings to be in the range of $1 trillion annually. Thus, this amount of risk reduction will be worth around $50 billion (1986) in each year of the 2025

Table 1–1
Projection of the U.S. Population by Broad Age Groups

Year	Population (in thousands) as of July 1				65 and Over		Ratio of Persons Under 18 to Persons 18–64
	Under 18	18–64	65 and Over	Total	Percent of Total	Ratio to 18–64	
Assumption A—2.1 fertility							
1975	66,273	124,847	22,330	213,450	10.5	0.18	0.53
2000	71,079	160,815	30,600	262,494	11.7	0.19	0.44
2025	74,857	176,751	48,105	299,713	16.1	0.27	0.43
2050	78,701	188,448	51,247	318,396	16.1	0.27	0.42
Assumption B—2.7 fertility							
1975	66,273	124,847	22,330	213,450	10.5	0.18	0.53
2000	91,152	165,255	30,600	287,007	10.7	0.19	0.55
2025	121,054	212,852	48,105	382,011	12.6	0.23	0.57
2050	158,987	283,767	56,575	499,329	11.3	0.20	0.56
Assumption C—1.7 fertility							
1975	66,273	124,847	22,330	213,450	10.5	0.18	0.53
2000	57,322	157,176	30,600	245,098	12.5	0.19	0.36
2025	49,938	152,378	48,105	250,421	19.2	0.32	0.33
2050	44,146	135,532	47,024	226,702	20.7	0.35	0.33

Source: U.S. Bureau of Census, Current Population Report, Series P-25, No. 601, "Projections of Population of the United States: 1975–2050."

to 2045 retirement period. Discounting this to the present at a social discount rate of 2 percent per year, we have a present value of the policy, for this cohort alone, of $19 billion annually.

A similar calculation for the generation that will be working in these same years reveals an equally substantial gain to be made from risk-reducing social insurance policies. The 22 percent fluctuation in the capital stock, when combined with the correlated influence of their own variable numbers, gives a range for the capital-labor ratio of about 29 percent. This produces a 22 percent variation in the real wage, using the same Cobb-Douglas assumptions as above. Again, we can estimate the amount of consumption that these workers, most of whom are not yet born, would be willing to forgo to reduce this risk substantially. A risk premium of 2 percent of their labor income is not unreasonable. There will be approximately 2 million households in each year's cohort, using the average assumptions about population growth. If each of these households has a real income of $40,000 (1986), this means that they would be willing to pay, in aggregate, $1.6 billion to avoid the risk. Thus, with an average working life of forty-six years, the entire working population would be willing to reduce their income by almost $60 billion annually to substantially reduce the risk we are considering. Again, discounting this to the present, the present value of this policy of population-contingent income transfers is about $23 billion annually.

Needless to say, the calculations above are very crude. The aggregate possible benefit in present value terms, restricting our attention to the 2025 to 2045 interval, is $42 billion per year. This is a substantial sum. The purpose of this chapter is to see whether a population-contingent intergenerational transfer policy could be designed to capture at least part of these potentially large gains, and whether the gains that are captured can be spread equitably across individuals so that all would agree that the policy has been beneficial to them.

I cannot imagine that any policy could reduce the risks of population fluctuations to zero. Nevertheless, it is the nature of risk analysis that the most benefit is to be gained from mitigating the most extreme aspects of the variation. Based on the calculations above, it would seem that there are gains to be had in the multibillion-dollar-per-year range, if even part of the risk could be insured. Thus, we now turn to the more precise economic models in which the feasibility of a risk-reduction policy can be evaluated.

Mitigating the Risks of Demographic Fluctuations through Social Insurance

Two-Period Lifetime

In this section, I consider the principal risk for which social insurance is particularly well suited—the risk of fluctuations in the population size as caused by changes in the birthrate. Separate considerations are necessary for individuals who are already alive and for those in cohorts to come because, as we shall see, the risks they face are different.

An individual in a previous cohort has certain expectations about the prices and interest rates that will prevail in the future, conditional on the population size. If the next cohort, whose size is at present uncertain, turns out to be larger than expected, the older cohort will experience an increase in the real return on its savings as soon as the younger cohort joins the work force.

Now let's imagine ourselves as individuals in the younger cohort. If our generation is larger than expected, we will earn lower wages than expected throughout our lifetime. The return on a unit of retirement savings might be higher or lower, depending on how elastic the supply of savings is with respect to the wage during our working years and with respect to the interest rate. Whether interest rates in our retirement years rise or fall, we will surely be worse off by having been born into a larger cohort.

Thus, individuals in younger and older cohorts have negatively correlated risks with respect to variation in the size of the cohort in question. Negatively correlated risks create a prima facie case for mutually beneficial insurance. Moreover, under my assumption that individuals in the same cohort must act simultaneously, the private sector cannot pool these risks effectively, for the younger agent, who should be a party to this insurance, cannot contract for it until he or she and all the members of his or her cohort are born. And once the size of the cohort is known, it is too late to insure this risk, as the relevant uncertainty has been eliminated.

In this chapter, I examine whether some social insurance contract might be mutually beneficial to present and future cohorts. A contract of this form would bind the as yet unborn to a system of income transfers contingent on the size of their cohort. In any realization, the members of the younger generation would be either taxed or subsidized by these transfers when they are young. Thus, a large generation would be subsidized when young because the invested capital of their elders would have been highly profitable and the elders would be subject to taxation on this basis. Later in life, they would be on the other side of the same contract. There would be a new risk to insure: the size of the next generation to come.

Let's first look at the situation in the absence of a social insurance system and under the further simplifying assumption of a two-period lifetime, with working years in the first period and retirement in the second. Population growth is random. In an equilibrium of this model, a typical generation's savings depend on the amount of capital in place when it is born and its size relative to the size of the immediately preceding cohort. The evolution of the capital stock over different generations can be obtained by applying this savings policy function to the distribution of successive generation sizes.

On this laissez-faire system we superimpose a social insurance scheme as follows. A pay-as-you-go system is one in which each retiree receives a transfer from the government that is financed by a tax on the workers in an amount dependent on the size of their respective generations, and perhaps on the size of the capital stock. This transfer may be either positive or negative.

Given the considerations mentioned above, it is natural to consider transfers to retirees that depend negatively on the size of the succeeding generation. Let's suppose that the typical member of the retired generation is willing to accept the transfer, prospectively, before learning the size of the next generation. Would the unborn generation be willing to accept the other side of this gamble were it able to express its desires? If so, our argument is that a social insurance system that can commit future generations to such a policy is mutually beneficial to all concerned, even though in actuality some generations will be subsidized and others taxed.

The answer depends on the way in which we treat the members of the future generations. Imagine an individual who knows that he or she will surely be born as a member of the next generation but is unsure of exactly how many others will be born. His or her expected utility is determined by averaging over all possible population sizes.

In contrast to this, imagine an individual who does not know whether he or she will be born. His or her expected utility should be calculated conditional on this event. Thus, for an individual who will be born only if the rate of population growth is very high, expected utility will depend on the circumstances in which the social insurance scheme as envisioned would pay him a subsidy. Such individuals surely would prefer that this type of social insurance scheme be implemented. Conversely, under this view of the world, the individuals least likely to benefit from social insurance are those most likely to be born. To be universally beneficial, a social insurance scheme would have to keep these individuals at least as well off as they would be in the laissez-faire state.

If a social insurance system could be found that would pass this test and keep the older generation at least as well off, in expectation, it would benefit all. The individuals who are less likely to be born would receive more positive benefits. By being "absent" sometimes, they are "missing" in situations in which they would have been taxed. Thus, conditional on being born, they are doing better than they would be under laissez-faire.

Another approach is to treat all individuals as equally likely to be born. The actual composition of the population would then be determined in two stages. First, the actual size of the population would be fixed, but we would still be unsure about who, among all the potential individuals, will be present in the population. Second, the set of individuals comprising the population would be determined. Modeling random population growth in this way allows us to have a variable population size and individuals who are *ex ante* identical, without running afoul of the law of large numbers.

Under this set of hypotheses, only a single calculation need be made, because all individuals in the same cohort are identical at the time our policy evaluation is made. Each individual assesses the possible worlds into which he or she might be born by forming a posterior belief about the size of his or her generation, given that he or she will be a member of it. The average population size computed in this fashion is larger than the *ex ante* mathematical expectation of the distribution of population sizes because of the positive correlation of the births across potential people. Since the large cohorts are the ones that are to be subsidized, the typical individual will assign more weight to them in his or her probabilistic judgment if he or she forms conditional beliefs in this way, as compared to the estimate of an outside observer who is not conditioning his or her expectations on the event of his or her own birth. Therefore, under this approach the use of social insurance to mitigate the risk of population fluctuations is more likely to succeed than it would be under the hypothesis that individuals' births are ordered.

In the ordered births model, one can improve the welfare of the retirees and an individual who will surely be born into the succeeding generation if the risks they face are sufficiently severe relative to the surplus that will, of necessity, go to the less likely to be born members of the latter's generation. The conditions for this are developed mathematically later in this chapter. They turn on the relationship between the individual's risk aversion and the elasticity of substitution between labor and capital in production. The less substitutable are the factors of production, the more their relative prices will have to vary in the equilibrium in order to absorb the inelastic supply of labor that will be present at that time. Thus, social insurance will be universally beneficial if the coefficient of risk aversion and the elasticity of substitution are both high. Quite surprisingly, perhaps, these conditions for mutually beneficial social insurance will not hold under the commonly estimated values for these parameters. Therefore, although this type of social insurance might be thought to be socially beneficial when its effects on all individuals in the population are taken into account, it is unlikely to be beneficial to everyone.

This rather negative conclusion is partially a by-product of the assumption of a two-period lifetime. In the next section, I will show that under more general specifications of the demographic structure, there is a greater chance for universally beneficial social insurance to mitigate the risks of population fluctuations, even under the ordered births hypothesis.

Under the symmetric births hypothesis posited by de Bartholome and Brandts (1986), there is a much better outcome, even in the two-period lifetime model. Social insurance provides the individuals in question with an actuarially fair bet that is perfectly negatively correlated with the risk they face. The reason that this bet is exactly actuarially fair, whereas it is at less-than-fair odds in the ordered births specification, is that the members of the younger generation put more probability weight on the event that they will be born into a larger cohort than do the typical members of the older cohort. This is not because of a difference in beliefs or information. It is due simply to the fact that the younger agents neglect all those circumstances in which they themselves are not born, while the older agents do not care *who* is born, just *how many* are born.

More Than Two-Period Lifetime

In this section, I reconsider the above results in cases where agents live for more than two periods. If interpreted in economic terms, a two-period model ignores the part of life before one works and divides the remainder into two equal intervals. This distorts the analysis in several respects. A more realistic model must allow for the difference in length between the working and retirement periods and account for the first twenty or so years of life, which fall into neither category. Although theoretically interesting, it is not of practical relevance unless we can determine that the analysis is robust when the number of periods is extended.

Three-Period Model. Let's begin with a three-period model in which the working part of an individual's lifetime is modeled as being twice as long as retirement—work in the first two periods and retirement in the last. Thus, the ages involved are roughly 20–39, 40–59, and 60–80. Childhood and education are still neglected.

The economic difference between this and the two-period model is twofold. First, it allows for two periods within which each generation coexists with its immediate successor and its immediate predecessor, rather than the one period in the model discussed above. Second, because of this, adjacent generations can base the transfers between them on the size of the generation that follows them both. When this generation's size is known, the two contracting generations are at different times of life—one is retired, and the other is still working. Thus, their interests are opposed with respect to changes in the subsequent cohort's size. The retirees are hoping that they are more numerous so that the capital-labor ratio is lower, and the workers are hoping that they are less numerous so as not to depress their own wages. This effect is partially offset by the fact that the retirement income of the original workers will be higher if the generation following them is larger. Overall, however, it can be shown that this effect is overridden by the effect on the initial period's wages; the interests of the two generations in question are indeed opposed.

Under these conditions, there will be a mutually advantageous social insurance scheme if the retirees receive transfers from the immediately following generation. This will remain true under either of the assumptions about how the size of subsequent generations is determined, for unlike the case of the two-period lifetime, there is no uncertainty about the size of one's own generation. All the uncertainty pertains to a risk that is external to the two generations that are parties in the contract.

A contract between the retirees and the immediately following generation of workers would require age-specific taxation of the working population. The youngest generation of workers is, in this scheme, left out. If all workers have to share the burden of taxation because the older workers cannot be taxed or subsidized without the same being done to the youngest group, then this youngest group is placed in a position similar to the younger generation in the two-period lifetime case and my conclusions in the previous section still apply.

In summary, if the transfer scheme can distinguish between individuals of different generations, then a mutually beneficial social insurance system can be designed for all generations regardless of the modeling of demographic uncertainty. However, if the transfer policy can distinguish only between working-age and retirement-age individuals, it can benefit all generations only under the assumption that all individuals are *ex ante* identical.

Four-Period Model. The idea behind a four-period lifetime model is not simply that four is one more than three and that it is good to generalize the model further. The reason for exploring this model is that the three-year model omits the first twenty years of life. Even though individuals are not economically active in these years, they are important because accounting for them eliminates uncertainty about the size of the next working generation, even though there might still be uncertainty about the rate of population growth. The four periods are a period of economic inactivity, which serves only to model the size of future generations, then two working periods, and finally a retirement period of half the length of the working interval.

The results of the four-period model are qualitatively similar to those of the three-period model. Let's label the generations according to the period in which they are born and imagine that we are in period 4, just before the size of generation 4 is announced. Since these individuals will not be working, this announcement will have no impact on the capital-labor ratio or on the rate of return or the wage in the present period. Therefore, generation 1, which is now retired, experiences no real uncertainty on this account. Any transfer policy involving generation 1 that is conditional on the size of generation 4 will be welfare reducing for generation 1, unless it is more than actuarially fair. Therefore, the hope for a policy that is capable of being [Pareto improving] will have to rely on generations 2 and 3.

Generations 2 and 3 are both working at present. Their interests are opposed, however, because generation 3 will be retired when generation 1 starts working, whereas generation 2 will not. Thus, in a four-period model, mutually beneficial insurance is possible even though the size of one future generation is known in advance of its entering the work force because the working part of one's lifetime is twice the length of the retirement or the pre-working period. Note that this would not be true in a three-period model with all three phases of life of equal length. The retirees and the workers face no uncertainty about the capital-labor ratio during their lifetime. The uncertainty that any one generation faces is present only during its first period of life. But at that stage members of the cohort are not yet economically active, and they have no income of their own. We assume that they are sharing in their parents' consumption without effectively diminishing it.

Mathematical Analysis

Two-Period Lifetime: Ordered Births Hypothesis[1]

Let the initial capital stock be K_0 and the consumption of the current young generation (generation 0) be c_{y0}. Their savings for their retirement are equal to their wages, w_0, minus this current consumption. If n_1 is the population growth factor, then their retirement consumption is

$$c_{r0}(n_1) = (w_0 - c_{y0})(1 + f')\left(\frac{w_0 - c_{y0}}{n_1}\right) \qquad (1.1)$$

where f is the production function, as it depends on the capital-labor ratio. We assume that c_{y0} is chosen to maximize the agent's lifetime expected utility, holding other people's saving behavior constant and regarding n_1 as a random variable.

A population-contingent, pay-as-you-go, intergenerational transfer scheme is modeled as a term, $b(n_1)$, to be added to equation 1.1. If it is beneficial to all members of generation 0, we must have:

$$\sum_{n_1} u'_r(c_{r0}(n_1)) b(n_1) > 0 \qquad (1.2)$$

where u_r is their retirement period utility function.

Now we look at the members of generation 1. Their lifetime utility is affected by the social insurance scheme in two ways. First, they must pay for generation 0's transfer (recall that this may be positive or negative). Second, the result of this transfer affects their own savings and hence their own retirement consumption, even in the absence of transfers between themselves and generation 2. The magnitude of this second effect depends on the sensitivity of future interest rates to the capital-labor ratio. As savings are predetermined, the capital-labor ratio depends only on n_1. The magnitude of this dependence is a function of the elasticity of substitution of the production function, f.

The higher this elasticity, the less dependent is the future interest rate and therefore the less risky is retirement consumption as it is influenced by the first period's transfer. Thus, generation 1 will benefit from the transfer if they are very risk tolerant and if the elasticity of substitution is high.

Specifically, if

$$1 < \frac{f'(f - n_1 f')}{f\sigma(1 + f')} R_r$$

$$+ \frac{\frac{k_1}{n_1} f'}{f\sigma} R_y \qquad (1.3)$$

where R_r and R_y are coefficients of relative risk aversion in the retirement and young periods, then the worst treated member of generation 1 will benefit from a social insurance scheme for which equation 1.2 holds with equality (i.e., generation 0 will accept it as well).

Examining equation 1.3 in more detail, we see that it is quite unlikely to hold. When utility is logarithmic, $R_y = R_r = 1$. And if production is Cobb-Douglas, the entire right side of equation 1.3 reduces to capital's share in this production function, which is necessarily less than unity. Hence, equation 1.3 is surely violated in this case.

More Than Two-Period Lifetime

In the more than two-period lifetime models developed earlier in this chapter, the parties are generations whose size is known when the random event upon which they are contracting is determined. Therefore, we know from the basic theory of behavior in the presence of risk[2] that there exists a sufficiently small gamble, which, if negatively related to exogenous random wealths, will be acceptable to both sides. The future savings behavior of the labor generation might be affected by these transfers. To the extent that savings increase and the elasticity of substitution is small, future interest rates, and hence their own retirement consumption, will be lowered. However, under typical conditions, this interest rate effect will be dominated by the direct risk-reduction benefits of the population-contingent transfer.

Note, however, that to implement this plan, generations 0 and 1 must be able to make a contract that excludes the members of generation 2, even though in the three-period model generation 2 is working, just as generation 1 is, in its first period of life. If we were to accept as a constraint on the social insurance compact that taxes or subsidies be common across workers and retirees, not only constant across members of the same generation, then the same set of considerations that made the two-period model unlikely to succeed for members of the youngest cohort would apply here as well.

Summary

This chapter has addressed three questions: Is the uncertainty inherent in the rate of population growth a serious source of inefficiency that is worth overcoming, if possible, by a system of contingent intergenerational transfers? Can these benefits actually be realized by a pay-as-you-go system? And how are the gains distributed over the population and across successive generations?

I have shown that the risks are substantial, though silent. My best estimate of the annual value of eliminating the income risks attendant to population fluctuations is $42 billion. Of this, $19 billion is the value to future retirees, and $23 billion is the value to future workers.

I also have shown that many of these benefits can be captured by a system of implicit, or governmentally guaranteed, contingent income transfers. This calculation is hard to make precise, but it is likely that half of the $42 billion annual benefit is, in fact, recoverable.

The forgoing discussion has focused on the negative side of these results. Under typical economic assumptions, it might be impossible to distribute these benefits to all members of the contracting generations. The answer depends on how we model individuals' lifetimes, on whether the size of future working generations can be approximated by knowing their numbers as children, and on whether age-specific, as well as generation-specific, transfers are possible within the pay-as-you-go system.

Notes

1. This section is based on Green 1977.
2. See, for example, Arrow 1965.

References

Arrow, K.J. 1965. *Aspect of the Theory of Risk-Bearing*. Helsinki: Yrjo Jahnssonin Saatio.

Boskin, M., and D. Puffert. 1987. "Social Security and the American Family." National Bureau of Economic Research Working Paper No. 2117.

de Bartholome, C., and J. Brandts. 1986. "Social Security and Population Uncertainty: The Full Nature of Demographic Bias." Unpublished manuscript.

Green, J. 1977. "Mitigating Demographic Risk through Social Insurance." National Bureau of Economic Research Working Paper No. 215.

2
Why is the Government in the Pension Business?

Alan S. Blinder

> I advise you to go on living solely to enrage those who are paying your annuities.
>
> —Voltaire

The Social Security system involves almost every American, consumes about one-third of the federal budget, and enjoys political support that is broad, deep, and resilient. You might, therefore, suppose that the rationale for Social Security is evident, compelling, and widely shared. But such is not the case.

This chapter asks why the state provides mandatory public pensions and why these pensions have the particular features they do. Reasons, we shall see, are not hard to find. But the supporting arguments are not always lucid or of obvious practical importance. Although the Social Security system provides a variety of services, including life insurance, disability insurance, and, through Medicare, health insurance, I will focus exclusively on the largest program: old age pensions.

At first, the reason for a public pension system seems obvious. As a prosperous and humane society, we want our elderly to enjoy a decent standard of living without having to work until their dying day or rely on handouts from relatives. Social Security achieves that goal for many. But a second thought may give pause. The current elderly presumably had that very goal in mind for themselves when they were younger and fully capable of saving for their retirement. Why, then, does the state play such a prominent role in the provision of old age pensions? After all, though our society deems it desirable that people own their own homes, the government does not provide home mortgages and certainly does not compel home ownership. It leaves these decisions to individual choice and, for the most part, to the market.[1]

I thank Andrew Abel and Michael Hurd for useful suggestions and John Ammer for research assistance.

But the government has not been content to leave provision for retirement to the market. Instead, we have public old age pensions with the following characteristics (among others):

1. *Universal participation.* Almost every American worker participates. The principal exceptions are public employees, who are, of course, already covered by a government pension. Not only is participation mandatory, but individuals are given no discretion over the scale of their participation. Instead, a prescribed portion of their earnings is taxed away in return for a prescribed level of retirement benefits.

2. *Compulsory longevity insurance.* At retirement, benefits can be drawn only in the form of annuities, not as a lump sum. This amounts to a requirement that people insure themselves against the contingency that they will outlive their accumulated savings. And it means, among other things, that those who die young wind up subsidizing those who live long.

3. *Pay-as-you-go financing.* Unlike most private pension plans, which are funded, Social Security pensions are financed more or less on the pay-as-you-go principle.[2]

4. *Redistributive benefit formula.* The relationship between contributions and benefits is progressive, meaning that low earners receive more annuity per tax dollar than high earners.

This chapter asks two related questions. The first is descriptive/historical: Why does the United States have a social security program with these and other characteristics? The second is normative: Are these reasons valid? As I run down the long list of reasons that have been offered for public pensions, I pay particular attention to the ones that might rationalize a system with the features we observe. My perspective is clearly that of an economist. We are an odd bunch who find it unnatural to think that government compulsion can make people better off. In our peculiar way of thinking, there are two main categories of reasons for state intervention in economic decision making: market failure and redistribution. Each of these plays a role in rationalizing social security pensions, but, as we shall see, they cannot be the whole story and may not even be the most important parts. That nasty word *paternalism* will creep in late in the chapter.

Social Security as a Correction for Market Failure

The Need for Longevity Insurance

One argument for social security rests on the proposition that pensions are a desirable but risky asset. According to this argument, people would like to rid themselves of the risk of poverty due to underprovision for old age. A private pension plan organized by the employer can do this, but only by foisting other risks on the employee—such as the risks that he or she will not hold the job long enough to collect pension benefits or that the firm will go bankrupt and renege on its pension obligations. State-provided pensions avoid all such firm-specific risks and so provide a safe way to insure against the risk of longevity.

On second thought, however, it becomes clear that this reasoning is fallacious. The state can eliminate such risks from private pensions with statutes such as the Employee Retirement Security Act of 1974 (ERISA) that impose prompt vesting requirements and rigorous fiduciary standards. Alternatively, it can compel companies to carry sufficient pension fund insurance. The state need not provide the insurance itself. It can simply mandate purchase from a private insurer, as it now does with auto liability insurance. Thus, the desire to make longevity insurance available cannot rationalize a public pension system—and certainly cannot rationalize compulsory participation.

The Failure of the Private Annuity Market

Strictly speaking, organized pension plans are not necessary at all. Workers can simply save for their own retirement and use the proceeds to purchase annuities from private insurance companies. This does not seem to happen much, however. In this country, there is hardly any market for individually purchased annuities,[3] and the alleged failure of this market is often interpreted as a reason to provide annuities publicly. But is the low volume of transactions really evidence of market failure? Although few mink diapers are produced and sold, no one interprets that as a market failure. We think, instead, that the demand is not there. So before we declare that the market has failed, we should delve a bit more deeply into the reasons for the alleged failure.

In this case, there is a potentially good reason—a reason common to all lines of insurance—adverse selection. If people have better information about their life expectancies than insurance companies do, companies offering to sell individual life annuities will find that their customers have better longevity than the population as a whole. If so, policies offered at what appear to be actuarially fair premiums will bring losses to the companies.

How serious is this problem in the case of annuities? Fortunately, we need not merely speculate about this because Benjamin Friedman and Mark Warshawsky (1985) have recently tabulated the data. They compared the mortality experience of purchasers of individual annuities with that of the general population and found significant differences. For example, the probability of surviving from age sixty-five to age seventy-five was about 10 percentage points higher for those who bought annuities. That is certainly enough to matter to an insurance company. But is it enough to destroy the viability of the market? After all, the life insurance market is beset by a comparable adverse selection problem.

Calculations presented by Friedman and Warshawsky (1985) suggest that the adverse selection problem, though genuine, is not by itself severe enough to rule out a thriving market. Using the twenty-year U.S. government bond rate and life tables for the general population, they found that the annuity prices of the ten largest companies during the period 1968 to 1983 embodied an average load factor of 32 percent; that is, the premiums exceeded the actuarially discounted present value of benefits by 32 percent. When that same actuarial computation was performed using the superior mortality experience of annuity purchasers, however, the load factor dropped to 18 percent. Hence, 14 percent was necessary to compensate for adverse selection, leaving the other 18 percent to cover the companies' operating expenses, taxes, and profit.

The market could almost certainly survive a 14 percent load factor for adverse selection. But a 32 percent load factor, though not out of line with charges for other insurance products, leaves the typical rate of return offered on annuities below that of government bonds. That means that a potential annuitant would be better off purchasing a 30-year bond, forsaking the principal, and living off the interest. If there is any bequest motive at all, the dominance of conventional bonds over annuities is increased. In addition, annuitized wealth is locked in and hence unavailable if, say, ill health leads to a sudden need for cash.

Thus, we should think of the high prices of individual life annuities—which might not be a result of adverse selection—as damaging and perhaps even devastating to the private market. The question is: Does this leave any role for publicly provided annuities, which, by virtue of their universality and uniformity, avoid the adverse selection problem entirely? The answer from some recent economic theory appears to be yes. Theoretical models in which the private annuities market is plagued by adverse selection show that a fully funded social security program providing actuarially fair annuities to all can under certain circumstances improve social welfare.[4] The basic idea is that, because insurance companies cannot distinguish between people who are likely to be long-lived and people who are likely to be short-lived, the former impose an externality on the latter by driving up annuity prices. By insuring everyone, the state avoids the adverse selection problem and hence can offer a better deal.

Notice that this rationale for public annuities explains not only why the government gets in the business, but why participation is mandatory and why individuals are given no discretion over how much they buy. These models also are descriptively accurate in several important respects. They allow for the coexistence of social security and a small private market in individually purchased annuities in which prices will appear actuarially unfair if general mortality tables are used. And they predict that competition from social security will drive up the load factor on private annuities. They do, however, have two shortcomings. First, they provide a rationale only for a fully funded social security program, and so cannot explain why almost all countries opt for something approximating pay-as-you-go financing. Second, they do not allow for private group annuities. This seems a more important omission because group policies exist precisely to circumvent (or at least substantially reduce) the adverse selection problem. That social security can still raise welfare in the presence of private group annuities is far from evident and probably dubious.

At this point, I think the safest conclusion is that adverse selection *might* provide an intellectual justification for social security, but it certainly cannot be the whole story. And I doubt that it helps much in explaining why social security programs were actually established. It does, however, make economists feel better.

Desirability of Indexed Annuities

A different sense in which the private market for annuities can be said to fail is that it does not offer indexed annuities. A pension plan, be it public or private, does not provide safe longevity insurance if it offers only nominal annuities. Because no one can predict what the price level will be many years in advance, a purchaser of a nominal annuity simply trades longevity risk for inflation risk. Only indexed annuities get rid of both risks.

Here, it would seem, the state has a big advantage over private insurers, especially if it uses the pay-as-you-go method of financing. Under pay-as-you-go, the income of the social security trust fund is proportional to total earnings in the economy, which makes it straightforward and natural to link benefits to wages. It is worth looking briefly at the simple arithmetic. Let w be the average covered money wage, W be the number of covered workers, R be the number of retirees drawing benefits, and t be the payroll tax rate. Payments into the system are twW, which can finance an average benefit payment of $tw(W/R)$. In a stable population, W/R will be constant over time. Thus, a fixed payroll tax rate will be able to finance benefits equal to a fixed percentage of average wages, which is roughly what the U.S. Social Security system has done. In the United States today, a payroll tax of about 12 percent and a worker/beneficiary ratio of about 3.3:1 finance a benefit payment equal to about 40 percent of average wages.

This little piece of arithmetic, by the way, shows how a pay-as-you-go system can run into trouble when benefits are indexed to prices instead of wages and the population is not stable. Real revenues per beneficiary are $t(w/p)(W/R)$, where p is the price level. If wages grow more slowly than prices and the number of retirees grows more quickly than the number of workers, the payroll tax must be raised to maintain real benefits. Alternatively, a fixed payroll tax can finance only dwindling real benefits. During the 1970s, real wages fell, high unemployment limited the growth of employment, and labor force participation among the elderly declined. So the U.S. pay-as-you-go system encountered difficulties.

Indexing poses a tougher problem for funded systems, whether public or private. A funded defined contribution plan such as Teachers Insurance and Annuity Association—College Retirement Equities Fund—(TIAA-CREF) invests contributions at market interest rates, which certainly are not insured against inflation. It cannot guarantee a fixed real annuity unless it has indexed assets in which to invest, which it does not. If a social security system were run on the same principles, it would have precisely the same problem. Defined benefit plans that base benefits on earnings during, say, the last ten years of employment are naturally indexed during the working career, but they cannot provide indexed benefits after retirement without exposing themselves to great risks. Similarly, a funded defined benefit social security system could offer indexed benefits only by having a payroll tax rate that varied from year to year.

I used to think of the provision of indexed annuities as a major argument in favor of pay-as-you-go social security. It seemed to provide the "missing asset" in people's portfolios. The private sector could provide such contracts if the government issued indexed bonds, so perhaps this is just an argument for issuing indexed bonds,[5] not for social security. In addition, Lawrence Summers (1983) has argued that the demand for indexed annuities is not nearly as large as I have supposed because:

1. Errors in real benefits attributable to poor forecasts of inflation are unlikely to grow very large because discretionary adjustments can be made. In fact, U.S. Social Security benefits were tacitly (and irregularly) indexed by periodic congressional action long before they were explicitly indexed.

2. If indexing is seen as a device to make it difficult to cut real benefits, the social consensus might be to set real benefits at a lower average level.

3. The risk embodied in an asset depends on how that asset's returns correlate with those of other assets. Households heavily invested in housing might want their annuity income to correlate negatively with inflation and so might actually prefer nominal annuities.

To this list of conceptual problems, we must add the possibility—which turned out to be a reality in the United States—that indexing will be done poorly. Social Security benefits in the United States are indexed to the Consumer Price Index, which exaggerated inflation in the 1970s due to its flawed treatment of home ownership costs.[6] And the original indexing formula adopted in 1972 inadvertently overindexed, thereby accidentally raising real benefits for certain age cohorts until the error was corrected in 1977.

On balance, I continue to believe that indexed annuities would be a welcome addition to individual portfolios and that, therefore, public pensions have an edge over private pensions unless and until indexed bonds become available. But the case is not nearly as strong as I once thought and would be no case at all if the government issued indexed bonds. Furthermore, this certainly cannot be the main rationale for Social Security, which, after all, was not indexed until 1972. And, frankly, I think Social Security was indexed to rid Congress of political risks, not to rid retirees of inflation risks.

Economies of Scale

There is another sense in which the private market for annuities might be said to malfunction, though not fail. Capitalist production is supposed to keep costs down, but it appears that the administrative costs of running the Social Security program (expressed as a percentage of receipts) are far lower than the costs of private life insurance companies.[7] If this is interpreted as evidence of genuinely greater efficiency in the public sector, it can be used to build a case for public enterprise. It is not clear, however, that this evidence should be so interpreted.

It is hard to believe, for example, that there are huge economies of scale to be exploited by moving from a private company with, say, a mere million policyholders to a social security program with more than 100 million. The lower costs must derive from other factors. In fact, the major reasons for higher operating costs in the private sector are that private insurers must advertise and pay sales commissions to agents and must earn a return on their capital. Social security programs, of course, need no agents or advertising because participation is mandatory, and such programs need virtually no capital because they operate almost on a pay-as-you-go basis. I would never claim that the number of life insurance agents in the United States is socially optimal, but we do not normally accept such cost differences as arguments to engage in government production. Hertz and Avis, for example, would certainly rent automobiles more cheaply if they spent nothing on advertising and kept no profits for their stockholders. But no one thinks that a good reason for the government to go into the car rental business. So I am inclined to dismiss this rationale for public pensions.

Superior Risk Diversification

One final argument has been made for social security programs on market-failure grounds. Robert Merton (1983) noted that, for almost all of us, human capital is our biggest asset. But because it cannot be bought or sold, we cannot diversify our portfolios properly. So we wind up holding too much human capital—and therefore bearing too much risk—when we are young and too little when we are old. By taxing away some of the returns to human capital (via the payroll tax) when we are young, and giving retirees a share of the economy's total earnings, the government helps us diversify our portfolios better.

The argument seems conceptually valid—and note that it makes a case for a pay-as-you-go system linked to wages (like the one I discussed above), not a funded one. The importance of the portfolio diversification motive in practice, however, is unknown and might not be great. We know, for example, that individuals do not generally hold well-diversified financial portfolios, even though mutual funds make it easy to do so. This suggests that the efficiency gains from greater diversification are either not terribly important to, or not well understood by, most people. Second, most of the risk of human capital is idiosyncratic, while Merton's plan only diversifies away the economy-wide risk. Furthermore, it is not apparent that people are scurrying around trying to unload their human capital risks. Income-contingent educational loans, such as Yale's student loan system, are not widespread.

It seems unlikely that the risk-diversification argument is a major factor underlying the actual Social Security program. It is, however, an intellectually respectable one.

Social Security as a Redistributive Program

I mentioned earlier that economists, or at least liberal economists, recognize that government has a legitimate role in equalizing the distribution of income. Social security programs cause major redistributions, both across generations and within any single generation.

Redistribution across Generations

It is important to remember that the U.S. Social Security system was a child of the Great Depression. If we conceptualize the Depression as a terrible random event that severely damaged the economic well-being of those alive at the time, it makes sense to design a social mechanism to transfer income from generations yet unborn to the victims of the Depression. No private pension scheme can do this, since it cannot write contracts between people living and imagined. But a public pension system can, if it is organized on the pay-as-you-go principle and begins paying benefits right away.

People who retired in the early years of the Social Security system—say those who reached age sixty-five in 1940—were fifty-four or so when the Depression began. For many of them, the Depression represented a huge and irreparable loss of lifetime income for which they could not have prepared and from which they had little time to recover. Because this generation contributed almost nothing and drew substantial benefits, it received significant transfers from the Social Security system, which handed the bill to their grandchildren. That seems like an egalitarian redistribution to me.

Moving down a generation or so, to people who reached sixty-five in, say, 1960, we find people who were thirty-four to forty-five years old during the Depression years. Normally, these are life's prime earning years, but prospects for this particular age cohort must have been bleak. They, too, suffered enormous losses from the Depression and received huge transfers from Social Security.

Even those a decade or two younger were victims of the Depression to a significant degree. The 1905 birth cohort was twenty-four to thirty-five years old, and the 1915 birth cohort was fourteen to twenty-five. The incidence of unemployment must have been particularly severe for them, depriving them not only of earnings but of valuable work experience. Many of these people are still alive. By the time they die, they too will have received huge transfers from Social Security. In fact, two recent studies allow me to be less vague about these particular cohorts. Hurd and Shoven (1985), using individual data from the Longitudinal Retirement History Survey, estimate that the median real rate of return on Social Security contributions for the 1905 birth cohort was a sensational 8.5 percent. Boskin et al. (1986) calculate real rates of return for hypothetical couples in the 1915 birth cohort that range from 5.2 to 6.6 percent, depending on income. These rates of return are less generous, but they still dwarf, say, the real returns on government bonds.

Intergenerational transfers from a pay-as-you-go system end only when the system is mature, and that takes a long time. And then, of course, a new set of intergenerational transfers is set in motion each time benefits are increased. Using a 3 percent benchmark real interest rate, Boskin et al. (1986) estimate that positive transfers from Social Security ended only (approximately) with the 1935 birth cohort.[8] Thus, roughly speaking, every generation alive during the Depression was helped by Social Security.

According to this view, our pay-as-you-go system is something of an accident of history. Economists, most of whom are closet physicists, shy away from such explanations; they want an equilibrium theory. But there is a deep kind of hysteresis here, for if you start with a pay-as-you-go system, switching to a funded system is extremely difficult. To make the switch, some birth cohorts must pay taxes not only to finance the retirement benefits of older generations, but also to finance their own. What generation will volunteer for the honor? For this reason, pay-as-you-go social security, once started, is a durable social institution.

The founding of the U.S. Social Security system was not unique in this respect, except in its magnitude. Every subsequent increase in the benefit structure—such as the bonanza paid when benefits were generously increased in 1972—can be thought of as the start-up of a new mini pay-as-you-go system. This is the main reason, I think, why Hurd and Shoven (1985) found that the median member of the 1910 birth cohort saw his implied rate of return from Social Security rise from 7 percent to 8 percent between 1969 and 1975. The transfers being made to old people whenever Social Security benefits are increased are, I think, well understood and politically popular. Whether or not they are good social policy is, of course, another question entirely. In a society that anticipates long-run secular increases in living standards, however, transfers from later generations to earlier ones are in the egalitarian direction.

As a descriptive matter, I think the intergenerational redistribution that naturally arises whenever a pay-as-you-go system is started goes a long way toward explaining not only why Social Security began when it did, but also why it is unfunded. Furthermore, from the normative standpoint, this redistribution might even have been appropriate.

Redistribution within a Generation

The redistributive aspects of a social security system within a generation are more controversial. The first aspect is redistribution from rich to poor. Owing to the progressive benefit formula of the U.S. system, lower-income families earn more annuity benefit per dollar of Social Security contribution than do upper-income families, both on average and at the margin. To cite just one example, Boskin et al. (1986) calculate that, for the cohort born in 1945, implicit rates of return on Social Security will be 3.74, 2.3, and 1.95 percent for single-earner couples with low, moderate, and high incomes. Obviously, no private, voluntary pension plan could redistribute income in this way, for the rich would simply opt out. If the desirability of egalitarian redistribution within each generation is granted, we seem to have another argument for a mandatory, public pension scheme like social security. Who doubts that New Dealers had something like this in mind?

One can legitimately ask, however, why the pension system should be used to redistribute income rather than, say, the progressive income tax. I think there are two reasons. First, lower-income people have shorter life expectancies than upper-income people, so they must be given a bigger annuity per dollar of contribution just to make the system actuarially fair. In fact, Hurd and Shoven (1985) found that Social Security's progressive benefit structure just about compensates for mortality differentials, leaving rates of return roughly equal across wealth groups. That means that the apparent redistribution from rich to poor is an illusion; to be distributionally neutral, a pension system needs a progressive benefit structure. Since no private or voluntary system can post such a benefit structure, we have a reason for public intervention.

Second, Social Security is the one mechanism we have that redistributes lifetime rather than annual income. All other redistributive programs, at least in part, take from the transitorily rich to give to the transitorily poor. While current and lifetime incomes are positively correlated, the correlation is imperfect. So, if we want to reduce inequality in lifetime incomes, a redistributive social security program has much to recommend it.[9] Of course, a comprehensive income tax with lifetime income averaging might be even better, since it also would tax "uncovered" earnings and the returns on inherited wealth,[10] but we do not have such an income tax.

Social Security also redistributes income across different types of demographic units. The simplest way to summarize this is to say that Social Security subsidizes married women who do not work. Thus, couples get a better deal than single people, and single-earner couples do better than couples with two earners. Boskin et al. (1986) recently made extensive calculations documenting these redistributions. Taking the 1945 birth cohort as an example, they found the following implied rates of return:

	Low Income	*Middle Income*	*High Income*
Single-earner couple	3.74%	2.30%	1.95%
Two-earner couple[11]	3.30	1.75	0.80
Single man	1.42	−0.25	−0.60
Single woman	2.55	1.13	0.68

The higher returns for single women than for single men are attributable to the use of unisex life tables, which private insurers also must use. All the other differences favor nonworking wives.

The root of the problem, if indeed it is a problem, is that special benefits are provided for spouses.[12] Wives have the option of receiving either one half of their husband's benefit while he lives and his full benefit after he dies or the benefits to which their own earnings entitle them. A wife opting for the latter gets the same treatment as a single woman, but a wife who draws benefits as a spouse receives two transfer payments from the government. The first is the extra 50 percent benefit paid to couples while both are living, for which she paid nothing. The second is the survivor benefit. While a survivor benefit is standard in private annuity contracts, private insurers charge an actuarial fee; Social Security gives it away for free.

The subsidization of nonworking wives through Social Security is highly controversial, but the important point here is that these transfers are not inherent in the idea of running a public pension plan. They derive, instead, from the answer to a quite different question of social policy: Should society subsidize full-time motherhood?[13] Our society has answered this question in the affirmative. But the reasons—good or bad—for doing so have little or nothing to do with the rationale for having a mandatory public pension system.

Of the two types of intragenerational redistribution, the one from rich to poor seems to have the most to do with the establishment of Social Security. Social Security was meant to ensure that old people with no other means of support would not starve. It was not the rich that the founders of Social Security had in mind, which might, for example, be why there is neither a marginal payroll tax nor further accrual of benefits once a certain high level of earnings is surpassed.

Paternalism and Related Explanations for Social Security

I come at last to paternalistic rationales for Social Security. Although paternalism makes economists squirm, I doubt that we can understand either the founding of Social Security or its continued popularity without facing up to the common view that too few people will voluntarily provide enough for their old age. There are three different levels at which the paternalistic argument for Social Security can be made, and, fortunately, only one of them is predicated on outright irrationality.

Dictionary Paternalism

I call the version of paternalism founded on irrationality *dictionary paternalism,* since it means that the government treats people more or less as a father treats a child: with care but condescension. Knowing that some individuals are too shortsighted, too ill-informed, or simply unwilling to face reality, the wise and benevolent government makes sure that everyone reaches retirement age with at least a minimal portion of lifetime earnings left.

Economists are right to be wary of such arguments, for almost anything can be—and has been—rationalized by this type of argument, usually to no good end. When a feeling is so widespread, however, we should at least consider the possibility that it might be right. First, we know from psychological findings on cognitive dissonance that people sometimes stubbornly refuse to believe that unpleasant contingencies, such as a future inability to work, can happen to them.[14] Second, the actuarial and financial calculations necessary for intelligent retirement planning are difficult and probably beyond the capabilities of most people, even if we ignore the pervasive uncertainties, which put them beyond everyone's capabilities. For example, an experimental study of retirement savings by business and economics students by Johnson, Kotlikoff, and Samuelson (1987) found that errors and inconsistencies were the rule, not the exception. Third, myopia is probably one of the most common, and least pernicious, of all human failings. It has often been pointed out that most people reach retirement age with little in the way of financial assets, and many have interpreted this as evidence of myopia. Interestingly, however, the subjects in Johnson, Kotlikoff, and Samuelson's experiment typically oversaved.

Yet it is not clear that any of these arguments is really compelling. First, cognitive dissonance certainly applies to death and ill health at least as much as to retirement. Yet with only a few exceptions, the government does not provide life and health insurance.[15]

Second, while actuarial calculations are admittedly complex, so too are many other calculations that we leave to individuals. (We know, for example, that you need to be a keen intuitive physicist to play billiards well.) And besides, insurance and pension fund experts have computers programmed to perform the necessary calculations for us.

Third, Martin Feldstein (1985) has argued that, even if the myopia argument is granted, it alone can rationalize only a small social security system.[16] Furthermore, the fact that so many people arrive at age sixty-five with few financial assets may not be evidence of underprovision for old age because almost all these people have pensions from Social Security, many have private pensions, and many still have considerable earning power. In fact, Kotlikoff, Spivak, and Summers (1982) argued that most people in the Retirement History Survey had accumulated savings that were adequate to finance their retirement spending. The key question, of course, is whether these people would have had adequate savings in the absence of Social Security. Kotlikoff, Spivak, and Summers suggest not.

In any case, the irrationality arguments for paternalism are not the only, nor even necessarily the strongest, ones.

Ulysses Paternalism

I call the second concept of paternalism *Ulysses paternalism,* after the ancient mariner of mythology who had himself tied to the mast so as not to be lured by the Sirens' song. The general idea is that people sometimes find it useful to precommit themselves to rules of behavior because they fear they will lack the necessary self-control when the time comes. This need not be considered irrational. Indeed, it is not even paternalism according to the dictionary definition. It is a way for rational adults, making their own decisions, to assure themselves that they will not give in to temptation and do something they will subsequently regret. Unwilling to rely on self-control, they voluntarily and rationally set up a mechanism that locks them into what they deem to be the appropriate long-run decision.[17]

Examples abound: The smoker trying to quit throws away his cigarettes rather than leave himself a choice for later. People deposit money into Christmas clubs at unattractive (once zero) interest rates to ensure that they will have the money when Christmas shopping season rolls around. Millions of Americans voluntarily and knowingly allow the Internal Revenue Service of overwithhold their income taxes in order to receive a refund after April 15.

By perfect analogy, we can imagine that fully rational, but frail, individuals voluntarily arrange for a government institution to tax away some of their earnings while young and give it back with interest when old. According to this interpretation, no one imposes a social security program on young workers. They want it as a way of institutionalizing the self-control they fear they lack.

Superficially, this seems an attractive explanation for some form of social security, but there are problems. First, Ulysses paternalism rationalizes funded systems; the intergenerational transfers that come from pay-as-you-go must find their rationale elsewhere. Second, self-control would seem to rationalize only a voluntary pension system, not a mandatory one. Ulysses was not lashed to the mast by the Greek government; he made the arrangement by himself for himself. But people who claim they save enough without Social Security are not allowed to opt out. Again, redistributional motives might help explain why.

Nonetheless, I think the self-control idea helps explain the broad support the U.S. Social Security system enjoys. People find it a useful way to precommit themselves to retirement savings.

Filialism as an Externality

My third form of paternalism is really the opposite of paternalism. I will display the limits of my Latin scholarship by calling it *filialism,* meaning that the young make decisions on behalf of the old.

The central hypothesis behind filialism is that the young are distressed by seeing the old live in penury, even if their elders have brought the problem on themselves by undersaving. This is more than just a plausible hypothesis; it captures, I think, at least one of the main motives behind the founding of social security programs. Filial devotion creates an externality, for consumption by the old bestows benefits not just on the old, but also on the young. And, as usual, an externality creates a free-rider problem with which voluntary exchange through markets cannot cope. In this case, members of each generation know that succeeding generations will care for them in old age if necessary and so have an incentive to undersave. Since every generation has the same incentive, society winds up saving too little if all saving decisions are left to the free market.

Social security is a way out, for it provides for the sustenance of each older generation by institutionalizing intergenerational transfers rather than relying on the individual generosity of the young. And notice that if the concern of the young is not just for their own parents but for the older generation in general, filialism justifies a mandatory, public program on which no one can free ride.

Furthermore, Michael Veall (1986) has argued that what I am calling filialism explains why social security systems are almost always financed on a pay-as-you-go basis. One reason is that when a pay-as-you-go system is started, members of the initial older generation receive transfers, which benefits both the young and the old. A funded system would not pay benefits until the current young were old. A second reason is that pay-as-you-go has a kind of social stability that a funded system lacks. In a funded system, each generation provides for its own retirement. It therefore retains the incentive to abrogate social security when young and free ride on the generosity of its successors. But under pay-as-you-go, each generation has (part of) its retirement consumption financed by younger generations. Any generation that abrogates the social compact when young will lose not only the benefits it derives from the consumption of the old, but also its own future claims to social security benefits.

Finally, as I suggested earlier, the externality argument explains why an event like the Great Depression might lead to the establishment of a social security system. The young are distressed by the underconsumption of the old, regardless of whether it stems from improvidence or from an adverse random shock that wipes out accumulated savings. When such a shock occurs, the need to create social security suddenly becomes more acute.

Summary

In the end, I can offer no monolithic explanation of, nor justification for, social security. Economists prefer explanations based on efficiency, and there is at least a live possibility that the market for private annuities fails because of adverse selection. Even if not, the government can offer indexed annuities that private insurers cannot, although a simpler solution would be to issue indexed bonds for private insurance companies to buy. Finally, a social security system indexed to wages helps individuals diversify their portfolios. Each of these arguments provides a potential economic rationale for public pensions on strict efficiency grounds. However, none is totally persuasive, none explains why the program is redistributive, only the first (adverse selection) explains why participation is compulsory, and only the last (risk diversification) calls for a pay-as-you-go social security system.

Redistributive goals, which can hardly be left to the market, take us farther in understanding social security. The desire to redistribute income across generations explains the attraction of pay-as-you-go financing and can also be rationalized on egalitarian grounds if the economy anticipates future productivity growth or has recently experienced an adverse event like the Great Depression. To make a pension system distributionally neutral, you must have a progressive benefit structure to compensate for mortality differentials by income class. And the state is probably the only institution that can enforce such a benefit structure. Furthermore, general egalitarian principles can easily rationalize a social security system that redistributes lifetime earnings in favor of the lower income classes. And who doubts that New Dealers held such principles dear?

Finally, many societies probably fear that people will not provide enough for their old age. If the reason is irrational myopia, social security is perhaps justified on paternalistic grounds. But this justification comes uneasily to a believer in democracy. Lack of self-control provides a more comfortable rationale for public pensions, since people are seen as voluntarily committing themselves to what then is a forced savings plan only *ex post,* not *ex ante.* Participation in social security is not voluntary, however. (Here the adverse selection problem is probably germane.) Finally, what looks like a paternalistic attitude toward those who do not save enough for their retirement can be viewed as a rational response to an externality from consumption of the old to utility of the young. This rationale for social security explains why participation is mandatory, why benefits are paid only in annuities (and only to those who earn little or nothing), and why financing is on a pay-as-you-go basis. Furthermore, it turns what seems to be a paternalistic motive for social security into an efficiency motive. That is bound to please economists; no one else cares.

Notes

1. It does, however, intervene to support home ownership in a variety of ways.
2. The currently projected buildup of the OASDI trust fund is a major exception.
3. Only about 2 percent of the people in the Longitudinal Retirement History Survey owned individual annuities. See Friedman and Sjogren 1980.
4. See Eckstein, Eichenbaum, and Peled 1985; Abel 1985.
5. This argument is made by Blinder (1986) and by Munnell and Grolnic (1986).
6. See, for example, Blinder 1980.
7. See Diamond 1977, 296.
8. This is my interpolation from their Table 1A, based on a single-earner, middle-income couple.
9. Of course, we would rather redistribute lifetime well-being. Lifetime income is an imperfect proxy for lifetime well-being for a variety of reasons, including limits on the ability to borrow against future income. Still, it seems likely to be a better proxy than current income.
10. For example, Social Security pays transfers to double-dippers who, since they work in covered employment only a few years, look poor by Social Security's definitions even though they might be quite prosperous according to a more comprehensive definition of lifetime income.
11. The man is assumed to earn two thirds of the family total.
12. The Boskin et al. (1986) calculations omit some special benefits for children of deceased fathers.
13. Actually, it is not quite full-time motherhood that is subsidized, since childless wives receive the subsidies, while full-time mothers without husbands do not.
14. See, for example, Akerlof and Dickens 1982, which contains several references to the research of psychologists.
15. Significantly, the major exceptions are part of the Social Security program: the survivor death benefit and Medicare.

16. Interestingly, a bigger social security system is warranted in Feldstein's model if a portion of the population is 100 percent myopic than if everyone is partly myopic. For details, see Feldstein 1985.

17. The basic idea is discussed in economic contexts in Thaler and Shefrin 1981.

References

Abel, Andrew B. 1985. "Capital Accumulation and Uncertain Lifetimes with Adverse Selection." National Bureau of Economic Research Working Paper No. 1664.

Akerlof, George A., and William T. Dickens. 1982. "The Economic Consequences of Cognitive Dissonance." *American Economic Review* Vol. 72 (June): 307–19.

Blinder, Alan S. 1980. "The Consumer Price Index and the Measurement of Recent Inflation." *Brookings Papers on Economic Activity* 2: 539–65.

Blinder, Alan S. 1986. "A Way to Free Small Savers from the 'Casino Society.'" *Business Week* (December 8): 22.

Boskin, Michael J., Laurence J. Kotlikoff, Douglas J. Puffert, and John B. Shoven. 1986. "Social Security: A Financial Appraisal Across and Within Generations." National Bureau of Economic Research Working Paper No. 1891.

Diamond, Peter A. 1977. "A Framework for Social Security Analysis." *Journal of Public Economics* 8: 275–98.

Eckstein, Zvi, Martin Eichenbaum, and Dan Peled. 1985. "Uncertain Lifetimes and the Welfare Enhancing Properties of Annuity Markets and Social Security." *Journal of Public Economics* 26, no. 3 (April): 303–26.

Feldstein, Martin. 1985. "The Optimal Level of Social Security Benefits." *Quarterly Journal of Economics* 100, no. 2 (May): 303–20.

Friedman, Benjamin, and Mark Warshawsky. 1985. "Annuity Prices and Saving Behavior in the United States." National Bureau of Economic Research Working Paper No. 1683.

Friedman, Joseph, and Jane Sjogren. 1980. "Assets of the Elderly as They Retire." Mimeo: Social Security Administration.

Hurd, Michael D., and John B. Shoven. 1985. "The Distributional Impact of Social Security." In *Pensions, Labor, and Individual Choice*, edited by David A. Wise. Chicago: University of Chicago Press, 193–221.

Johnson, Stephen, Laurence J. Kotlikoff, and William Samuelson. 1987. "Can People Compute? An Experimental Test of the Life Cycle Consumption Model." Mimeo: Boston University, January.

Kotlikoff, Laurence J., Avia Spivak, and Lawrence Summers. 1982. "The Adequacy of Savings." *American Economic Review* 72, no. 5 (December): 1056–69.

Merton, Robert C. 1983. "On the Role of Social Security as a Means for Efficient Risk Sharing in an Economy Where Human Capital Is Not Tradable." In *Financial Aspects of the United States Pension System*, edited by Zvi Bodie and John B. Shoven. Chicago: University of Chicago Press, 325–58.

Munnell, Alicia H., and Joseph B. Grolnic. 1986. "Should the U.S. Government Issue Index Bonds?" *New England Economic Review* (September/October): 3–21.

Summers, Lawrence H. 1983. "Observations on the Indexation of Old Age Pensions." In *Financial Aspects of the United States Pension System*, 231–58.

Thaler, Richard H., and H.M. Shefrin. 1981. "An Economic Theory of Self-Control." *Journal of Political Economy* 89, no. 2 (April): 392–406.

Veall, Michael R. 1986. "Public Pensions as Optimal Social Contracts." *Journal of Public Economics* 31, no. 2 (November): 237–51.

Comment

Andrew B. Abel

Jerry Green and Alan Blinder have provided us with interesting perspectives on the reasons for a social security system. Although the details and style of their chapters are quite different, they deal with some of the same basic themes. Each sets out to explain, within the paradigms of economic analysis, why so many countries have social security systems, and in particular why these systems are run on a pay-as-you-go basis rather than on a fully funded basis.

Blinder's chapter is an extremely well written critical survey of several strands of the academic literature on social insurance in general and the social security systems in particular. The chapter displays the broad perspective and is laced with the wit that readers of Blinder's work have come to expect. Blinder's mission was to explain and evaluate the existing literature rather than to develop and analyze a new model. While there are nits that could be picked, I find myself in general agreement with Blinder's assessments of several aspects of the literature.

In contrast to Blinder's broad-brush approach, Green focuses on a specific aspect of pay-as-you-go social security that has received little attention to date. In particular, Green develops a theoretical model to analyze the role of social security in mitigating the risk associated with being part of a large cohort rather than a small cohort. As members of the baby boom generation know all too well, there are costs associated with being part of an unusually large cohort. Green's model captures two aspects of these costs: Members of a large cohort tend to have low real wages because the capital-labor ratio tends to be low when this cohort is of working age; when they are old, members of a large cohort earn a low rate of return on capital because the capital-labor ratio is high. An additional disadvantage of being part of a large cohort is that when this cohort is retired, the younger generation of workers might not be willing to continue to support a pay-as-you-go social security system. This particular cost is alluded to by Blinder when he shows the dependence of the social security tax rate on the ratio of retirees to workers. The prospect of high social security taxes threatens the continued viability of the system. Whether the U.S. Social Security system will continue to be viable is the fundamental question facing us as we look to the twenty-first century. Unfortunately, Green's analysis does not touch on this aspect of demographic uncertainty.

Both chapters stress the important role of the pay-as-you-go social security system as a system for transferring resources across generations. In contrast, a fully funded social security system would not transfer resources across generations. The particular reasons given for intergenerational transfers differ in the two chapters: Blinder's explanation is based on what he calls *filialism*, which is the notion that people obtain utility from the consumption of their parents. He cites an interesting paper by Michael Veall that examines social security in the context of filialism. Green motivates intergenerational transfers as a type of insurance against the bad luck of being born into a large cohort.

While both chapters focus on the intergenerational resource sharing or risk spreading of pay-as-you-go social security, they do not emphasize an important macroeconomic aspect of pay-as-you-go social security—that social security policy is an important component of national saving policy. This point is made emphatically in a famous article by Martin Feldstein (1974). The link between social security and savings is quite simple. A transfer of income from workers to retirees allows retirees to increase their consumption but does not necessarily induce workers to reduce their consumption. The reason that workers might not reduce their consumption is that they anticipate receiving social security payments when they are old and hence have a reduced need or incentive to save. The precise response of workers to a social security tax depends on the details of the economic environment, but the increased consumption of the beneficiary retirees will usually exceed any decrease in consumption of the workers. Thus, national consumption is increased, which means that national saving and national capital accumulation are decreased.

As a matter of economic theory, Feldstein's conclusion that social security crowds out the capital stock is not as clear cut as I make it sound. In an equally famous paper, Robert Barro (1974) argues that fiscal policies such as pay-as-you-go social security would not affect national saving or indeed any aspect of behavior. His argument rests on the assumption that each person is altruistic in the sense that he or she obtains utility directly from his or her own consumption and from the utility of his or her heirs. Thus, if a dollar is taken from each worker and a payment is given to each retiree, Barro has argued that each retiree will maintain his or her originally planned consumption and will simply pass along the increased social security benefit to his or her heir(s) in the form of a bequest. In this way, individuals are able to undo the effects of social security, and Barro argues that they would choose to do so.

Barro's argument invites the following question: What is it in the models of Blinder and Green that makes it possible for the government to effectively transfer resources intergenerationally? The answer in Green's model is obvious. He has simply assumed that individuals are selfish and do not care about anything except their own consumption. He states that accounting for altruism would require a reformulation of his analysis. [Although I have not seen Green's formal model,[1] my hunch is that altruism of the Barro variety would negate Green's results.] The argument is that if individuals care about the utility of their heirs as well as about their own consumption, they will take it upon themselves to share cohort risks across the generations of their own families.

The reason for the effectiveness of governmental redistribution across generations in Blinder's model (i.e., Veall's model) is more subtle. I think that the reason, if valid, has something to do with binding nonnegativity constraints on private intergenerational transfers.

A strength of Blinder's chapter is that it presents a plausible economic explanation, based on the concept of filialism, of why the U.S. Social Security system was introduced during the Great Depression. His explanation is that the cohorts of older workers were especially hard hit by the Depression. This loss in income came near the end of their working lives and thus did not allow them a sufficient time to recoup the unexpectedly large losses in lifetime income associated with the Depression. Because these workers, and indeed several later cohorts of workers, were substantially hurt by the Depression, the introduction of an intergenerational transfer system made all cohorts better off. It permitted the cohorts of older workers to increase their consumption and thus directly raised their utility. In addition, the cohorts of younger workers benefited both from the increased consumption of the older workers (as a consequence of filialism) and from the prospect of future Social Security benefits.

There is an alternative explanation, which is also based on private intergenerational transfer motives, but in the opposite direction of Blinder's filialism. Suppose that individuals have altruistic bequest motives of the type discussed by Barro. That is, individuals obtain utility from the utility of their heirs (rather than from their parents) as well as from their own consumption. Provided that individuals are planning to make positive bequests to their heirs, an intergenerational transfer of resources will have no effect because the older generation will simply offset the transfer by adjusting its bequests. However, this irrelevance of transfer policy (which Buchanan (1976) has dubbed the Ricardian Equivalence Theorem) depends on the fact that older consumers are planning to leave positive bequests.

It is quite possible that individuals with so-called altruistic bequest motives would like to leave negative bequests. For instance, even though an individual cares about the utility of his children, it might be that his children will be sufficiently richer than he is and that the extra utility of a dollar's consumption by the older consumer exceeds the extra utility he could get by giving a dollar to his heirs. Not only is this outcome a theoretical possibility, it was probably a widespread actuality during the Depression. That is, individuals who had been planning to save for their retirement and leave the residual to their heirs saw their tangible wealth and lifetime earning prospects dramatically reduced with the onset and long duration of the Depression. It then became optimal for these people to leave negative bequests, but there is no developed mechanism for leaving negative bequests to one's own heirs—or to anyone else's heirs, for that matter.

Now introduce pay-as-you-go Social Security, which is a device by which consumers can effect their desired negative bequests. Any consumers who planned to leave positive bequests would not consume the newly introduced Social Security benefits. But those consumers who wanted to leave negative bequests in order to consume more themselves could increase their consumption to the extent of their Social Security income, and thus enjoy a higher level of utility.

An added dimension to the political economy of national saving policy has been stressed in a paper by Alex Cukierman and Allan Meltzer (1986). Cukierman and Meltzer point out that if fiscal policy reduces capital accumulation, it will tend to reduce real wages and increase the rate of return to capital. As I mentioned above, social security is an example of a fiscal policy that reduces capital accumulation, and hence tends to reduce real wages and increase the return to capital. The reduction in real wages will tend to make people with a relatively large amount of human capital opponents of social security; the increase in the return to capital would tend to make people with relatively large amounts of physical capital supporters of social security. In addition, of course, those consumers who would like to leave negative bequests would favor social security. During the Depression, many consumers were thrust into the position of wanting to leave negative bequests, and thus the constituency for social security was greatly increased.

Green's chapter does not appear to offer a satisfactory explanation of the introduction of Social Security during the Depression. His paper is about the risks associated with cohort size. While the Depression was undeniably a terrible event, Green's model focuses on a different bad event—being born during a baby boom. More substantively, Green's model is presumably a model of selfish consumers. In this model, older consumers would always vote to initiate a pay-as-you-go social security system. Whether younger workers would vote to institute social security depends on a cost-benefit calculation comparing the taxes paid when young with the prospective benefits to be received when old. Roger Gordon and Hal Varian (1985) have argued that a system of fiscal transfers designed to share intergenerational risk among selfish consumers would be most likely to end, rather than begin, in periods requiring large payments from the young to the old, such as the Depression. Although Green's model is not identical to the Gordon-Varian model, it does analyze intergenerational risk sharing among selfish consumers. It is difficult to see how this model could be used to explain the fact that Social Security began, rather than ended, during the Great Depression.

Finally, let me suggest some evidence to help choose between the gift motive from children to parents arising from filialism emphasized by Blinder and the bequest motive from parents to children that I discussed above. Blinder points out that very few individual life annuities are sold in the United States and claims that adverse selection could not be severe enough to account for this fact. A simple explanation is that people have bequest motives, and thus even if annuities were offered on an actuarially fair basis, individuals might not purchase them. Therefore, as suggested in the study by Friedman and Warshawsky (1985), which is cited by Blinder, the fact that there is very little participation in the individual life annuity market is suggestive of a bequest motive on the part of consumers. In the absence of a bequest motive of some sort,[2] consumers would choose to fully annuitize their wealth. Furthermore, consumers with Blinder's filialism would not buy life insurance, but consumers with a bequest motive would buy life insurance. Thus, while I agree with Blinder that some form of intergenerational altruism or filialism is important, I think that the fact that annuity markets are thin while life insurance thrives points to a bequest motive rather than filialism.

Notes

1. These comments are based on the incomplete draft of the paper that was available at the time of the conference.

2. Bernheim, Shleifer, and Summers (1985) analyze a manipulative bequest motive in which parents do not care about the utility of children but use the prospect of a bequest as a means for inducing children to behave as the parents desire.

References

Barro, Robert J. 1974. "Are Government Bonds Net Wealth?" *Journal of Political Economy* 82, no. 2 (November/December): 1095–1117.

Bernheim, B. Douglas, Andrei Shleifer, and Lawrence Summers. 1985. "The Strategic Bequest Motive." *Journal of Political Economy* 93, no. 6 (December): 1045–76.

Buchanan, James. 1976. "Barro on the Ricardian Equivalence Theorem." *Journal of Political Economy* 84, no. 2 (April): 337–42.

Cukierman, Alex, and Allan Meltzer. 1986. "A Political Theory of Government Debt and Deficits in a Neo Ricardian Framework." Mimeo, Carnegie Mellon University.

Feldstein, Martin S. 1974. "Social Security, Induced Retirement, and Aggregate

Capital Accumulation." *Journal of Political Economy* 82, no. 5 (September/October): 905–26.

Freidman, Benjamin M., and Mark Warshawsky. 1985. "Annuity Prices and Saving Behavior in the United States." National Bureau of Economic Research Working Paper No. 1683.

Gordon, Roger H., and Hal R. Varian. 1985. "Intergenerational Risk Sharing." Mimeo, University of Michigan.

Comment

Robert D. Paul

Professors Blinder and Green have eloquently spelled out a number of reasons why the U.S. Social Security system has worked so well as a method of delivering retirement income to the many millions of people who are now receiving benefits. This intergenerational transfer mechanism has worked because the U.S. population has been growing in all the years since 1935, when the program was enacted. Accordingly, every retired generation has received benefits that are much larger than could have been purchased by the employee payroll taxes allocated to finance the program. Sometimes this has been described as a rate of return on these taxes. That rate of return has been very competitive with other investment opportunities. As the growth rate of the U.S. population slows, and in anticipation of the baby boomers beginning to retire early in the next century, some new questions arise. It is these questions that must be reflected upon as this century draws to a close.

As a matter of policy, we are departing from a strict pay-as-you-go method of financing by accumulating reserves for the next twenty-five years or so in order to lessen the impact of the baby boomers' retirement on the payroll tax. The Social Security tax is now higher than it needs to be to pay current retirement benefits. The excess is being invested so that the reserve will grow even larger. The expectation is that the reserve will be used, beginning in 2010, to help pay benefits to the much larger cohort of retirees who will then begin to retire. If all were to proceed as planned, that reserve would be depleted, and the Social Security system would revert to pay-as-you-go financing well into the next century when the last baby boomer dies.

Do we have the political will to accumulate these reserves? Will there be pressure to spend these reserves on other socially desirable needs? Will there be an attempt to reduce the payroll tax instead? What are the economic consequences of these alternatives? A detailed analysis of these questions would be a welcome addition to the literature.

While arguments have been offered as to why Social Security is best funded on a pay-as-you-go basis, there has been little study of the advantages of prefunding retirement income in the private sector, thereby creating investment capital for our savings-starved economy. Many scholars believe that Social Security reduces savings. If so, should more of the responsibility for retirement income be shifted to the private sector? What are the economic trade-offs of these two alternatives?

Neither chapter acknowledges the existence of a growing network of pension and other tax-deferred methods of accumulating retirement income, including thrift and saving plans, 401(k) plans, profit-sharing plans, and Employee Stock Ownership plans. These plans have grown rapidly since the end of World War II and now cover nearly 60 percent of all the workers in private industry and virtually all state, local, and federal government employees. In private industry, coverage is the highest in unionized industries, in more prosperous industries, and among workers whose earnings are at or above the national average wage. Workers earning less than $15,000 a year are much less likely to be covered by a pension plan than those earning more than that. By itself, Social Security does not provide adequate income to keep a retired worker who has earned wages at the $15,000 level during his or her career off the poverty rolls.

Suggestions have been offered that the Social Security program should be amended to increase the benefits for lower-paid workers. That would require a higher payroll tax, general taxation financing, or a combination of both. Others have pointed out that this would place an additional burden on those employers who already sponsor a private pension plan for their workers and who do not need additional Social Security benefits. In response, others have proposed that the federal government mandate that all employers provide a minimum level of pension benefit for their workers. It would work much like a minimum wage. That alternative would not impose any additional cost on those employers who already provide a private pension plan but would impose a cost on those employers who do not.

Filling this gap in retirement income for lower-paid workers could remove many more retirees from the poverty rolls. The gap is about 15 percent of pay that should be replaced in retirement but is not now being replaced. The burden falls unevenly on women, who are both more likely to be in the lower-wage category and more likely to live longer in retirement. More and more women in retirement are slipping into poverty. Mandating a minimum layer of private pensions or improving Social Security benefits at the lower wage levels would do much to improve the situation. But if the choice is to improve Social Security, another look at how it treats women is in order.

A married woman who does not work is treated more favorably than one who does work but does not earn enough to qualify for a benefit that is more than one half of her husband's. In addition, women who are divorced can be left with an inadequate retirement income. Various solutions to this problem have been offered, including earnings sharing between wives and husbands for Social Security purposes and establishment of a two-tier system. A two-tier system would break the current Social Security payments into two pieces or tiers. The first tier would not be related to earnings. Instead it would be a flat monthly payment of perhaps $400 a month for all retirees. Both women and men would receive the $400 monthly payment when they retire at age 65 or later or upon attaining age 65, if they have not been working. The second tier, based on earnings, would permit a woman with an intermittent career to supplement the $400 a month minimum based on her career earnings. The two-tier approach would break the link between benefit payments and marital status. A woman would be paid $400 a month even if she is not married or has not been employed or both. Now a woman who is married gets an amount equal to one half her husband's benefit even if she never worked. A woman would also get an earnings related benefit if she had been employed for any length of time prior to age 65. A discussion of these issues would be a worthwhile agenda for future scholarship.

Part II

Financial Status of the Elderly: Current and Twenty-first Century

3
Forecasting the Consumption and Wealth of the Elderly

Michael D. Hurd

Forecasts of the economic status of the working-age population mainly depend on the trend of wages because the major economic asset of workers is their human capital. If the trend in wages is stable, a good forecast can be made from the economic status of today's workers. To forecast the economic status of the elderly requires further consideration because the economic status of the elderly today is probably not a good guide to their future economic status. Each cohort of the elderly faces different economic conditions during their working lives, which affect not only their lifetime incomes, but also their savings. For example, the current elderly had substantial increases in Social Security and Medicare/Medicaid, whereas future cohorts will probably have much more stability. In addition, each cohort has a different rate of return on savings, and changes in mortality rates probably have some effect on the rate of wealth decumulation.

For all these reasons, a forecast of consumption and wealth based on an extrapolation of trends is likely to be unreliable. Even if such a forecast were reliable, it would not be as interesting as one based on an economic model because it would be difficult to investigate how future wealth will vary as the economic environment varies. For example, forecasts based on past trends of economic variables cannot be used to learn how consumption will change if Social Security benefits are changed because there is no economic model for consumption. Similarly, trend analysis cannot forecast how a change in mortality rates will affect consumption.

In this chapter, I study the future consumption and wealth of the elderly by projecting what the consumption and wealth of the retirement-age elderly will be. The projections are based on an economic model of the consumption behavior of single elderly. The model has been estimated from the Longitudinal Retirement History Survey (RHS), a panel data set that spans the years 1969 to 1979. (See Appendix 3A for a discussion of the RHS.) Given the model,

Financial support from the Commonwealth Fund is gratefully acknowledged. Many thanks to Bryan Boudreau for superb research assistance.

initial economic variables, and parameter values, I can forecast the consumption and wealth paths of each individual in the data set. By changing the initial economic variables to reflect steady growth in wealth at retirement, the consumption and wealth paths of future cohorts also can be estimated. Taken together, all the forecasts generate the distribution of consumption and wealth over all ages in future years.

This method of forecasting has a number of advantages. First, it is based on a behavioral model, so one can study the reaction of the elderly to changes in the economic environment. Second, it automatically accounts for differences across cohorts in economic resources. It produces distributions of consumption and wealth rather than just averages, allowing one, for example, to study the fraction of the population in poverty. Third, because the RHS has an almost exhaustive accounting of economic resources, the wealth and consumption measures are more complete than those from other sources. Finally, the estimated consumption paths allow one to define welfare measures that are based on consumption rather than on income. These measures are certainly more appropriate for the elderly than income-based measures.

Consumption and Wealth of the Elderly

The future economic status of a cohort of the elderly depends on initial conditions, the future economic environment, the choices the individuals make, and stochastic events. Studying the future consumption and wealth of retirement-age rather than preretirement-age elderly is simplified because the RHS provides a solid estimate of the resources of the retired; whereas determining the resources of preretirement-age elderly requires an estimate of the date of retirement. Further, many of the elderly have a rather stable economic environment because most of their assets (housing, Social Security, and Medicare/Medicaid) are indexed. Indeed, the elderly apparently were better protected against the fall in real income during the 1970s than the rest of the population (Hurd and Shoven 1983).

In this chapter, I give two kinds of forecasts. In the first, I concentrate on how the economic status of the elderly changes with age as a result of their consumption decisions; initial conditions are given. In the second kind of forecast, I change the initial conditions of each cohort to reflect future economic growth.

The initial conditions for the first set of forecasts are the distribution of resources, age, and household structure in the 1979 RHS. Using a utility-based model of consumption behavior that I have estimated over the ten-year panel data of the RHS, I forecast the consumption and wealth trajectories of each household in the RHS. Because of mortality, each household will, with a certain probability, produce households of different composition in each future period. Thus, the number of households defined by composition and assets will grow in each time period, but the weight attached to each type will shrink. From the forecasts, a standing population of the elderly is generated based on a steady-state economy in which each cohort will reach the age of the 1979 RHS population with the same distribution of assets and household composition as the 1979 population. From this standing population, I study the distribution of assets, consumption, and poverty status at each age. One might say that I am forecasting the condition of the 1979 RHS population at each future age.

This forecasting method has the advantage of distinguishing initial conditions from life cycle behavior after retirement. It has the further advantage that the calculations produce a consumption-based measure of economic well-being. This is especially important for the elderly because income, the usual measure of economic well-being, is not a good measure of their economic position, as life cycle considerations indicate that at some age they will consume part of their capital. Therefore, their consumption can be very different from their income. Although wealth is probably a better measure of economic position than income, it is not completely satisfactory either because of the importance of Social Security and other annuities. When these sources of income are exogenous, it is not obvious how to aggregate them with other forms of wealth.

The model that is used to forecast consumption and wealth is based on utility maximization under mortality uncertainty. The model works for single people but not for couples because the utility function of the household changes according to future mortality realizations. Although the model of singles is appropriate for studying the future economic status of the single people in the RHS, it is not complete because the couples will generate new singles as they age, and in order to project the economic status of the new singles, their initial condition must be known. My ad hoc solution is to assume that couples will consume their bequeathable wealth at the average rate that was observed for retired couples in the ten-year RHS. This rate was 0.016 per year.

The second set of forecasts comes from changing the initial conditions in a way that is consistent with steady growth in household wealth and annuities, and from changing the assumptions about mortality rates. The first of these forecasts, to be discussed in more detail below, generates the wealth and consumption distributions that would be found in an economy with steady productivity growth. In such an economy, the younger cohorts will enter retirement with more wealth than the older cohorts had when they entered retirement. Although the growth rates are necessarily ad hoc, they seem to be consistent with historical growth rates. When mortality rates change, the age structure and the distribution of households between single people and couples will change. In addition, consumption will change because of the change in mortality uncertainty.

Because all the forecasts depend on the quality of the model and the parameter estimates, I discuss in Appendix 3A the specification and estimation of the economic model in a condensed form. More details can be found in Hurd 1986. I also outline the ideas behind the model in Appendix 3A.

Suppose a retired individual wants to maximize lifetime utility when the date of death is uncertain. Utility depends on consumption during each time period and on any bequests the person might leave should he or she die. Economic resources are initial bequeathable wealth and annuities, which include Social Security, Medicare/Medicaid, and private pensions. It can be shown that the solution to this utility maximization problem implies that desired consumption will depend on the parameters of the utility function, mortality rates, bequeathable wealth, entire time path of annuities, and strength of the bequest motive. I used the solution to the utility-maximization problem along with data from the ten years of the RHS to estimate the parameters of the utility function. Given the parameters, the economic resources, and the utility-based model, I can forecast the future consumption and wealth paths of each individual in the RHS.

Forecasting Consumption and Wealth

Before discussing the forecasts, I give the rationale behind the measures of economic welfare and poverty that are found in the tables. The most common measure of economic well-being is income. This measure is appropriate for someone with few resources except human capital, but it is not appropriate for the elderly because almost all their resources are nonhuman wealth, including annuities and pensions. Any definition of well-being or poverty should take this into account. For example, the Bureau of Labor Statistics (BLS) defines poverty according to observed nominal income. For the elderly, there are at least two weaknesses in this definition. First, if the rate of inflation is positive, using nominal income from capital implies real capital decumulation because the interest rate that is used to calculate the income is nominal. Thus, the welfare implications of nominal income are obscured. Second, according to the life cycle hypothesis, the income of the elderly is not a good welfare indicator because some wealth should be consumed at an advanced age. I use two measures of well-being. The first, an income-based measure, is the sum of annuities and real income from capital rather than nominal income from capital. I use a real rate of return on capital of 0.03. The second measure of well-being is based on estimated consumption. From these measures, I calculate the fraction in poverty by comparing each individual's real income and real consumption to the poverty level. I use the poverty levels given by the BLS: $3,479 for one person over the age of sixty-five and $4,388 for two persons over the age of sixty-five, both figures in 1979 dollars.

Any measure of the welfare of the elderly must address the problem of placing a value on Medicare/Medicaid. It certainly is of some value to the elderly; were there no such program, the elderly would spend more of their own wealth on medical care. Rather than speculate about the value, I present two sets of consumption and income measures. The first follows Hurd and Shoven (1983); it includes a value roughly equal to the average transfer through the Medicare/Medicaid system to each eligible person. The idea is that the transfer is the value of a fair medical insurance policy given each year to those who are eligible. The second set of results excludes any valuation for Medicare/Medicaid.

Steady-State Forecasts

The first kind of forecast allows no change in economic resources as successive cohorts reach retirement age. Each cohort has the distribution of resources found in the 1979 RHS. For example, the cohort reaching seventy years of age in 1983 is assumed to have the same resources as the cohort reaching seventy in 1979. This steady-state forecast is useful as a base case with which forecasts based on changes in initial conditions can be compared. Of course, given the essentially static nature of the economy over the past decade and the stabilization of Social Security, the base case might be of interest in and of itself.

Table 3–1 includes forecasts of the consumption, income, and wealth of elderly couples in the year 2003. Consumption is defined to be income plus the change of wealth. The simple model of the wealth decumulation of couples and the constant rate of interest of 3 percent imply that consumption in each time period will simply be the annuity flow plus 4.6 percent of wealth. As discussed in the appendix, wealth includes all the usual financial components plus human capital and net housing equity. In the table, the base year is the year in which the simulation began; the final year of the simulation is 2003.

The first line in the table shows what the economic variables of the 1979 RHS couples will be in 2003. Initially there were 2,418 couples; according to the 1979 mortality tables, by 2003 there will be just 16 surviving couples. The mean age of the husbands will be 94.1 years and of the wives 91.5. According to the forecast, mean wealth will be $60,890 in 1979 dollars. Annual consumption and income, including an imputation for the value of Medicare/Medicaid, will be $11,638 and $10,519, respectively. The other entries in the first line are consumption and income, excluding any value for Medicare/Medicaid, and estimates of the fraction in poverty.

The second line of table 3–1 forecasts the economic variables in 2003 when the initial year of the forecast is 1983. In that initial conditions are unchanged from the forecast based on 1979, the forecasts in lines 1 and 2 differ only because the 1979 and 1983 inflation rates differ and because the

Table 3–1
Forecasts for Couples: Base Case
(consumption, income, and wealth in 1979 dollars)

| Base Year | Mean M | Age F | Total # Households | Wealth | Mean ($1979) | | | | | | | |
| | | | | | Medicare/Medicaid Included | | | | Medicare/Medicaid Excluded | | | |
					Consumption	%	Income	%	Consumption	%	Income	%
1979	94.1	91.5	16	60,890	11,638	1	10,519	2	9,845	5	8,725	6
1983	90.4	87.9	79	65,388	11,989	1	10,787	2	10,176	4	8,974	5
1987	86.6	84.2	260	70,416	12,332	1	11,038	2	10,505	4	9,211	5
1991	82.8	80.4	611	75,915	12,699	1	11,303	1	10,863	4	9,467	5
1995	78.9	76.6	1,139	81,545	13,069	1	11,570	1	11,228	4	9,728	5
1999	75.0	72.7	1,777	87,368	13,454	1	11,847	1	11,608	3	10,002	4
2003	71.1	68.8	2,418	93,714	13,877	1	12,154	1	12,029	3	10,306	4
Total	75.9	73.6	6,299	86,600	13,404	1	11,812	1	11,561	4	9,969	4

forecasts in line 1 are over twenty years rather than twenty-four. Of the initial 2,418 couples, 79 will survive until 2003. The mean age of husband and wife will be 90.4 and 87.9 years, respectively.

When the base year is 2003, the forecast begins and ends in 2003; thus, the entries in that line are the actual data of the 1979 RHS couples. Taken together, the lines give an estimate of the wealth, consumption, and income of couples in 2003 under the assumption that in each base year, couples will reach approximately seventy years of age with the distribution of assets that the 1979 RHS couples had. Because of the assumption of steady-state resources, the results also can be interpreted as the expected paths of the economic variables of the 1979 RHS couples as they age.

The last line gives average values over all the age groups. Average consumption and income levels are quite high. Whether or not Medicare/Medicaid is included in consumption and income, the fraction of couples in poverty averaged over all the age groups is small, between 1 and 4 percent. These are smaller fractions than would be found in official statistics on the poverty of the elderly, but the measures used here are different. They include housing, they use a real rate of return, and they are defined over a limited age group. I would argue that these measures are more appropriate for the elderly. According to these measures, the future economic status of elderly couples is good even if there is no upward trend in the initial economic position of the cohorts as they reach retirement age.

The forecasts for singles are based on the consumption model discussed in the appendix. Given the estimated model and initial conditions, the consumption and wealth of each single person in the 1979 RHS can be projected by solving equations 3.5a–3.5d of the appendix. The initial conditions are real annuities, which include Social Security benefits and Medicare/Medicaid; nominal annuities, which include pensions; bequeathable wealth; and the path of mortality rates, which are defined by age, race, and sex. A typical solution is shown in figure 3–1. The wealth and consumption paths of all the 1979 single people will, when weighted by the probabilities of living, give the expected distribution of wealth and consumption not only at each year but also across years.

In a steady-state or static economy, each cohort will reach retirement age with the same resources as the 1979 RHS population. But simply projecting the economic variables of 1979 RHS singles to the year 2003 does not give us a good idea of the economic status of a steady-state population of singles because such a forecast does not take into account that as husbands or wives die, new singles will be added. In that couples are substantially more wealthy than singles, the new singles will be more wealthy than the original singles. During each time period, each couple will generate three other households: a widow, a widower, and a couple, each with a probability that is calculated from the mortality tables. The new widows and widowers have initial conditions that are related to the wealth and annuities of the couple from which they came. This situation is shown in figure 3–2. For example, a couple in

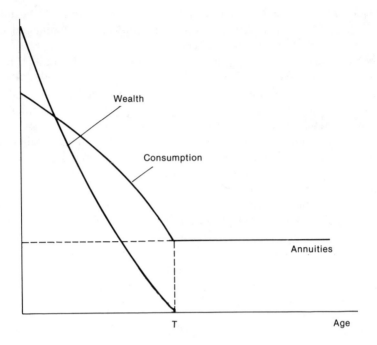

Figure 3–1. Consumption and Wealth Trajectories

1979 will, by 1984, generate four additional households, each of which will have a different wealth level because each is identified by the sex of the survivor and the date of creation.

The wealth of couples will decline each year by 1.6 percent, which is the average rate of real wealth decumulation over the ten years of the RHS. Evidence from the RHS indicates that a number of changes in economic status occur when a husband dies. I assume that all nominal annuities are lost; this is roughly confirmed in the RHS data, as most nominal annuities apparently are pensions without survivor benefits (Hurd and Wise 1987). Human capital also is lost, as it is almost exclusively due to the husband's working. Social Security benefits become 0.67 percent of their former level, which assumes the family's benefit is based on the husband's earnings record. Medicare/Medicaid becomes half its former level. I assume that bequeathable wealth decreases by 32 percent when the husband dies, as this is the average figure over the ten years of the RHS (Hurd and Wise 1987). When the wife dies, I make all the preceding changes in resources except the loss of nominal pensions and human capital.

Table 3–2 lists the projections for all singles, including widows, widowers, and original singles. The table includes compositional changes

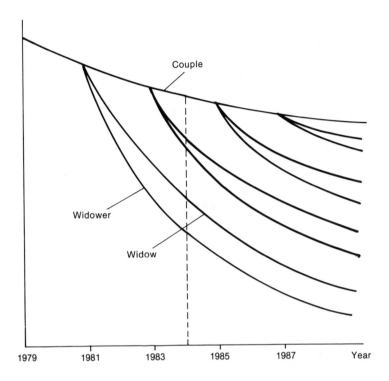

Figure 3–2. Consumption Trajectories of a Couple and Surviving Widow and Widower

caused by the mortality of both husbands and wives. To simplify the discussion, I concentrate here and in the results to follow on the results that exclude Medicare/Medicaid. Singles will have much less wealth than couples: Averaged over all ages, their wealth will be only 21 percent of the wealth of couples. Their income will be about half the income of couples because Social Security, which is a very important component of their income, is much more evenly distributed than wealth. Consumption by singles will average 70 percent of the consumption of couples. This is a consequence of the much more rapid decumulation of singles' wealth. Mortality differentials suggest that a couple will survive, possibly not intact, much longer than a single, meaning that a couple's wealth should decrease more slowly than a single's wealth. Even though average consumption by singles will be quite high, a large fraction of singles will be in poverty. Apparently the distribution of consumption will be highly skewed. The results also point out the important difference between an income-based and a consumption-based measure of poverty: At

Table 3–2
Forecasts for Singles: Base Case
(consumption, income, and wealth in 1979 dollars)

Base Year	Mean M	Age F	Total # Households	Wealth	Mean ($1979)							
					Medicare/Medicaid Included				Medicare/Medicaid Excluded			
					Consumption	%	Income	%	Consumption	%	Income	%
1979	94.3	92.5	762	2,245	5,959	21	5,059	22	5,071	40	4,170	42
1983	90.6	88.9	1,501	4,655	6,731	21	5,140	22	5,829	38	4,239	42
1987	86.8	85.3	2,335	8,000	7,523	20	5,227	23	6,611	36	4,315	42
1991	83.0	81.6	3,001	12,178	8,258	19	5,318	23	7,340	33	4,400	42
1995	79.1	77.9	3,348	13,797	8,993	17	5,411	24	8,068	29	4,486	42
1999	75.1	74.2	3,376	25,321	9,931	14	5,552	23	9,000	24	4,621	42
2003	71.2	70.5	3,179	39,589	11,399	11	5,859	22	10,462	20	4,922	40
Total	79.5	79.2	17,501	18,367	8,963	16	5,441	23	8,041	29	4,519	41

the youngest age, the income-based definition will have twice as many in poverty as the consumption-based definition. According to the income-based definition of poverty, the incidence of poverty will be much higher than the official statistics indicate. In 1983, the official poverty rate for unrelated individuals over the age of sixty-five was 22 percent for men and 28 percent for women. These figures may be compared with the average of 41 percent in table 3–2 based on the income measure of poverty.

At older ages wealth will become small and, of course, average consumption will approach average income. The fractions in poverty in the oldest group will be almost the same by either measure, which implies that a large fraction of singles will have no remaining bequeathable wealth.

Dynamic Forecasts

In the rest of the forecasts, I change the initial conditions of the successive cohorts to reflect economic changes or changes in mortality. I first consider the growth in bequeathable wealth that would accompany steady economic growth. According to Wolff and Marley (1987), real average household wealth, excluding claims to pensions and Social Security, grew by about 2 percent per year from 1949 to 1983. I take this to be the expected growth rate in initial bequeathable wealth of the retirement-age elderly. In principle, the economic status of the elderly in 2003 can be found as follows. The consumption and wealth of 95-year-olds in 2003 can be forecast by the economic model from the initial conditions of the 71-year-olds in the 1979 RHS population. To find the consumption and wealth of 94-year-olds in 2003, I increased the bequeathable wealth of the 71-year-olds in the 1979 RHS population by 2 percent and forecast from 1980 to 2003 their consumption and wealth. This represents the consumption and wealth in 2003 of the cohort that reached seventy-one in 1980. Increasing initial bequeathable wealth by 2 percent and forecasting from 1981 to 2003 yields the distributions of consumption and wealth of 93-year-olds. Continuing in this way, the initial retirement-age conditions of consumption and wealth in 2003 of all cohorts that will be seventy-one through ninety-five years old in 2003 is generated. This method produces the distribution of consumption and wealth by age in 2003. Because of the highly nonlinear response of consumption to changes in bequeathable wealth, the resulting distribution of consumption and wealth is not a simple geometric projection of the original forecasts.

To reduce the very extensive computations, I increased the initial bequeathable wealth of each couple by $(1.02)^4$ every four years and began the forecasts at each of the years 1979, 1983, 1987, and so forth, as in table 3–1. The results, which represent the economic status of couples in the year 2003, are given in table 3–3. Because the increases began after 1979, the oldest cohort has exactly the same economic variables as in the base case. Of course, the greatest change is found in the youngest cohort: Average wealth will be 59 percent higher than in the base case. Because most couples are

Table 3–3
Dynamic Forecasts for Couples: Growth in Bequeathable Wealth
(consumption, income, and wealth in 1979 dollars)

Base Year	Mean M	Age F	Total # Households	Wealth	Mean ($1979)							
					Medicare/Medicaid Included				Medicare/Medicaid Excluded			
					Consumption	%	Income	%	Consumption	%	Income	%
1979	94.1	91.5	16	60,980	11,638	1	10,519	2	9,845	5	8,725	6
1983	90.4	87.9	79	70,575	12,240	1	10,942	2	10,427	4	9,129	5
1987	86.6	84.2	260	82,072	12,896	1	11,387	1	11,069	4	9,560	5
1991	82.8	80.4	611	95,580	13,650	1	11,893	1	11,815	3	10,057	4
1995	78.9	76.6	1,139	110,930	14,491	1	12,451	1	12,650	3	10,610	4
1999	75.0	72.7	1,777	128,443	15,441	1	13,079	1	13,596	3	11,234	4
2003	71.1	68.8	2,418	148,904	16,548	1	13,810	1	14,700	2	11,961	3
Total	75.9	73.6	6,299	127,138	15,366	1	13,028	1	13,523	3	11,184	4

young, average wealth changes averaged over all ages also are large, about 46 percent. Mean consumption, excluding Medicare/Medicaid, will be 16 percent higher; mean income will be 11 percent higher. The large differences between the increase in wealth and the increase in consumption and income reflect the important role annuities, especially Social Security, play in consumption and income. The fractions in poverty, which were already low in table 3–1, will be reduced slightly.

Table 3–4 has the forecasts for singles under growth in the bequeathable wealth of both couples and singles. A comparison with table 3–2 shows a substantial growth in wealth over all ages by 55 percent. Excluding Medicare/Medicaid, average consumption will be 19 percent higher and average income will be 6 percent higher. Poverty levels will not change much because most people near the poverty line have little bequeathable wealth, so proportional increases in wealth have little effect. The older elderly also will not be appreciably affected, as this group has a high poverty rate and comprises a sizeable fraction of the singles. The conclusion from these simulations is that unless economic growth causes more than a proportional change in bequeathable wealth at retirement, there is little hope for large improvements in the poverty rate of singles over the next thirty years.

In a growing economy, one would expect increasing productivity to cause increases in Social Security benefits; that is, as real wages increase, real Social Security taxes and real Primary Insurance Amount (PIA) will increase. It is difficult to know what a reasonable assumption is for increases in real PIA. In line with the results of Wolff and Marley (1987) on household wealth, I assume a growth rate of 2 percent per year, although due to the progressivity of the benefit schedule and the cap on taxable earnings, this might be an overestimate of the effect on PIA. Tables 3–5 and 3–6 have simulations that incorporate the 2 percent growth in PIA.

With a growing PIA, the youngest cohort will have much higher Social Security benefits than the oldest cohort because once an individual's PIA is fixed he or she will have no future increase in benefits. Results for couples are in table 3–5. A comparison with table 3–1 shows a much higher income and consumption on average, which is a reflection of the importance of Social Security benefits in the economic resources of the elderly. Very few will be in poverty, except among the oldest cohort, which under this experiment had no increase in benefits.

Table 3–6 shows the corresponding results for singles. The increases in income and consumption will be substantial in the younger cohorts, and poverty will fall by more than 50 percent. Overall, poverty will fall substantially, especially according to the income measure. Average wealth will be almost unchanged, as the increase in benefits will be almost completely consumed. This result has two causes: First, according to the model, when annuities increase, the rate of consumption from bequeathable wealth increases; second, the effect of a bequest motive is small.

Changes in mortality will have a number of effects in this model. The rate

Table 3–4
Dynamic Forecasts for Singles: Growth in Bequeathable Wealth
(consumption, income, and wealth in 1979 dollars)

Mean ($1979)

Base Year	Mean M	Age F	Total # Households	Wealth	Medicare/Medicaid Included				Medicare/Medicaid Excluded			
					Consumption	%	Income	%	Consumption	%	Income	%
1979	94.3	92.5	762	2,245	5,959	21	5,059	22	5,071	40	4,170	42
1983	90.6	88.9	1,501	5,116	6,877	20	5,154	22	5,976	38	4,252	42
1987	86.8	85.3	2,335	9,655	7,973	19	5,276	22	7,061	35	4,365	41
1991	83.0	81.6	3,001	16,130	9,156	18	5,437	23	8,238	32	4,518	41
1995	79.1	77.9	3,348	25,459	10,489	15	5,645	23	9,565	27	4,720	40
1999	75.1	74.2	3,376	39,161	12,130	12	5,967	22	11,200	21	5,036	39
2003	71.2	70.5	3,179	63,118	14,996	10	6,565	20	13,559	17	5,628	35
Total	79.5	79.2	17,501	28,480	10,553	15	5,722	22	9,541	27	4,800	39

Table 3–5
Dynamic Forecasts for Couples: Growth in Social Security
(consumption, income, and wealth in 1979 dollars)

Mean ($1979)

Base Year	Mean M	Age F	Total # Households	Wealth	Medicare/Medicaid Included				Medicare/Medicaid Excluded			
					Consumption	%	Income	%	Consumption	%	Income	%
1979	94.1	91.5	16	60,890	11,638	1	10,519	2	9,845	5	8,725	6
1983	90.4	87.9	79	65,338	12,688	1	11,485	2	10,725	4	9,523	5

	Mean M	Age F	Total # Households	Wealth	Consumption	%	Income	%	Consumption	%	Income	%
1987	86.6	84.2	260	70,416	13,794	1	12,499	1	11,653	3	10,359	4
1991	82.8	80.4	611	75,915	14,990	1	13,594	1	12,662	2	11,266	3
1995	78.9	76.6	1,139	81,545	16,260	1	14,760	1	13,732	2	12,232	2
1999	75.0	72.7	1,777	87,368	17,616	0	16,010	1	14,874	1	13,267	2
2003	71.1	68.8	2,418	97,314	19,091	0	17,368	0	16,119	1	14,395	2
Total	75.7	73.4	6,299	87,982	17,448	0	15,856	1	14,734	13,141	2	

Table 3–6
Dynamic Forecasts for Singles: Growth in Social Security
(consumption, income, and wealth in 1979 dollars)

					Medicare/Medicaid Included				Mean ($1979)	Medicare/Medicaid Excluded			
Base Year	Mean M	Age F	Total # Households	Wealth	Consumption	%	Income	%		Consumption	%	Income	%
1979	94.3	92.5	762	2,245	5,959	21	5,059	22		5,071	40	4,170	42
1983	90.6	88.9	1,501	4,579	7,128	17	5,543	18		6,152	32	4,567	35
1987	86.8	85.3	2,335	7,749	8,347	13	6,055	15		7,279	28	4,987	31
1991	83.0	81.6	3,001	11,614	9,526	11	6,590	13		8,362	24	5,425	28
1995	79.1	77.9	3,348	16,339	10,739	8	7,132	11		9,469	19	5,863	25
1999	75.1	74.2	3,376	23,957	12,316	6	7,727	9		10,933	14	6,344	22
2003	71.2	70.5	3,179	39,589	14,875	5	8,527	9		13,277	9	7,020	18
Total	79.5	79.2	17,501	18,454	10,750	10	7,037	12		9,485	20	5,789	26

of transition from couples to singles will change; the mortality rates of singles will change; and the consumption paths of singles will change. To investigate these effects, I substituted for the 1979 mortality table an estimated mortality table for the year 2000. The base case was simulated again so that I could make *ceteris paribus* comparisons. Table 3–7 shows the new results for couples. Comparison with table 3–1 shows that the mean age will increase by about 0.6 years and the number of households by about 12 percent. The effects on the oldest households will be larger: The fraction of the elderly population in the three oldest categories will increase from 5.6 percent to 9.1 percent. Even though more of the population will live longer, the fraction in poverty will increase only slightly, and the mean wealth will be only marginally lower.

Table 3–8 shows the corresponding results for singles. The mean age will increase by 0.6 years, and the number of households will increase by 11 percent. The fraction of the single population in the three highest age groups will increase from 26 percent to 32 percent. Average wealth will decline only slightly. The fraction in poverty will increase marginally—by 1 percent according to the income-based measure and by about 2 percent according to the consumption-based measure. The increase in life expectancy will cause only a 1 percent decrease in annual income. Consumption, however, will drop by almost 10 percent. The difference in these changes points out, again, that income is probably not a good measure of the economic well-being of the elderly. The large change in consumption that results from using mortality tables that are just twenty-one years apart indicates the importance of accounting for the reactions of individuals to mortality changes. This cannot be done in forecasting methods that rely only on trends, as those methods change only the age and marital status distributions in response to changes in mortality rates.

Conclusions

The economic prospects of elderly couples seem good through the end of the century, as young elderly couples have enough assets and claims to Social Security. Only a small fraction can expect to be in poverty. The prospects of singles, most of whom are widows, are not nearly so bright. On average they can expect to have low wealth and a high incidence of poverty. This is especially true of those who will be very old by the turn of the century. Their economic resources are already fixed, and unless there is an across-the-board increase in Social Security benefits, little can happen to change them. If there is an increase in productivity leading to higher Social Security benefits, the young elderly will benefit considerably by the turn of the century. Under such an assumption, poverty rates among that group can be expected to be low.

Table 3-7
Dynamic Forecasts for Couples: Mortality Changes
(consumption, income, and wealth in 1979 dollars)

Base Year	Mean M	Age F	Total # Households	Wealth	Medicare/Medicaid Included				Mean ($1979)				Medicare/Medicaid Excluded			
					Consumption	%	Income	%					Consumption	%	Income	%
1979	94.3	91.8	48	60,486	11,639	1	10,527	2					9,831	5	8,719	6
1983	90.5	88.1	169	65,047	11,990	1	10,793	2					10,166	4	8,970	5
1987	86.7	84.4	424	69,998	12,319	1	11,032	2					10,486	4	9,198	5
1991	82.8	80.6	820	75,279	12,665	1	11,281	1					10,825	4	9,441	5
1995	78.9	76.7	1,320	80,985	13,037	1	11,547	1					11,193	4	9,704	5
1999	75.0	72.8	1,876	87,114	13,439	1	11,837	1					11,592	4	9,990	4
2003	71.1	68.8	2,418	93,714	13,877	1	12,154	1					12,029	3	10,306	4
Total	76.5	74.2	7,073	85,124	13,310	1	11,745	1					11,466	4	9,901	5

Table 3-8
Dynamic Forecasts for Singles: Mortality Changes
(consumption, income, and wealth in 1979 dollars)

Base Year	Mean M	Age F	Total # Households	Wealth	Medicare/Medicaid Included				Mean ($1979)				Medicare/Medicaid Excluded			
					Consumption	%	Income	%					Consumption	%	Income	%
1979	94.5	92.8	1,280	3,190	6,191	21	5,057	23					5,294	40	4,160	43
1983	90.7	89.2	2,092	5,724	6,848	21	5,131	23					5,941	38	4,224	42
1987	86.9	85.5	2,819	8,801	7,400	20	5,197	24					6,486	36	4,283	43
1991	83.0	81.8	3,274	12,473	7,890	19	5,267	24					6,970	34	4,347	43
1995	79.1	78.0	3,437	17,513	8,530	17	5,363	24					7,604	30	4,437	43
1999	75.1	74.3	3,374	25,524	9,461	15	5,529	24					8,530	25	4,598	42
2003	71.2	70.5	3,179	39,589	10,890	12	5,859	22					9,953	21	4,922	40
Total	80.2	80.3	19,454	18,189	8,471	17	5,388	23					7,549	31	4,466	42

The projections produce four measures of economic well-being, with substantial differences among them. They are summarized in the following table, which gives poverty rates over the 2003 population of elderly. These rates are calculated from those found in tables 3–1 and 3–2.

	Poverty Rate	
	Income-Based	*Consumption-Based*
Medicare/Medicaid Included	17%	12%
Medicare/Medicaid Excluded	31%	22%

The variation in poverty rates is from 12 percent in poverty to 31 percent, depending on the definition. It seems that the consumption-based measure is preferable to the income-based measure because the latter gives no weight to the stock of wealth that is consumed. The differences between the measures that include and exclude Medicare/Medicaid indicate the importance of research into a reasonable valuation of Medicare/Medicaid.

Appendix 3A[1]

I assume that individuals maximize in the consumption path $\{c_t\}$ lifetime utility.

$$\int U(c_t)e^{-\rho t}a_t dt + \int V(w_t)e^{-\rho t}m_t dt \qquad (3.1)$$

in which

$$U(c_t) = c_t^{1-\gamma}/(1-\gamma), \text{ and}$$

$$a_t = 1 - \int_o^t m_s ds$$

is the probability that the individual is alive at t: m_t is the instantaneous mortality rate; ρ is the subjective time rate of discount; r is the real interest rate, which is taken to be known and fixed; and $V(.)$ is the utility from bequests. This formulation of utility maximization with bequests is due to Yaari 1965. The resources available are bequeathable wealth, w_t, and annuities, including pensions, Social Security, and Medicare/Medicaid. Annuities are distinguished from bequeathable wealth in that they cannot be borrowed against and are not bequeathable. The conditions on the utility maximization are that initial wealth, w_0, is given, and that

$$w_t = w_0 e^{rt} + \int_o^t (A_s - c_s)e^{(t-s)r} ds \geq 0 \text{ for all } t, \qquad (3.2)$$

where A_s is the flow of annuities at time s. This formulation differs from the usual intertemporal utility maximization problem in that the annuity stream cannot be summarized by its expected present value. It turns out that because many of the elderly have large annuities relative to their bequeathable wealth, the corner solutions are important. I parameterize the bequest function by assuming that the marginal utility of bequests is constant. This assumption may be defended in several ways. First, from a practical point of view, without such an assumption the model cannot be solved, and the estimation requires a model solution. Second, in other work I have found that the strength of the bequest motive does not seem to depend on the wealth level.[2] Third, variations in the level of wealth cause only small variations in the wealth level of heirs; therefore, the marginal utility of the wealth of heirs will be roughly constant over variations in wealth of the older generation, and one would expect the marginal utility of bequests to be constant.

The Pontryagin necessary conditions associated with this problem are that

$$c_t = A_t, \text{ if } w_t = 0, \tag{3.3}$$

and that

$$c_t^{-\gamma} a_t = c_{t+h}^{-\gamma} a_{t+h} e^{h(r-\rho)} + \alpha \int_t^{t+h} e^{(s-t)(r-\rho)} m_s \, ds \tag{3.4}$$

over an interval $(t, t+h)$ in which $w_t > 0$; α is the constant marginal utility of bequests.

If $\rho > r$, these conditions generate consumption trajectories that slope downward and, unless wealth is very large, wealth trajectories that also slope downward. A typical example is shown in figure 3–1: The consumption path follows equation 3.4 until bequeathable wealth is exhausted at T; then it follows equation 3.3. The present value of the area under the consumption path and above the annuity path equals initial bequeathable wealth. The solution is implicitly defined by:

$$C_T = A_T \tag{3.5a}$$

$$c_0^{-\gamma} = c_t^{-\gamma} a_t e^{t(r-\rho)} + \alpha \int_0^t e^{(r-\rho)s} m_s \, ds \tag{3.5b}$$

$$w_T = w_0 e^{rT} + \int_0^T (A_s - c_s) e^{(T-s)r} \, ds \tag{3.5c}$$

$$w_T = 0 \tag{3.5d}$$

If initial wealth is very large, wealth will never go to zero, and the nature of the solution is different. Although these cases are taken care of in the estimation, I will not discuss them here because empirically they are not important.

The data are from the Longitudinal Retirement History Survey (RHS). About eleven thousand households whose heads were born in 1906–1911 were interviewed every two years from 1969 through 1979. Detailed questions were asked about all assets (except a meaningful question on life insurance), and the data were linked with official Social Security records so that one can calculate exact Social Security benefits. There are some data on consumption, but they are not complete, so I estimated the parameters of the model over wealth data. Bequeathable wealth includes stocks and bonds, property, businesses, and savings accounts, all less debts. As suggested by King and Dicks-Mireaux (1982), I excluded housing wealth because the costs of adjusting housing consumption are substantial, and people might not follow their desired housing consumption path. As long as the consumption of other goods follows its desired path, the parameters can be estimated over bequeathable wealth excluding housing wealth. Annuities include pensions, Social Security benefits, an estimated income value from Medicare/Medicaid, privately purchased annuities (which are very small), welfare transfers, and transfers from relatives. See Hurd and Shoven (1985) for a detailed description of the data.

The estimation method is to use equations 3.5a–3.5d to solve for the consumption path as a function of an initial choice of the parameter values.[3] This requires numerical integration and a search for T. The solution will depend on initial wealth. Wealth in the next survey, w_2, is predicted from equation 3.2. That is, the necessary conditions and the boundary conditions, equations 3.5a–3.5d, implicitly define

$$w_2 = f(w_0, \{A\}, \theta),$$

in which w_0 is initial wealth, $\{A\}$ is the annuity stream, and θ is the parameter vector $(\gamma\ \rho\ \alpha)'$. The parameter space is searched to minimize a function of $(w_2 - f)$.

Although α is, in principle, identified through nonlinearities in the functional form, the identification is very weak. Therefore, I specify that α is zero if a household has no living children.[4] The interpretation of α is the increase in the marginal utility of bequests across households according to whether they have living children or not.

The parameter estimates come from solving

$$\min \Sigma (w_2 - f(w_0, \{A\}, \theta))^2$$

The estimated parameter values, to which I refer later as the nonlinear least squares (NLLS) estimates, are

γ	ρ	α
0.729	0.0501	5.0×10^{-7}
(0.004)	(0.091)	(1×10^{-4})

Number of observations = 5,452

Because $\rho > r$, estimated consumption trajectories will slope downward, as shown in figure 3–1. Bequeathable wealth will decline sharply. This decline and the fact that many singles in the RHS have little bequeathable wealth imply that many people will rapidly spend all their bequeathable wealth. In fact, according to the parameter estimates, the average time to the exhaustion of bequeathable wealth is, for the single people in the RHS, just 6.7 years.

The estimate of γ is much smaller than what has typically been assumed in the literature. For example, Kotlikoff, Shoven, and Spivak (1983, 1984) and Kotlikoff and Spivak (1981) use a value of 4 in their simulations. Hubbard (1984) uses values of 0.75, 2, and 4. Davies's (1981) "best guess" for his simulations is 4. Large values of γ mean that the slope of the consumption trajectory is not sensitive to variations in mortality rates; my estimates imply that the consumption paths of the elderly will have substantial variation with mortality rates.

The marginal utility of bequests, α, is estimated to be very small, which is consistent with other estimates I have made in a model that is almost free of functional form restrictions.[5] The small estimate of α is caused by the fact that in the data, there is no difference between the saving rates of households with children and households without children.

Notes

1. This section is drawn from Hurd 1986.
2. See Hurd 1987.
3. The estimation is over all singles observed in any two-year period. The real interest rate, r, is taken to be 0.03.
4. Although the RHS does not have information about the ages of the children, because of the ages of the RHS population, the median age of the children would be about thirty in the first year of the survey. Thus, almost all the children will have their own households.
5. See Hurd 1987.

References

Davies, J. 1981. "Uncertain Lifetime, Consumption and Dissaving in Retiremment." *Journal of Political Economy* 86 (June):561–577.

Hubbard, R.G. 1987. "Uncertain Lifetimes, Pensions, and Individual Saving." In *Issues in Pension Economics,* edited by Z. Bodie, J. Shoven, and D. Wise. NBER and the University of Chicago Press, 175–206.

Hurd, M. 1986. "Mortality Risk and Bequests." in process.

Hurd, M. 1987. "Savings of the Elderly and Desired Bequests." *American Economic Review* 77 (June):298–312.

Hurd, M., and J. Shoven. 1983. "The Economic Status of the Elderly." In *Financial Aspects of the United States Pension System,* edited by Z. Bodie and J. Shoven. NBER and the University of Chicago Press, 359–397.

Hurd, M., and J. Shoven. 1985. "Inflation Vulnerability, Income, and Wealth of the Elderly, 1969–1979. In *Horizontal Equity, Uncertainty, and Economic Well-Being,* edited by M. David and T. Smeeding. NBER and the University of Chicago Press, 125–172.

Hurd, M., and D. Wise. 1987. "The Wealth and Poverty of Widows: Assets Before and After the Husband's Death." Paper presented at the National Bureau of Economic Research Conference on the Economics of Aging, New Orleans, March.

King, M., and L-D. Dicks-Mireaux. 1982. "Asset Holdings and the Life-Cycle." *The Economic Journal* 92 (June):247–267.

Kotlikoff, L., J. Shoven, and A. Spivak. 1983. "Annuity Markets, Saving, and the Capital Stock." National Bureau of Economic Research Working Paper No. 1250.

Kotlikoff, L., J. Shoven, and A. Spivak. 1984. "The Impact of Annuity Insurance on Savings and Inequality. National Bureau of Economic Research Working Paper No. 1403.

Kotlikoff, L., and A. Spivak. 1981. "The Family as an Incomplete Annuities Market." *Journal of Political Economy* 89 (April):372–391.

Wolff, E., and M. Marley. 1987. "Long-Term Trends in U.S. Wealth Inequality: Methodological Issues and Results." Paper presented at the National Bureau of Economic Research Conference on Research on Income and Wealth, Baltimore, March.

Yaari, M. 1965. "Uncertain Lifetime, Life Insurance and the Theory of the Consumer." *Review of Economic Studies* 32:137–150.

4

Future Sources of Retirement Income: Whither the Baby Boom

Emily S. Andrews, Ph.D.
Deborah Chollet, Ph.D.

T he improved economic status of today's elderly, relative to the preceding generation and to the nonelderly, has become a matter of record. Today, fewer elderly live in poverty than ever before; although the elderly comprise a growing proportion of the entire population, they are now less than 10 percent of the poor population, compared to 13 percent a decade ago.

Despite the progress made in moving the elderly out of poverty, many remain near poor. Health and personal care needs that rise with age, therefore, can readily thrust many elderly back into poverty. In fact, today's elderly are still more likely than the nonelderly to be poor or near poor.

This chapter analyzes the retirement income prospects of the baby boom generation using a microsimulation model of retirement income: the Pension and Retirement Income Simulation Model (PRISM). Based on generally conservative assumptions about real wage and pension coverage growth, PRISM projections of retirement income among the baby boom cohort are optimistic. Average real Social Security income is projected to rise, largely as a result of rising real wage growth and significantly greater rates of labor force participation among women.

Pension recipiency among baby boom retirees is projected to be much greater than among today's retirees, making pension income an increasingly important source of retirement income. The five-year vesting rule enacted in the 1986 Tax Reform Act is an important impetus to higher rates of pension recipiency, particularly among women. This higher projected recipiency, with more short-tenure workers and women with lower average career earnings vesting in pension plans, reduces average pension income among some groups (in particular, women who are single at retirement), while adding to aggregate pension income among the baby boom cohort as a whole.

The projected average rate of preretirement earnings replacement from Social Security and pensions is lower for the baby boom cohort than for

The authors are, respectively, Research Director and Senior Research Associate of the Employee Benefit Research Institute, Washington, D.C.

workers retiring today. In part, this lower replacement rate reflects scheduled reductions in Social Security payments; it also reflects Social Security's generally lower wage replacement at higher levels of preretirement earnings.

Our PRISM model also projects an important source of noncash retirement income—health insurance benefits continued from an employer plan. Assuming a status quo environment for employer-sponsored retiree health benefits and assuming that employers continue the eligibility standards for retiree health insurance that existed before the shorter pension vesting became law, recipiency rates among the baby boom are projected to be about the same as among workers retiring today.

Movement to a five-year eligibility standard to parallel pension vesting rules would almost double projected retiree health benefit recipiency among baby boom retirees compared to workers retiring now. The magnitude of this change, and the uncertain legislative future of retiree health insurance benefits, suggests the intensity of employer incentives to modify or terminate retiree health insurance benefits for future retirees.

Higher real retirement income is expected to reduce the poverty rate among baby boom retirees below that of workers retiring today. Although all retirees across gender and marital status are less likely to be poor or near poor than today, the poverty rate among women who are single at retirement remains higher than for other retirees. Among baby boom retirees, poverty will become even more distinctly a problem of single women than it is today.

The projected changes in income among baby boom retirees—lower preretirement earnings replacement coupled with higher real retirement income—might force a public policy review of retirement income goals. The issues that arise in defining these goals were last addressed in the context of the debate over indexing Social Security benefits. Definition of retirement income goals for the baby boom might help to clarify directions for further modification of the Social Security system to address, in particular, the foreseeable insolvency of the Medicare program.

The Elderly in Perspective

With the introduction of Social Security and the emergence of a system of employer-sponsored pensions, we have witnessed a striking change in the provision of income to the elderly over the past half century. In 1940 more than 2 million of the 9 million individuals age sixty-five or over were workers. Another 2 million relied on public assistance. Relatively few retirees had income from an employer-sponsored pension.

By the 1980s, these building blocks of retirement income remained, but their relative importance changed substantially. As of 1983, Social Security's Old Age and Survivors Insurance (OASI) provided benefits to more than 32 million retired workers and their dependents and survivors. Employer-sponsored pension plans (including private and government-sponsored retirement and railroad retirement plans) served 15 million beneficiaries. These included mostly retirees and their dependents and survivors, but also the disabled. Social Security and employer-sponsored pensions have become much more important sources of retirement income relative to welfare and earnings.

A preponderance of evidence indicates that the income of the elderly today is generally comparable to that of the nonelderly (Andrews 1985). In 1984 the mean per capita income of elderly households (where the householder was age sixty-five or older) was, before taxes, 101 percent of the mean per capita income of younger households before taxes. After taxes, the per capita income differential was greater; the after tax mean per capita income of elderly households was nearly 113 percent of that among nonelderly households in 1984.

This after tax differential reflects several tax preferences available to elderly taxpayers but not to younger taxpayers. Most Social Security benefits, amounting on average to about one third of total income, are tax exempt. Also, prior to the 1986 Tax Reform Act, the federal income tax code accorded the elderly an additional personal exemption. Finally, the elderly commonly receive property tax preferences under state and local laws.

Public insurance programs that serve the elderly are also an important source of real retirement income. Medicare serves primarily the elderly population and provides average service benefits to elderly enrollees that exceed $2,000 per year in value. Medicaid, designed to serve specific segments of the poor, including the elderly, has become the elderly's principal financier for nursing home and other long-term care services. In fiscal year 1985, Medicaid spending for elderly beneficiaries averaged $4,605 — nearly 38 percent of the federal-state Medicaid budget. Adjusting income among both the elderly and the nonelderly for the value of Medicare, Medicaid, and workers' employer-provided health insurance, the elderly's mean per capita real income was an estimated 111 percent of real per capita income among nonelderly households in 1979 (Smeeding 1986).

Improvements in Social Security benefits and the expansion of employer-sponsored pensions have been important factors in the elderly's improving economic status. The elderly have benefited from indexation of their Social Security income while, during the first half of the decade, real income among nonelderly households declined (Moon and Sawhill 1984). In 1982, 33 percent of married retired couples reported income from one or more private pension plans and 15 percent reported income from a public employer pension; these proportions are twice the rate of private and public pension recipiency reported two decades earlier.

Improvements in the elderly's economic status also are reflected in declining poverty rates among the elderly. In 1959, 35 percent of the elderly lived in poverty. With the advent of Social Security and the emergence of private and public employer pensions, the elderly's poverty rate dropped below 19 percent in 1972 and continued to decline below 15 percent in 1974. During the last ten years, the percent of elderly in poverty hovered between 14 and 16 percent, but declined to nearly 12 percent in 1984. The elderly now constitute less than 10 percent of the population in poverty.

Although summary income statistics indicate significant improvements in the elderly's economic well-being, they hide considerable variation in economic status among the elderly, as well as the vulnerability of many elderly to substantial expenses for health care. Although fewer elderly live in poverty, many elderly live near poverty. In 1984 more than 20 percent of the elderly were near poor, reporting income above poverty but within 125 percent of the poverty level (Chollet 1987). Single elderly women and all elderly over age seventy-five are disproportionately poor and near poor. In 1984 nearly 28 percent of the elderly over age seventy-five were poor and near poor, compared to 17 percent of the elderly age sixty-five to seventy-four. Nearly two thirds (60 percent) of poor and near-poor elderly are single women.

Despite continuing economic vulnerability among important segments of the elderly, the retirement income system has achieved signal success for this generation of retirees compared to earlier generations. Some wonder, however, whether such success can continue or improve in the future. Interest centers on what will happen to the baby boom—that generation born in the high-birthrate years between 1946 and 1964—when they reach retirement. Will the baby boom generation be burdened by the costs of the current generation and then face a crumbling retirement income system at age sixty-five? The answer to this question depends on many variables we cannot forecast (including the nation's commitment to a pay-as-you-go Social Security system), as well as some that we can. This chapter uses the findings from a microsimulation model, the Pension and Retirement Income Simulation Model (PRISM), to address the question of retirement income among future retirees.

PRISM Simulation Model

PRISM is a long-range microsimulation model developed by ICF, Inc., in part for the 1979 President's Commission on Pension Policy. Under contract to the Employee Benefit Research Institute and others, PRISM has been enhanced and periodically updated to reflect provisions of new legislation. Since PRISM relies on a one-time match of the Current Population Survey (CPS) to actual Social Security earnings histories, PRISM's input data base remains the May 1979 CPS, but the model's parameters have been recalculated and its projections benchmarked to the 1984 CPS.

PRISM simulates individuals' work experience based on detailed demographic, labor force, and economic assumptions. Each individual's earnings, periods of employment, and marital status are simulated between 1979 and the date at which the individual reaches age sixty-seven. The model attributes pension coverage, participation, and vesting for each job an individual holds. For jobs with pension coverage, actual pension provisions are selected from a representative sample of private and public pension plans. The model incorporates the liberalized vesting standards of the 1986 Tax Reform Act by assuming that all private single-employer defined benefit plans and all primary defined contribution plans have five-year cliff vesting, unless the actual plan provisions include a shorter vesting period. All multiemployer plans and public plans retain their actual vesting provisions, typically ten years. PRISM calculates pension benefits at retirement based on preretirement simulated earnings. Other simulated sources of income include Social Security, earnings, and Supplemental Security Income (SSI).

PRISM's assumptions about future labor force structure and economic growth are based on projections made by the Social Security Administration (SSA) and the Bureau of Labor Statistics (BLS). PRISM is constrained to simulate aggregate levels of employment consistent with BLS forecasts of labor force participation rates for 1982–1995 (Fullerton and Tschetter 1983). Real wage growth is constrained to Social Security's low-growth, alternative III assumptions; the assumed rate of wage growth is about 1 percentage point more than inflation. Use of these assumptions probably produces somewhat conservative estimates of pension benefits in particular.

The assumed rates of inflation and interest are consistent with the alternative II-B rates in the 1985 report of the Trustees of the Social Security Trust Funds. That is, all defined contribution plans and all investments in individual retirement accounts (IRAs) accrue interest at a 7.1 percent average rate.

Pension coverage within industry groups is assumed to remain constant at 1983 levels. This assumption leads to a slight decline in the aggregate pension coverage rate during the simulation period compared to the 1983 rate, due to BLS-projected shifts in employment. Employment in industries with high pension coverage rates (such as manufacturing) is projected to decline relative to employment in industries with lower coverage rates (such as retail trade and selected services).

PRISM simulates defined benefit and/or defined contribution pension recipiency at age sixty-seven among the population age twenty-five to sixty-four in 1979. Workers with vested defined contribution plan benefits who change jobs may, based on probability assumptions derived from Atkins (1986), roll their preretirement distributions into an IRA. Distributions that are not rolled into an IRA are not included in future benefit calculations. (For job changers over age fifty-five, PRISM assumes that all distributions above $1,750 are rolled into an IRA.)

Finally, this version of PRISM simulates the continuation of employer-sponsored health insurance into retirement. The receipt of continued health coverage assumes that (1) the individual retires from a job that offers retiree health insurance benefits; (2) the retiree is vested in a defined benefit plan from that job; and (3) the retiree leaves the job eligible for immediate pension benefits.

In this study, we compare real retirement income at age sixty-seven among workers who are now retiring (age fifty-five to sixty-four in 1979) to that among baby boom retirees (age twenty-five to thirty-four in 1979) based on full simulations for these cohorts. The retirement income recipiency and benefit amounts simulated for the cohort of workers now retiring have been checked against, and are comparable to, actual survey and program data on new retirees. In fact, as relatively few years of work were simulated for this oldest cohort of workers, the primary task of the simulation was calculating the probability of pension coverage and benefit amounts accruing to workers from actual jobs. Rather than using actual statistics for current retirees, however, simulation estimates are presented to ensure that the generational comparisons are based on consistent data. Also, actual data are not always available in the exact form needed for comparison with the baby boom simulations.

Projected income among baby boom retirees is based almost entirely on simulated job histories, since these people had relatively few years of actual work-history data in 1979. This means that the accuracy of retirement income among this cohort depends almost entirely on the accuracy of the model. For that reason, the model was tested to determine its sensitivity to key assumptions. In particular, the effects of different wage growth and pension-coverage growth assumptions were investigated. Other changes, such as increased rates of labor force participation or changes in public policy toward pensions and retiree health benefits, also could affect PRISM's projections.

Sources of Retirement Income for Current and Future Retirees

Using PRISM, several important properties of retirement income can be compared for workers now retiring versus baby boomers retiring in the twenty-first century. We analyze differences in the prevalence of particular retirement income sources among future retirees compared to those retiring today and compare retirement income for the two cohorts in constant dollar terms. We compare projected income replacement from Social Security and employer-sponsored pensions as a percentage of preretirement earnings. Finally, the share of income each source provides is investigated for each cohort.

Sources of Income

When the baby boom retires, 97 percent of retired families (married couples and single retirees) can expect to receive income from Social Security's OASI program (see table 4–1). This represents an increase from a projected recipiency rate of 86 percent amont current retired families. As the Social Security system has matured over the past thirty years, growth in benefit recipiency has naturally declined. Projected increases in Social Security benefit recipiency among new retirees stem from the additional coverage provided under the 1983 Social Security amendments and from increases in recipiency among women workers.

The decline in welfare recipiency among retirees is projected to continue into the twenty-first century. Only 3 percent of baby boom retirees are projected to qualify for SSI benefits, compared to 10 percent of current new retirees. Some of this decline might be attributable to increased labor force participation of women in the baby boom generation and subsequent eligibility for Social Security and employer pension benefits in their own right.

Projected pension recipiency among retirees in the twenty-first century is considerably higher than among current new retirees. Among workers now

Table 4–1
Percent of Retired Families of Different Generations with Retirement Income at Age Sixty-seven from Various Sources

Income Source	Workers Currently Retiring[a]	Baby Boom Retirees[b]
All Retiree Families		
Social Security	86	97
Employer-sponsored pensions	48	71
Earnings	35	29
Supplemental Security Income	10	3
Married Couples		
Social Security	94	98
Employer-sponsored pensions	59	83
Earnings	44	39
Supplemental Security Income	2	—
Single Individuals		
Social Security	77	95
Employer-sponsored pensions	36	60
Earnings	25	21
Supplemental Security Income	21	5

Source: Employee Benefit Research Institute tabulations of the Pension and Retirement Income Simulation Model (PRISM) (EBRI 1986).

[a]Age fifty-five to sixty-four in 1979.

[b]Age twenty-five to thirty-four in 1979.

retiring, 48 percent are projected to receive pension income at age sixty-seven (assuming lump-sum distributions at retirement are annuitized). Among baby boom retirees, 71 percent are projected to receive pension income.

Based on static, within-industry coverage rates assumed throughout the simulation period, growth in pension recipiency among baby boom retirees reflects their longer tenure in the workforce after the passage of the Employee Retirement Income Security Act (ERISA) (Andrews 1987), as well as their longer work histories with the recently enacted five-year vesting rule. Although vested benefits may be small for young workers who vest after only five years of credited service, these benefits accumulate to produce higher recipiency rates from a greater number of pension plans (Employee Benefit Research Institute 1987b).

Strong growth in labor force participation among baby boom women also raises pension recipiency among baby boom retirees, compared to earlier generations. The marked increase in labor force participation among married women has been a dominant socioeconomic trend of the post–World War II period, rivaled only by the income-induced decline in labor force participation among older workers as they retire earlier.

The trend toward earlier retirement is expected to continue, barring significant changes in public and private sector policies. Growth in the relative wages of older workers (as the baby boom nears retirement and the size of the labor force shrinks) is not expected to offset preferences and incentives for earlier retirement. As a result, while 35 percent of workers retiring today are projected to have earnings at age sixty-seven, only 29 percent of the baby boom cohort are projected to have earnings when they reach the same age. Nonetheless, earnings are expected to remain an important source of retirement income for elderly families, and particularly for married couples, when the baby boom retires.

Real Income Levels

Among baby boom retirees, average real family income from major sources — Social Security, employer-provided pensions, and IRAs — is projected to exceed that received by today's new retirees. Among married couples in the baby boom, real Social Security income (in 1985 dollars) is projected to average $12,800 per year, compared to average benefits of $9,500 among married couples now retiring (see table 4–2). Among single baby boom retirees, Social Security benefits are projected to average $6,800, compared to $4,800 among single workers retiring today.

The higher real Social Security income projected for baby boom retirees results from both real wage growth and increased labor force participation among women. Social Security's benefit formula translates higher preretirement wages into higher postretirement benefits; as a result, economy-wide

Table 4-2

Average Income at Age Sixty-seven from Selected Sources among Recipient Families of Different Generations

(1985 dollars in thousands)

Income Source	Workers Currently Retiring[a]	Baby Boom Retirees[b]
Married Couples		
Social Security	$9.5	$12.8
Employer-sponsored pensions, total	7.1	14.3
Defined contribution plans	4.4	11.3
Defined benefit plans	6.5	8.7
Single Individuals		
Social Security	$4.8	$6.8
Employer-sponsored pensions, total	5.3	9.6
Defined contribution plans	3.3	8.5
Defined benefit plans	5.1	6.5

Source: Employee Benefit Research Institute tabulations of the Pension and Retirement Income Simulation Model (PRISM) (EBRI 1986).

[a] Age fifty-five to sixty-four in 1979.

[b] Age twenty-five to thirty-four in 1979.

productivity gains that produce higher real wages also generate improved real Social Security benefits. Increased labor force participation among women raises the probability that women will receive Social Security benefits in their own right and in excess of the 50 percent spousal benefit they might otherwise receive. In addition, more divorced women can expect higher Social Security benefits at retirement than today, since divorce settlements will more commonly divide Social Security benefits between long-time spouses.

Average real income from private and public employer pensions among married baby boom couples is projected to exceed $14,000 per couple (compared to $7,100 among couples now retiring), surpassing average Social Security benefits among the baby boom cohort. Gains in average pension income amounts among baby boom retirees reflect increases in income from defined benefit plans and even greater increases in income from defined contribution plans. For instance, average defined contribution plan income is projected to rise from $4,400 among current retired couples to $11,300 among retired couples in the baby boom.

Despite projected increases in Social Security and pension income, wage replacement from those two sources of income is expected to decline slightly relative to current levels. While Social Security benefits and pension income replace 49 percent of preretirement average earnings among married men currently retiring, that replacement rate is projected to fall to 45 percent as the baby boom reaches retirement age. Projected replacement rates for unmarried women decline from 77 percent among women now retiring to 53 percent among single women in the baby boom. These declining replacement rates reflect scheduled reductions in the Social Security benefit formula, as well as Social Security's lower wage replacement for workers with higher life-time earnings.

Share of Income by Source

Although Social Security is likely to continue as the average retiree's single most important source of retirement income, the importance of Social Security relative to other income sources is projected to decline. Among today's new retirees, Social Security provides, on average, 46 percent of the personal income of couples and single individuals; among baby boom retirees, Social Security is projected to provide 40 percent of income (see table 4–3). The declining relative importance of Social Security benefits primarily reflects the increasing relative importance of pension income. Among baby boom retirees, pensions are projected to provide 37 percent of average income, compared to 23 percent among workers now retiring.

Table 4–3
Percent of Total Retirement Income at Age Sixty-seven from Various Sources among Retired Families of Different Generations

Income Source	Workers Currently Retiring[a]	Baby Boom Retirees[b]
All Retired Families		
Social Security	46.1	39.7
Employer-sponsored pensions	22.7	37.8
Earnings	28.8	22.2
Supplemental Security Income	2.1	0.3
Married Couples		
Social Security	47.1	37.7
Employer-sponsored pensions	22.7	36.6
Earnings	29.8	25.7
Supplemental Security Income	0.3	—
Single Individuals		
Social Security	43.8	43.8
Employer-sponsored pensions	22.7	40.2
Earnings	26.0	15.3
Supplemental Security Income	7.4	0.7

Source: Employee Benefit Research Institute tabulations of the Pension and Retirement Income Simulation Model (PRISM) (EBRI 1986).

[a] Age fifty-five to sixty-four in 1979.

[b] Age twenty-five to thirty-four in 1979.

Assuming an unabated trend toward earlier retirement, fewer retired families in the twenty-first century are projected to have earnings. As a result, the average importance of earnings as a source of income is projected to decline. Among today's new retirees (including married couples and single individuals), earnings provide 29 percent of income; among baby boom families in retirement, earnings are projected to provide 22 percent of income.

Five-Year Vesting and the Baby Boom

The higher pension recipiency and pension income that we project for baby boom retirees relative to workers retiring today result in part from ongoing trends (such as increased labor force participation among women), but they also reflect a new influence, the five-year vesting standard required under the 1986 Tax Reform Act. The effect of more rapid vesting under the Tax Reform Act can be observed by comparing projected pension recipiency and income under actual vesting standards in force before the Tax Reform Act to our basic PRISM simulation, which incorporates five-year vesting.

Our analysis of the effects of the Tax Reform Act on pension benefits focuses on the entitlement of individual workers under their own job-related pension plans. While the family is a more appropriate unit for analyzing income recipiency and evaluating the elderly's well-being, changes in individual pension recipiency provide a clearer indication of actual benefit determination, since labor force participation drives pension entitlement.

Workers might be covered by either or both of two types of pension plans, resulting in retirement benefits from either defined benefit plans or defined contribution plans or from both. Shorter vesting requirements might lead to changes in pension recipiency from either or both plan types. Shorter vesting also might lead to changes in levels of retirement income in each category.

Pension Recipiency

Women accrue the greatest gains in pension recipiency with five-year vesting. (Appropriately, shorter vesting standards were in part promoted as a policy change that would benefit women, who typically have shorter careers in paid employment than men.) Much of the ultimate benefit of five-year vesting is apparent among baby boom women who will spend much of their careers under the new, shorter vesting standard. Our projections indicate that 56 percent of women in the baby boom generation who are married at retirement will receive income from an employer-sponsored pension plan. This rate represents a 13-percentage point increase from the 43 percent rate projected using the earlier ten-year ERISA standard (see table 4–4). Women who are unmarried at retirement achieve comparable gains. Although men also benefit from five-year vesting in terms of pension recipiency, their gains are smaller, ranging from 4 to 6 percentage points, raising pension recipiency to 74 percent for married men and 69 percent for single men.

Gains in defined contribution pension recipiency are particularly strong among baby boom retirees, both from primary (stand-alone) defined contribution plans and from defined contribution plans that are secondary to a defined benefit plan. These findings suggest that some defined contribution plans must shorten their vesting periods to comply with the changed tax code; the need for this adjustment is most apparent among primary defined contribution plans, which are more likely to be established by smaller employers.

Table 4–4

Future Pension Recipiency Rates among Baby Boom Workers[a] at Age Sixty-seven under Different Vesting Standards, by Sex and Marital Status at Retirement

(*in percent*)

	Total Recipiency	Defined Benefit Plan Only	Defined Contribution Plan Only	Both Plan Types
Married Men				
Five-year vesting	73.8	32.0	15.0	26.7
Vesting before 1986 Tax Reform Act	69.4	34.2	12.7	22.5
Single Men				
Five-year vesting	69.1	33.0	11.5	24.6
Vesting before 1986 Tax Reform Act	63.4	36.3	10.5	16.6
Married Women				
Five-year vesting	55.7	25.2	16.8	13.7
Vesting before 1986 Tax Reform Act	42.7	24.4	10.6	7.9
Single Women				
Five-year vesting	54.9	24.1	16.8	14.0
Vesting before 1986 Tax Reform Act	43.7	21.7	11.5	10.5

Source: Employee Benefit Research Institute tabulations of the Pension and Retirement Income Simulation Model (PRISM) (EBRI 1986).

[a]Age twenty-five to thirty-four in 1979.

Pension Income

Five-year vesting also raises real retirement income from public and private employer sponsored pensions among some baby boom retirees—from $13,900 to $15,400 for married men age sixty-seven, and from $12,500 to $15,400 for single men (see table 4–5). This increase derives primarily from projected increases in benefits from defined contribution plans.

The story for women is quite different. Although substantially more women are projected to receive pension income under five-year vesting, their average total benefits are projected to change very little. For both married and single women, lower average projected benefits from defined benefit plans offset higher average projected benefits from defined contribution

Table 4–5
Future Average Pension Income at Age Sixty-seven among Baby Boom[a] Pension Recipients under Different Vesting Standards, by Type of Pension Plan, Sex, and Marital Status at Retirement
(1985 dollars in thousands)

	Total Pension Replacement Rate	Defined Benefit Plan Only	Defined Contribution Plan Only	Both Plan Types	
				Defined Benefit Plan	*Defined Contribution Plan*
Married Men					
Five-year vesting	$15.4	$10.7	$13.4	$7.8	$14.7
Vesting before tax reform	13.9	10.5	10.9	8.2	13.0
Single Men					
Five-year vesting	15.4	9.8	13.3	6.5	17.3
Vesting before tax reform	12.5	9.4	8.0	7.6	14.2
Married Women					
Five-year vesting	3.7	3.1	3.9	1.9	3.9
Vesting before tax reform	3.6	3.5	2.4	2.1	3.5
Single Women					
Five-year vesting	5.7	5.9	5.2	3.2	5.2
Vesting before tax reform	6.0	6.6	2.5	3.7	5.2

Source: Employee Benefit Research Institute tabulations of the Pension and Retirement Income Simulation Model (PRISM) (EBRI 1986).
[a] Age twenty-five to thirty-four in 1979.

plans. Parenthetically, average defined benefit income among married men with benefits from both defined benefit and defined contribution plans also declines.

Decreased average real pension income among some recipient groups appears to result from the higher rate of pension recipiency among workers who would not otherwise vest in a pension plan. To the extent that five-year vesting ensures that workers will be entitled to benefits from pension plans from more jobs, average benefits are likely to increase. To the extent that five-year vesting provides new workers first-time pension benefits, average benefit amounts are likely to decrease, as they will be based on fewer years of service (and probably lower salaries), compared to pension entitlement among those qualifying under ten-year vesting.

The relative impact of these offsetting factors largely determines changes in average real pension income among baby boom retirees. On average, across all retirees, the shorter vesting standard raises real average pension income more for men than for women, but increases the number of women who receive pensions relative to men. In the aggregate, projected pension income among baby boom retirees rises with five-year vesting.

The Issue of Retiree Health Benefits

Employer-sponsored health insurance benefits are an important source of real income among retirees and workers alike. Our preliminary estimates using an annualized 1984 data file from the Survey of Income and Program Participation (SIPP) indicate that at least 21 percent of the retired (nonworking) population age sixty-five or older received health insurance benefits from a past employer in their own right or as a dependent in 1984. In estimating real income among future retirees, including the value of health insurance benefits would be desirable.

The difficulties associated with estimating the real value of health insurance among retirees are considerable, however. Little information is available about employers' costs for providing benefits to retirees. In any case, valuing health insurance benefits at employer cost is a hazardous business, as benefits provided by a small employer are likely to be more costly than comparable benefits from a large employer. Furthermore, estimating the present value of a health insurance benefit "promise" from a past employer involves estimation of future health care costs, a task that has confounded private business practice and public policy alike. Consequently, our PRISM projections of employer-sponsored retiree health insurance recipiency do not include valuation of the benefit received.

For those who might nevertheless seek to impute value to benefit recipiency, several warnings are in order. First, since retiree health insurance benefits typically "carve out" Medicare benefits, changes in Medicare coverage or regulation directly affect the value of plan benefits. Second, there is ample evidence that employers might seek to modify retirees' benefits over time to parallel changes in their plan for active workers. Finally, the mounting problem of employers' unfunded liability for retiree health insurance — and congressional attention to this issue — means that the probability of major public policy changes and employer plan modifications is substantial. Each of these considerations might affect not only the value of employer-sponsored health benefits for retirees, but also the likelihood of benefit recipiency.

Simulation models depend on predictable behavior to make reasonable projections; changes in important factors exogenous to the model raise the potential for radically wrong projections. This might be the case for retiree health insurance. Nevertheless, our projections of retiree health insurance benefit recipiency by necessity assume that the current employer environment will remain substantially the same.

Several other assumptions built into the model might make this overall assumption more tolerable. In particular, our projections assume that retiree health insurance benefits only (but not always) accompany recipiency of defined benefit pension income. In fact, our tabulations of 1984 SIPP data indicate that a significant minority of retirees with health insurance from a past employer receive no pension income at all. This finding suggests that our PRISM projections might understate total recipiency by ignoring recipiency among retirees without pension income or with pension income only from a defined contribution plan.[1] These plans, whether they are freestanding (without an accompanying pension plan) or associated with a primary defined contribution plan (and, therefore, potentially offered by predominantly smaller employers), might be most vulnerable to major public policy change.

Other assumptions used in projecting retiree health insurance recipiency among retirees are worth reviewing. The probability that an employer offers health insurance as a retiree benefit depends on (1) whether the employer offers health insurance benefits to active workers and (2) the industry and establishment size. Workers who vest in defined benefit plans on jobs and leave before retirement age are assumed to carry no vested health insurance benefits into retirement. While employers are in fact not tied to five-year vesting for their retiree health insurance plans, whether employers nevertheless maintain parallel standards for defined benefit pension vesting and retiree health insurance eligibility is critical to projecting eventual recipiency. In fact, no eligibility or vesting rules for retiree health insurance are established in law, and it is likely that no single employer practice predominates.

Using the ten-year ERISA vesting rule in place before tax reform to project retiree health insurance recipiency, recipiency rates among future cohorts of retirees remain substantially at the level of coverage projected among workers retiring today (24 percent). This result is due primarily to PRISM's assumption that rates of defined benefit pension coverage among workers in each industry group remain constant. By comparison, however, a five-year vesting rule applied to retiree health insurance benefits substantially raises recipiency rates among retirees, even assuming that workers who terminate employment before retirement retain no vested health benefit. Among workers now retiring (and largely unaffected by the shorter vesting standard), PRISM projects a retiree health benefit recipiency rate of 24 percent; projected recipiency among baby boom retirees ranges from 30 percent (among workers who are single at retirement) to 51 percent (among married retirees), assuming uniform five-year vesting for both health and pension plans (see table 4–6).

Five-year vesting has a greater impact on the number of retirees receiving benefits from their own employer's plan than on the number of retirees receiving benefits only as a dependent of a retired worker. About 10 percent of retirees with continued coverage in the baby boom are projected to receive employer-based health insurance as a dependent or survivor of a covered spouse under a five-year eligibility rule. The percent of retirees without either direct or dependent's coverage is projected to be much lower under five-year eligibility, dropping from 76 percent among workers retiring today to 58 percent among baby boom retirees.

Table 4–6
Projected Number and Percent of Retirees of Different Generations with Health Insurance Benefits Continued from an Employer Plan at Age Sixty-seven under Alternative Eligibility Rules

	Workers Currently Retiring[a]		Baby Boom Retirees[b]	
	Vesting before Tax Reform	Five-Year Vesting	Vesting before Tax Reform	Five-Year Vesting
	Number, in Millions			
Retirees with coverage	5.2	5.4	7.6	13.1
Benefits from own plan	3.8	3.9	5.5	10.1
Benefits as dependent only	1.5	1.5	2.2	3.0
Retirees without coverage	16.9	16.7	23.6	18.1
	Percent			
Retirees with coverage	23.7	24.5	24.5	42.1
Benefits from own plan	17.1	17.7	17.5	32.5
Benefits as dependent only	6.7	6.7	7.0	9.6
Retirees without coverage	76.3	75.5	75.5	57.9

Source: Employee Benefit Research Institute tabulations of the Pension and Retirement Income Simulation Model (PRISM) (EBRI 1986).
[a] Age fifty-five to sixty-four in 1979.
[b] Age twenty-five to thirty-four in 1979.

The magnitude of the projected increase in retiree health benefits using a five-year vesting rule provides an indication of the pressure employers might face to scale back the health insurance benefits offered to retirees, tighten eligibility rules, and/or alter their plan funding. Employers who use their pension plan vesting standard to establish service requirements for retiree health benefits now have a strong incentive to establish separate rules for health benefit eligibility. Given the current judicial, legislative, and regulatory uncertainties that beleaguer retiree health benefits, projections of strong growth in retiree health benefits might be best interpreted as the emergence of strong incentives for employers to modify or terminate their plans for future retirees.

Modification of employer-sponsored retiree health plans might take several forms, including (1) reduction in the share of plan cost that employers pay, (2) reduction of the service coverage provided by the plan, or (3) conversion of conventional service coverage to a cash benefit with access to a group insurance plan. In the last case, the cash benefit may (or may not) be gauged to the insurance plan premium. No data indicate that any employer now offers a cash-denominated health benefit distinct from their pension plans, nor is it clear that the present tax law would recognize such a benefit. Nevertheless, the U.S. Treasury has shown interest in allowing cash-denominated retiree health benefits (Ross 1985), an option that might be increasingly attractive to employers as they seek to limit out-year liability for retiree health benefits.

A Further Decline in Poverty

While PRISM simulates retirement income from major sources among future retirees, it does not simulate income from all sources. In particular, PRISM's income projections exclude personal income from assets other than pension accumulations and IRAs. This deficiency, however, is unlikely to strongly bias estimates of poverty and near poverty among future elderly.[2]

PRISM projections indicate that the proportion of elderly in poverty or near poverty will continue to decline, producing a poverty rate among baby boom retirees that is substantially lower than that among current elderly. Among workers now retiring, 25 percent are projected to be poor or near poor (see table 4–7). Among the baby boom cohort of retirees, 19 percent are projected to be poor or near poor. This improvement in the aggregate rate of poverty and near poverty among baby boom retirees is consistent across different family types. The projected percentage of married men and women who are poor or near poor declines from 11 percent among workers now retiring to 2 percent among baby boom retirees. Among single men, the projected percentage who are poor or near poor declines from 32 percent among

Table 4–7

Percent of Retirees of Different Generations in Poverty or Near Poverty[a] at Age Sixty-seven, by Sex and Marital Status at Retirement

	Workers Currently Retiring[b]	Baby Boom Retirees[c]
All individuals	25.1	18.6
Married men and women	11.2	1.6
Single men	31.5	5.4
Single women	64.9	43.3

Source: Employee Benefit Research Institute tabulations of the Pensions and Retirement Income Simulation Model (PRISM) (EBRI 1986).

[a]Retirees with family/personal income equal to 125 percent of poverty or less.

[b]Age fifty-five to sixty-four in 1979.

[c]Age twenty-five to thirty-four in 1979.

those currently retiring to 5 percent among baby boom retirees. Women who are unmarried at retirement are expected to remain at highest risk of poverty or near poverty (43 percent), despite the increase in the number of unmarried women projected to receive retirement income.

Part of the projected decline in poverty and near poverty reflects PRISM's economic assumptions. With nominal wages assumed to be growing faster than inflation (albeit by only one percentage point), real wage growth ensures that the standard of living of the population will increase into the twenty-first century. For the same reason, poverty rates will decline, since nominal adjustments to the poverty index are based on the Consumer Price Index (CPI). Much of the reduction in the percentage of retirees who are poor or near poor, particularly among single men, might stem from economy-wide productivity growth, as well as greater access to, and income from, employer-sponsored pensions.

Although single women also benefit from economy-wide productivity gains, the improvement in their economic situation might be more strongly related to longer work histories compared to women in earlier retiree cohorts. These longer work histories lead to greater Social Security entitlement in their own right. PRISM projections indicate that 97 percent of women in the baby boom cohort who are single at retirement will have Social Security benefits, compared to 77 percent among women retiring today. Nevertheless, the average retirement income among single women in the baby boom cohort is substantially less than that among couples and single men. As a result, single women are projected to comprise a larger percentage of the poor and near poor (87 percent) than they do among today's new retirees (60 percent). Poverty among single elderly women appears to be an enduring public policy problem; furthermore, poverty among the elderly will increasingly become a problem of poverty among single elderly women.

Retirement Income Modeling Gaps

The validity of microsimulation projections in providing an overall picture of the future is constrained both by the model's assumptions and by its omissions. This section provides some discussion of several of the model's major omissions, including (1) its inability to forecast property income, (2) the implication of projecting only a single year's income, and (3) its inability to anticipate public policy fully.

While PRISM projects major components of retirement income, it omits others, including real income from noncash retirement benefits (specifically, health insurance) and income from nonpension assets. In recent years, the importance of property as a source of income among the elderly has increased steadily. In 1983, 24 percent of the income of aged-headed family units was from property (Radner 1986),[3] compared to 15 percent in 1967. The real average value of property income (in constant 1983 dollars) among elderly families with property income increased from $1,370 in 1967 to $3,360 in 1983.

Furthermore, property income appears to be a relatively more important source of income among older cohorts of elderly family units than among younger cohorts of the elderly. In 1983, 19 percent of the total income of family units headed by someone age sixty-five to sixty-nine derived from property, compared to 31 percent of the total income of family units headed by someone age eighty to eighty-four.[4]

What can we expect in terms of the baby boom? Will the importance of property income continue to increase? The clearest answer to that question appears to be not necessarily. There are several reasons why the baby boom may be less reliant on income from assets than today's new retirees. While savings flows are difficult to measure or predict, both the Department of Commerce and the Federal Reserve Board report that the savings rate has been declining. Many consider these declines more than reactions to specific quarterly events or statistical discrepancies. Some feel they might be closely related to the savings behavior of the baby boom relative to the savings behavior of older cohorts in earlier years. Of course, predicting future savings behavior is hazardous at best, since empirical findings on how saving is determined are not robust.

Cohort size effects also might influence the return that the baby boom can expect to earn from investment, regardless of its savings rate. As the large baby boom cohort dominates the labor market, it is likely to receive lower real wages than previous generations; as capital becomes relatively scarce, the real rate of return to capital is likely to grow. As the baby boom's retirement reduces the size of the labor force, however, capital will become relatively more abundant and real returns to investment will decline. The size of these effects can be projected using a long-run macroeconomic model; in general, however, the fewer baby boomers who save should do relatively well on their investments during their working years but might still face lower average asset income in retirement.

A second omission of PRISM relates to its prediction of retirement income for only one year and for relatively young retirees (at age sixty-seven). Among today's elderly, average income is substantially lower for older cohorts than for the youngest cohort. While lower average income among older cohorts might reflect lower income at retirement, it also reflects the different gender and marital composition of the very old.

Adjusted for family size, median gross income among family units headed by householders age fifty-five to sixty-nine was $12,980 in 1983, compared to $7,110 among family units headed by householders age eighty-five or older (Radner 1986). The poverty rate among family units headed by a householder age sixty-five to sixty-nine in 1983 was 12.8 percent, compared to 26.9 percent among units headed by someone age eighty-five or older.

This pattern of lower income and greater poverty among older elderly families has been consistent over time and has been the result of a number of factors. First, older retirees are likely on average to have lower retirement benefits than younger retirees, since the benefits of older retirees reflect lower real earnings in earlier calendar years. Income from employer-sponsored pensions only partially kept up with inflation during the 1970s, depressing the real income of older retirees who have been retired longer. Rates of Social Security recipiency are lower for older retirees, as is employer-sponsored pension recipiency. Also, since women live longer than men, and single women are more likely to live in poverty, the proportion of individuals with low incomes increases as a cohort ages.[5] Finally, the need for health care and/or personal assistance tends to increase with age; the financial strain of greater health-related needs can lead to the depletion of assets and a reduction in property income.

These factors might affect baby boom retirees as they do current elderly, reducing their real income absolutely and/or relative to that of post–baby boom retirees. In addition, however, baby boom retirees might confront sources of declining real and relative income that are less important among current elderly. PRISM projections indicate that the baby boom will derive more of its retirement income from employer-sponsored pensions than do earlier cohorts. Unless employer practice changes, increases in defined benefit pensions will continue to lag behind the inflation rate. The actual amount of total income erosion will depend on the stability of the CPI and the relative importance of asset income, including the annuitized value of lump-sum pension distributions. Furthermore, if Social Security benefits are linked to the CPI and wages rise faster than prices, baby boom retirees will not share in productivity gains after retirement, reducing their real income relative to subsequent retiree cohorts.

Finally, microsimulation models must, by necessity, assume a generally stable policy environment exogenous to the model. Recent legislative activity, however, suggests that Congress might address perceived flaws in our system of retirement income, changing the environment for employer decisions about pensions and noncash retirement benefits. For instance, some members of Congress are currently interested in ways to increase portability across employer-sponsored pension plans. In addition, some would like to ensure that pension distributions received before retirement are not spent on consumption but are reinvested until retirement. Other changes in private sector pension legislation might eventually be considered, including changes in participation standards and mandated pension coverage.

Congressional interest in retiree health insurance benefits has been growing, as bankruptcy reorganizations and the termination of retiree health insurance benefits have left many early retirees (who are ineligible for Medicare) without access to affordable private health insurance. Congress has ordered the U.S. Treasury to report on possible vesting and funding rules for retiree health insurance; the Financial Accounting Standards Board (FASB) is investigating appropriate accounting rules that would require employers to disclose for the first time a conservatively estimated aggregate unfunded liability for retiree health benefits of more than $98 billion.

The Social Security system also might eventually resurface as a candidate for legislative change. Social Security's Old Age, Survivors and Disability Insurance (OASDI) trust fund is expected to accumulate a surplus in preparation for the baby boom's retirement. Some would use that surplus to finance benefits from the more imminently troubled Medicare Hospital Insurance (HI) trust fund; others would reduce the payroll tax, reverting to an entirely pay-as-you-go system. Some would significantly restructure the entire system.

While these and other changes are being discussed and some legislative initiatives might be close to action, some might never be introduced or acted upon. The enactment of any one change, including one of those mentioned above, would almost certainly have a significant impact on the baby boom in retirement.

Conclusion: Whither the Baby Boom

A gloomy prognosis for the baby boom in retirement seems unwarranted. Despite their greater numbers and relative handicaps in terms of earnings and career advancement compared to earlier generations, the baby boom's retirement years appear to be secure. They seem likely, perhaps more than any other generation, to reap the fruits of a mature employer-sponsored pension system. A greater proportion of baby boom retirees will receive pensions compared to workers now retiring, and their real pension income will be higher, as will their Social Security benefits. Improved pension and Social Security benefits, however, will encourage baby boom workers to retire at earlier ages, so fewer of the baby boom cohort are likely to work after age sixty-five, and fewer will rely on earnings.

These forecasts of trends in Social Security, employer-provided pensions, and earnings represent a continuation of trends that have emerged over the past five decades. Several factors drive these developments for the baby boom cohort. Economic growth, even at the relatively moderate rates we assumed in PRISM, raises real wages over time, subsequently raising Social Security benefits and employer-sponsored pensions. In addition, more baby boom retirees will be eligible for pension benefits than retirees in earlier cohorts, even assuming no future growth in within-industry pension coverage rates among workers. While these increases would have taken place under the vesting standards inaugurated by ERISA, they are multiplied by the 1986 Tax Reform Act's five-year vesting standard.

The projected economic security of the baby boom cohort is subject to the vicissitudes of the economy, however, and the perils of legislation. Although few economists now project slower growth than that reflected in Social Security's alternative III assumptions, a severe economic recession (comparable to the Depression of 1930s) would make economic projections of any type unreliable. Similarly, if current or future legislation discouraged pension plan continuation among small and medium-size employers, plan terminations might generate much lower rates of pension recipiency and the development of a two-tier retirement income system. Although, a two-tier system could in turn encourage an economy-wide increase in individual saving, such compensating reactions are uncertain.

Perhaps one of the most significant factors leading to increased pension recipiency and greater retirement income for the baby boom is the substantially higher labor force participation of women compared to the work history of today's elderly women. The projections yielded by our PRISM model probably underestimate the degree of market work undertaken by the baby boom generation. Nevertheless, the increase in labor force participation reduces the projected poverty rate among baby boom retirees and the reliance of future elderly on SSI.

Although a lower percent of women retirees are projected to be poor, significantly lower income and significantly higher poverty rates will persist among single older women in the twenty-first century. Current research suggests that substantially reduced income among older women is more likely a result of divorce than of either retirement or widowhood. (Of course, women without work skills who have never married are likely to have very low life-time income, regardless of age.) Census projections concerning the rate and incidence of divorce and marriage, as well as changes in labor force activity associated with childbearing, are incorporated as parameters in PRISM and drive the projections presented here.

The persistently higher rate of poverty that is projected to continue among women retirees in the baby boom cohort warrants the attention of public policymakers. The policy alternatives for addressing this poverty are both familiar and controversial. They include programs to train welfare mothers in employment skills, to help displaced homemakers enter the paid labor force, and to ensure that divorced husbands provide financial support (including benefits such as health insurance) for their children. How these programs are structured and enforced, however, is politically sensitive; the fact that different segments of the American public have very different values concerning childbearing and work might prohibit effective public policy in this area.

As an unresolved problem of retirement income security, the problem of health care financing for the elderly is becoming increasingly urgent. Medicare's HI trust fund is projected to be insolvent by the turn of the century or sooner. And while general revenues continue to finance 75 percent of the cost of Medicare Supplementary Medical Insurance (SMI, or Part B), the share of total costs that SMI pays for covered services continues to erode as its cost to the public and the elderly rises.

Perhaps the most difficult health care financing question for the elderly, however, relates to long-term care—that is, health and personal care provided in institutions or at home. The inability of most elderly to pay for nursing home care in particular is demonstrated by the high rate of Medicaid eligibility among nursing home residents and the high proportion of all nursing home care that Medicaid finances. For most elderly, the cost of long-term care is literally impoverishing, leading (in states that have a medically indigent program) to Medicaid eligibility.[6] The higher projected real income of baby boom retirees, as well as their higher average preretirement income, suggests that they might be somewhat better able than the current elderly to finance health care. But the absence of an adequate insurance market for the risk of long-term care precludes equating higher real income with improved ability to finance care for most baby boom retirees.

Absent the issue of financing health and personal care needs in retirement, the baby boom's current low marginal propensity to save does not adversely affect their projected retirement income. This projection is largely the result of substantial saving among this cohort in the form of employer-sponsored pensions that might in fact displace individual saving. Furthermore, while Social Security's partial funding might constrain current consumption and/or saving by transferring resources between generations, projected increases in Social Security (and pension) income might independently deter saving, if people are confident that target retirement income goals can be met without accumulating additional resources.

Setting income goals for retirees in the twenty-first century, as a matter of public policy, is problematic. Should future retirees live according to today's living standards or the standards of the twenty-first century? Unless economic growth stops altogether, living standards in the twenty-first century will be higher than those of today. Should retirees share some or all of the gains of economic growth? These issues were last addressed in the context of the Social Security indexing debate; benefits were indexed to prices rather than wages on the assumption that retiree living standards should keep pace with inflation but not necessarily with productivity gains. Since prices then unexpectedly outpaced wages, Social Security benefits kept pace with inflation, while wages and pensions did not. Lower projected pension and Social Security replacement rates, but higher projected retirement income among the baby boom cohort, might force a review of our retirement income goals. Only by defining a standard for future retiree income can we determine a public policy course to achieve retirement income goals for the baby boom.

Notes

1. The similarity of PRISM's projected retiree health benefit recipiency rate to the prevalence of retiree health benefits among all elderly reported in SIPP also suggests that PRISM underestimates retiree health coverage among new retirees.

2. Although about one third of poor or near-poor elderly reported asset income in 1984, average reported asset income among recipients was very low.

3. Radner (1986) used CPS data, which are not adjusted for underreporting. He notes in the report that the income of the elderly tend to be underreported. Earlier research by Radner (1982) suggested that underreporting of property income was particularly prevalent among the elderly.

4. Of course, property income is not equally distributed across income classes. Elderly family units in the second income decile receive 4 percent of their income from property, compared to 12 percent among elderly in the fifth income decile and 28 percent among elderly in the ninth income decile. In average real 1983 dollars, this translates to $180 for family units in the second income decile, $1,100 for the fifth decile, and $6,410 for the ninth decile.

5. While single women have lower projected retirement income than married couples or single men, recent research suggests that after widowhood, women do not face as severe a decline in income as previously suspected (Burkhauser, Holden, and Myers 1986). Nevertheless, the greater proportions of single women produce lower income averages in older cohorts.

6. A study of nursing home admissions in Massachusetts found that 63 percent of single people age sixty-six or older and 37 percent of couples with one spouse admitted to a nursing home were impoverished and qualified for Medicaid benefits

within thirteen weeks after the admission. Within one year of admission, 83 percent of individuals and 57 percent of couples were impoverished (U.S. Congress 1985).

References

Andrews, Emily S. 1985. "The Changing Profiles of Pensions in America." Washington, DC: Employee Benefit Research Institute.

Andrews, Emily S. 1987. "Changing Pension Policy and the Aging of America." *Contemporary Policy Issues* (April):84–97.

Atkins, G. Lawrence. 1986. *Spend It or Save It? Pension Lump Sum Distributions and Tax Reform.* Washington, D.C.: Employee Benefit Research Institute.

Burkhauser, Richard V., Karen C. Holden, and Daniel A. Myers. 1986. "Marital Disruption and Poverty: The Role of Survey Procedures in Artificially Creating Poverty." Working Paper No. 86–W11, Department of Economics and Business Administration, Vanderbilt University.

Chollet, Deborah J. 1987. "Financing Retirement Today and Tomorrow: The Prospect for America's Workers." In *America in Transition: Employee Benefits for the Future.* Washington, DC: Employee Benefit Research Institute.

Employee Benefit Research Institute. 1987a. "Long-Term Effects of Tax Reform on Retirement Income: Many Unanswered Questions." *EBRI Issue Brief* 64 (March).

Employee Benefit Research Institute. 1987b. "Pension Portability and What It Can Do for Retirement Income: A Simulation Approach," *EBRI Issue Brief* 65 (April).

Fullerton, Howard N., and John Tschetter. 1983. "The 1995 Labor Force: A Second Look." *Monthly Labor Review* (November):3–10.

Kennell, David L., and John F. Shiels. 1986. "Summary of Assumptions for PRISM Simulations." Submitted to the American Association of Retired Persons (AARP).

Moon, Marilyn, and Isabel V. Sawhill. 1984. "Family Incomes: Gainers and Losers." In *The Reagan Record,* edited by J.L. Palmer and I.V. Sawhill. Cambridge, MA: Ballinger Publishing Company, 334–35.

Radner, Daniel B. 1982. "Distribution of Family Income: Improved Estimates." *Social Security Bulletin* 45 (July):13–21.

Radner, Daniel B. 1986. "Changes in the Money Income of the Aged and Nonaged, 1967–1983." Washington, DC.: Social Security Administration *(Studies in Income Distribution,* No. 14).

Ross, Dennis E. 1985. Deputy Tax Legislative Counsel, U.S. Department of the Treasury. Statement before the Subcommittee on Savings, Pensions, and Investment Policy of the U.S. Senate Committee on Finance, September 9.

Smeeding, Timothy M. 1986. "Nonmoney Income and the Elderly: The Case of the 'Tweeners.'" *Journal of Policy Analysis and Management* 5, no. 4 (Summer): 707–24.

U.S. Congress. 1985. House Select Committee on Aging. "America's Elderly at Risk." Committee No. 99–508, July.

Comment

Richard A. Ippolito

Will income among the elderly be adequate at the turn of the century? This question, which was discussed by Emily Andrews and Deborah Chollet and by Michael Hurd, is a difficult one to address because the results are so predictable. Unless major economic institutions such as Social Security and private pensions are changed dramatically and soon, it is hard to imagine that the income and/or wealth position of the elderly vis-à-vis the working population could be anything other than what it is today, with an allowance for moderate improvements attributable to more female participation in the work force.

Essentially, these are the results reported in both chapters, although the authors do an admirable job of developing other interesting features of elderly income distribution as well. Andrews and Chollet concentrate on likely improved economic conditions, especially among widows. Hurd presents results that describe the erosion of wealth during retirement and derives useful economic measures of poverty. My only quibbles are that Andrews and Chollet dramatically overstate the role of the new five-year pension vesting rules on future retiree income (the impact will be inconsequential) and that both chapters understate the rate of growth of pension retirees over the next twenty years, which will be dramatic (Ippolito 1986).

Proper Role of Government

One problem with research efforts in the area of income adequacy is that they invariably ask the wrong question: Are income levels of the elderly sufficient? The question presumes (1) that there is a "right" level of retiree income and that it is known to government and (2) that individuals are unable to determine or attain it. There is an assumption in this research that researchers can characterize consumption functions, thereby allowing them to evaluate whether the optimal lifetime distribution is being achieved. Frequently, it is implicit that consumption during retirement ought to be about equal to consumption during the working years, perhaps being adjusted for changing spending patterns (less need for saving or expenditures for children, for example).

If elderly incomes are "inadequate," this field of research invariably assumes that the proper role of government is to regulate intertemporal consumption to attain the "proper" levels. Thus, the research concentrates on a discussion of whether Social Security (and other government programs such as ERISA) are sufficient to allow appropriate income levels. Often it is assumed that without government intervention, income during retirement would be lower by the amount of Social Security benefits.

The proper role of government is not to interfere with the allocation of resources between work and retirement periods, nor is it to determine the age at which the transition from work to retirement should occur. Its proper role is exactly the reverse: to minimize the distortions created by government activity on individuals' preferences to allocate their productive efforts and income over their lifetime. Government regulations and programs that interfere with this allocation of leisure and income reduce overall welfare.

There is one exception to this rule: Given that elderly individuals are guaranteed welfare benefits, if destitute, "spenders" can take advantage of "savers." That is, given the existence of one government program (the welfare system), an incentive is created for some individuals (presumably those with a high discount rate and low income) to spend all their income during the working years, then collect welfare during retirement at the expense of the rest of society. To reduce this potential, some kind of minimum forced savings program can be justified. While the Social Security system is not necessarily the best way to accomplish this goal (a mandatory savings program might be better), it is at least a way to eliminate the free-rider problem.

Given that such a program is in place, however, there is no reason to enforce additional constraints that interfere with individuals' preferences for consumption over their lifetime. I have treated these issues elsewhere in some detail (Ippolito 1986), but in essence, an efficient national retirement policy would include actuarially fair Social Security benefits, regardless of the age of first receipt, and the elimination of Internal Revenue Code discrimination rules, ERISA regulations, and mandatory pension insurance. In addition, tax policy toward pensions should not be restricted to pension plans offered by firms. This can be done by availing unlimited individual retirement accounts (IRAs) to all workers. Unrestricted IRAs would eliminate firm-offered pension plans unless these plans had clear economic advantages.

Current tax policy (extended to IRAs) is consistent with the proper role of government. Taxation of savings at the time of deposit and earnings as earned causes distortions in the choice of retirement age and the allocation of income to working and retirement years. In effect, the current tax policy is a consumption tax applied to income devoted to spending during retirement.

A government policy that embraced economic efficiency instead of income adequacy as its main principle would generate an unknown distribution of retirement ages and consumption. This distribution might not be "adequate" in a paternalistic sense, but it would be efficient (and adequate) to workers because it would represent decisions they made individually. (This is not inconsistent with the notion that, once retired, all individuals wish they had saved more.) In this sense, there is a fundamental irrelevance of income level and the notion of income adequacy.

Efficacy of Government Policy

Even if those concerned with income adequacy issues do not consider the notion of efficiency important, it would seem that the most interesting question has not been asked: Assuming that a goal of government is to increase income among the elderly, have programs designed to attain this goal been successful thus far?

As far as I know, this is an unanswered question. It is commonly believed that Social Security is responsible for higher income among the elderly. To be sure, for all generations to date, Social Security benefits have greatly exceeded contributions, conferring a so-called wealth effect on these cohorts. In addition, it is plausible that some workers have Social Security income instead of welfare benefits, although this has not been empirically demonstrated to my knowledge.

In general, however, there is much slippage between the Social Security program and higher retirement income. We have every reason to believe that individuals will undo the intent of the system, which is otherwise inconsistent with their preferences. They can do this simply by offsetting expected Social Security benefits with less private saving (Feldstein 1974) and by children transferring less to aging parents (Barro 1978). Moreover, workers might retire at an earlier age. In fact, the Social Security earnings test itself almost surely has induced some workers to retire prematurely (Burkhauser and Turner 1981). While these issues have been the subject of empirical study, all (except the earnings test impact) remain unsettled. Certainly it has not been demonstrated that the overall impact of Social Security has been to increase the income level of the elderly.

Government tax policy, however, is almost surely responsible for a sizable portion of current levels of retirement consumption and the growing length of the retirement period. Admittedly, this is a difficult proposition to test because it poses a counterfactual question: What would retirement age and income have been had the tax code not treated pension savings according to consumption tax principles?

Prior to 1940, almost no one paid income taxes, and those who did paid single-digit marginal tax rates. During World War II, the structure was changed dramatically. Virtually all workers paid income taxes, and the median marginal tax rate was almost 25 percent. After these changes, workers could no longer use private savings vehicles to efficiently save for retirement because interest earnings were taxed. This resulted in a double tax on earnings—once as wages are earned and again as workers try to translate a portion of these wages (savings) from today's dollars into tomorrow's dollars. Savings for retirement became more costly because a higher fraction of current wages had to be saved to attain the same level of income during retirement relative to the working years. Thus, workers were unable to save as much—that is, they could buy less retirement leisure and consumption. I have shown elsewhere (Ippolito 1986) that the magnitude of these effects is large.

Since the tax code was written in the 1920s to permit pensions to escape the double tax, the effective restructuring of the tax code in the 1940s did not make retirement savings less efficient. Rather, it ensured that these savings would be made through tax-exempt pensions offered by firms. In this sense, pensions might not be new savings for retirement; perhaps they merely reflect a displacement of other types of savings vehicles.

Summary

I think it is fair to say that a government tax policy designed to eliminate savings distortions might have had a dramatic impact on retirement age and income. If it were not for the special tax policy awarded pensions, the income tax structure created in the 1940s almost surely would have caused important distortions in the retirement decisions that otherwise would have been made freely. At the same time, it is likely that government efforts to generate higher rates of income for the elderly have been offset in an important way. A sound national retirement policy would recognize the benefits of creating rules and programs that are consistent with the preferences of the individuals it governs.

A sound research agenda for economists would include a systematic evaluation of the efficiency and efficacy of government policy and would devote less time to the notion of income adequacy. It would, however, pay attention to the theory of political economy. Although the literature on income adequacy presumes that the government is benevolent, it is doubtful that any important headway can be made in the evaluation of government policy without asking how the policy was originally put in place. Was Social Security enacted because the government wanted to accomplish some social purpose or because the electorate discovered that they could vote themselves intergenerational transfers in ways that would be difficult for subsequent generations to cancel? Was ERISA passed to improve the chances that workers would receive private pension benefits or to effect transfers to a predictable minority of workers at the expense of the majority of workers? Answers to these questions provide the requisite framework for understanding how and why government programs work the way they do and why they have the effects they do. Efforts along these lines represent exciting and productive areas of policy research.

References

Barro, Robert. 1978. *The Impact of Social Security on Private Saving.* Washington, DC: American Enterprise Institute.

Burkhauser, Richard, and John Turner. 1981. "Can 25 Million Americans Be Wrong? A Response to Blinder, Gordon and Wise." *National Tax Journal* 34 (December): 467–72.

Feldstein, Martin. 1974. "Social Security, Induced Retirement and Aggregate Capital Accumulation." *Journal of Political Economy* 82, no. 5 (September/October): 905–26.

Ippolito, Richard A. 1986. *Pensions, Economics and Public Policy.* Homewood, IL: Dow Jones-Irwin.

Comment

Robert M. Ball

I enjoyed the chapters by Chollet and Andrews and by Hurd and found them to be thoughtful work. Both agree, as do I, that those who are now young are very likely to be better off in retirement than those currently retired. This is a welcome change from the popular press notion that the baby boom bulge will make our present retirement income systems unworkable.

Both chapters highlight a problem that will continue into the next century—inadequate income for elderly women who are on their own, whether widowed, divorced, or never married. To a lesser extent, the problem also exists for single men. Married couples do quite well now and will do better in the future, and the survivors of marriages that last until late in life also do better than other singles. Nothing can be done through pensions or savings for those who are elderly and single today, as their saving days are largely over, but the Supplemental Security Income (SSI) plan—a means-tested federal/state general revenue supported plan—could be improved to at least bring these people up to the poverty level.

Andrews and Chollet and Hurd were not given the task of proposing program improvements to meet the needs of those who will become old in the future, but I do have a proposal that would improve Social Security in the future. Since the most pressing need is an improvement in the level of benefits for individuals living alone, I propose leaving benefits for married couples at the same replacement rate—that is, benefits as a proportion of earnings shortly before retirement—but increasing what is known technically in Social Security jargon as the primary insurance amount (PIA). In addition to providing additional money for older people living alone, this proposal would also improve the fairness of the system by improving benefits for two-earner couples as compared to one-earner couples.

A specific example of such a proposal would be a 7 percent increase in the PIA and a simultaneous reduction in the spouse's benefit from 50 percent of the PIA to 40 percent. Under this proposal, benefits to married couples with one earner stay the same, while benefits to widows rise by 7 percent, as they do for all single workers and for couples in which both persons work.

The proposal is not cheap. It would require about a 0.3 percentage point increase in the contribution rate for both employers and employees. This probably would not receive widespread support at this time because there is almost no interest in spending more on Social Security benefits, but it might be feasible at some later date.

Incidentally, under this proposal something special would have to be done to help women who did not have much paid employment experience and were divorced after a long marriage. The divorced wife's benefit is now the same as for the wife living with her husband, but is much less adequate for a person living alone than as an add on to a retirement benefit being received by a husband. The couple gets one and a half times the retirement benefit, a generous amount compared to a single retired person, but the divorced widow gets only half the amount a retired person's benefit. Perhaps earnings sharing at divorce ought to be considered as a way of improving this benefit. Another possibility would be to gradually increase the amount of benefit payable to a divorced wife according to the number of years the marriage exceeded the ten years now required for eligibility. Thus, if the increment were 1 percent a year, the proposed wife's benefit of 40 percent of the PIA would become 70 percent of the PIA for a divorced wife if the marriage lasted forty years before divorce. This benefit would be payable until the divorced wife remarried, at which time she would be eligible for a wife's benefit based on her former husband's or her new husband's benefit, whichever was larger.

Another major weakness in our retirement system (taken as the combination of Social Security, private pensions, and private savings) mentioned in the Andrews and Chollet chapter is the nearly total lack of assured inflation protection in private pensions and the quite limited protection in state and local plans. Reliable inflation protection is fully provided for only in Social Security and for federal military and civilian employees. Private pensions, almost never guarantee any protection, and when they do, the protection is very limited, say up to 2 or 3 percent a year. Such limitations are also the rule for state and local plans.

Yet inflation protection is critical in fulfilling the basic purpose of retirement pay. It makes no sense to supply a certain level of benefits on retirement that continually declines over the fifteen to twenty years of retirement. Why get less at age eighty than at age sixty-five? No one would deliberately plan such an arrangement, particularly when those who have assets at the beginning of retirement frequently use them up in whole or in part during the first fifteen years they are no longer working. Many find this necessary in order to maintain their previous level of living, and thus are forced later into total reliance on Social Security or Social Security plus pension income.

The Andrews and Chollet analysis is based entirely on an ICF model that has two major flaws. One big problem, which they recognize, is that income from property is omitted in the model. In 1983, 24 percent of the income of aged-headed families came from this source. The bigger flaw, though, is that the model predicts income for only one year after age sixty-seven. Because of the inflation factor, I think this makes some of Andrews and Chollet's conclusions invalid. The conclusion that the role of private pensions will expand at the expense of Social Security is certainly not valid over the whole period of retirement, even if it were valid at age sixty-seven, which I seriously question. This conclusion is not valid even in the far-off future, unless private pension plans develop a way to provide inflation protection.

Quite low rates of inflation are devastating to a pension over the years of retirement unless the income is inflation protected. Let me illustrate the dynamics of this situation for a working couple who are relatively well off—one earning the average wage in 1985 of $16,743 and one earning a wage halfway between the average and the maximum then covered under Social Security, $28,178. Suppose they plan to retire in the year 2000, when one earner is sixty-five and the other, sixty-two. They figure that in order to maintain about the same level of living in retirement as they had while working, they will require an income in 1985 dollars that is about 70 percent of their combined earnings. In 1985 dollars, their Social Security benefits will amount to $17,088 a year, and they are counting on private pension and other unindexed income amounting to $19,344 to give them the 70 percent they want. Thus, when they start out in retirement, their Social Security benefits account for 47 percent of their income, but since Social Security is indexed to prices after retirement and the rest of their income is not, Social Security plays an increasingly important role as the years pass. When they are seventy-five and seventy-two, the purchasing power of Social Security will still be $17,088, but assuming a modest average inflation rate of 4 percent, their other income will have a purchasing power of only $13,068. At the end of twenty years of retirement, the $17,088 in Social Security purchasing power will represent two thirds of their total income, which is now far below the retirement income goal they had in mind. This problem goes to heart of the future complementary roles of Social Security and private pensions.

I also have doubts about the projected changed roles even at age sixty-seven for two reasons. First, I do not understand the assertion in both chapters that higher wages reduce Social Security replacement rates at the time of retirement because of the weighted benefit formula and the cap on the benefit and contribution base. In Social Security, the wage brackets to which the weights in the formula apply and the maximum base are both indexed to increases in average earnings so that the weighting stays the same and, along with wage indexing, provides for stable replacement rates at the time of retirement indefinitely into the future (with purchasing power protected after retirement).

Second, it is not clear to me why an assumption of 1 percent in real wage growth produces such relatively small increases in real Social Security benefits when they are fully indexed to current wages—and why such growth produces so much larger increases in defined benefit plans of private pensions, which quite typically are geared to the highest five or the highest three years of earnings (also an approximation of wage indexing). A 1 percent increase in real wages would be expected to have the same effect on Social Security as on such defined benefit plans. For private pension plans of the career average type, a 1 percent increase in real wages would have less effect than it would on Social Security.

Both chapters take seriously the proposal to include a value for Medicare as income in determining the number of elderly in poverty. That is, they show the numbers both ways, counting and not counting Medicare. Michael Hurd goes so far as to suggest that ". . . at least half the widows will live off Social Security and Medicare." I hope it will be mostly Social Security, since it is pretty hard to see how one can live off an insurance program that pays part of your medical care bills.

The authors are not the first to consider this approach. The controversy has been going on some time now over whether or not to include the actuarial value of Medicare, or alternatively the average payment by Medicare, in the income of people over age sixty-five when measuring poverty or near poverty.

Nevertheless, I find the whole argument strange. The poverty measure, as we all know, is a very rough indication of the minimum amount of money needed to get along. It is based only on a food budget multiplied by variables that take into account family size and urban and rural differences. A lower food budget is used for the elderly than for the rest of the population. The multipliers are assumed to take account of all expenditures other than food. No allowance is made, for example, in comparing the poverty figures for the old and the young, for any specific type of expenditure. It seems odd, therefore, to include a value for Medicare on the income side but not to take into account on the measurement side the fact that medical expenditures are much higher for the elderly than for the rest of the population and that the elderly, even with Medicare, have much higher out-of-pocket medical expenses than does the rest of the population.

After all these years we should be developing better age-specific measures of poverty—and measures specific in other ways, too—rather than resting everything in the standard on a food budget and then arguing about what should be included on the income side alone.

Although Hurd recognizes the arbitrary and artificial nature of the poverty measure, his chapter would have been better if he had applied his analysis not only to those in poverty, but also, as Andrews and Chollet did, to those with incomes up to 125 percent of poverty. I would also like to see what happens up to 200 percent of poverty.

Both chapters make an important point that contradicts some generally held misconceptions. The authors point out that many elderly are near poor and that the elderly are more likely to be poor or near poor than the rest of the population.

Andrews and Chollet also make an important point in emphasizing that the health care plans for retirees sponsored by private industry are in difficulty and that one cannot realistically expect a voluntary expansion to long-term care insurance. It seems to me that if long-term care insurance is ever going to be available to most people, it will have to be a public program.

Finally, I feel a considerable sense of responsibility for the Retirement History Survey that is the basis for Michael Hurd's analysis, because it was started when I was commissioner of Social Security. A great deal of what he has done in his chapter would have been unnecessary if that survey had been continued. It is a great disappointment to me that the survey stopped after the ten-year period 1969–1979, just as the group born in the years 1906–1911 reached age sixty-eight to seventy-three. I understand that some thought has been given to going back and interviewing the sample, which would now be age seventy-six to eighty-one. I think this would be a very important thing to do, and if undertaken, I believe the survey then ought to be continued for another ten years or so.

Part III
Planning for the Twenty-first Century: Policy Options

5
Future Social Security Financing Alternatives and National Saving

Michael J. Boskin

While the short-run financial status of Social Security is quite secure, its long-run financial status is very uncertain. First, future economic and demographic trends will heavily affect revenues and outlays. Second, except under the Social Security Administration's (SSA's) optimistic economic and demographic scenario, the retirement and disability part of the system (OASDI) is projected to be in long-run actuarial deficit (small under the intermediate assumptions, large under pessimistic ones). Hospital Insurance (HI) is projected to run a large deficit beginning in the 1990s. Finally, the OASDI system is projected to accrue (under the intermediate assumptions) a very large surplus over the next thirty years. This surplus is projected to cumulate to almost 30 percent of the gross national product (GNP), close to the current national debt to GNP ratio. This surplus is designed to reduce the need for still larger tax increases or benefit reductions during the baby boom generation's retirement. Figure 5–1 presents estimates of these average annual (not cumulative) surpluses and deficits in Social Security, including and excluding HI, over the next seventy-five years to highlight this projected movement away from pay-as-you-go finance.

We have never been able to accrue a surplus this large in Social Security; the retirement surplus may well be dissipated for other purposes (for example, to bail out HI, fund other programs, raise benefits, or cut taxes). These possibilities involve major intercohort transfers relative to accruing the surplus, as do, of course, the alternative methods of dealing with the long-run deficit (see Boskin 1986). They also involve potentially major effects on net national saving in the United States, directly because of the role Social Security surpluses or deficits will play in government sector saving or borrowing and indirectly via whatever effects they have on private saving or the non–Social Security part of the federal government budget.

I would like to thank Douglas Puffert and Jessica Primoff for valuable research assistance, John Shoven for helpful comments, and the Stanford University Center for Economic Policy Research for financial support. The intergenerational transfers corresponding to the alternatives discussed herein are estimated in Boskin and Puffert 1987.

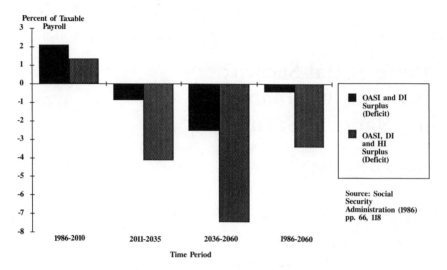

Figure 5–1. Projected Social Security Finances

The purpose of this chapter is to present calculations of the financial status of Social Security and its impact on net national saving under alternative economic, demographic, and future financing assumptions. Thus, the chapter is organized as follows: the first section describes the methodology and data and briefly discusses related analyses. Section 2 presents estimates under alternative economic and demographic assumptions of the long-run actuarial status of Old Age and Survivors Insurance (OASI). They indicate how the long-run financial status might vary from very large surpluses to very large deficits. The next section estimates the implications of alternative uses of the large surplus that is projected to accrue in the OASI trust fund. This section explores the difference, in the aggregate, if the surplus is used to raise benefits or reduce taxes or if it is spent on other programs.

Section 4 turns to the potential implications of these alternative scenarios for the level and time pattern of net national saving. The status of the Social Security system might affect the net national saving rate in several ways. First, the surplus (or deficit) in any year contributes directly to that year's net government saving (or dissaving). Second, a Social Security surplus or deficit might affect the surplus or deficit in the remainder of the federal government budget. Third, the status of Social Security might affect private saving. This chapter concentrates on the first two avenues through which Social Security affects national saving.

While I believe the weight of the evidence is that Social Security's expected evolution will affect private saving as well, this effect is somewhat more controversial and its magnitude subject to much dispute. (While much important work has been done in the past ten years, the classic debate on the subject is still found in Barro and Feldstein 1978.) Thus, the results reported in this chapter should be considered a large part of, but not all of, the story. The results are striking: Alternative scenarios with respect to accruing or dissipating the surplus have major effects on the net national saving rate. Under the SSA's intermediate assumptions, Social Security's long-term deficit (including HI) offsets almost 40 percent of the remaining net national saving. The time pattern is equally interesting: a surplus adding one sixth to net national saving in the period 1986 to 2010, but a deficit offsetting one half of all other net national saving in 2011–2035 and five sixths in 2036–2060. With tax increases and/or outlay reductions to cover the HI deficit, the surplus adds one quarter to net national saving in the period 1986 to 2010.

In the last section of the chapter, I discuss some of the implications of these results for investment, international capital flows, trade, and productivity growth, then present a brief conclusion concerning the results.

Data, Method, and Cursory Literature Review

Several studies analyze the long-run financial solvency of Social Security under alternative economic and demographic assumptions. The most important, of course, are the annual Social Security trustees' reports (formally, the Annual Reports of the Board of Trustees of the Old Age and Survivors Insurance and Disability Insurance Trust Funds). They present both short- and long-term actuarial projections of Social Security trust fund finances under alternative assumptions. The reports certainly have valuable information, but these data are presented only as fractions of taxable payroll (except, in one table, as fractions of GNP); dollar figures (whether discounted or not) are not presented for long-term projections. More importantly, the reports do not consider what the state of the retirement (OASI) trust fund might be at the end of the report's seventy-five-year horizon. Rather, it presents the *simple* average, over seventy-five years, of each year's surplus or deficit (that is, tax receipts minus benefit payments) as a fraction of that year's taxable payroll. The calculation considers neither the increase over time in taxable payroll nor the interest earned on the cumulated trust fund surplus. Thus, the 1986 report's claim that the OASI trust fund is in "close actuarial balance" because the average annual deficit is only 0.29 percent of taxable payroll is based on a fundamental misunderstanding of what that figure means. The report presents no sufficient basis for evaluating the long-run financial solvency of OASI.[1]

Boskin's (1986) estimates of the long-run financial solvency of OASI avoid these inadequacies by considering the annual flow of dollars and by projecting the actual accumulation and decumulation of the OASI trust fund. He also considers what will happen if the expected cumulative surplus of the next three decades is dissipated (for example, by raising benefits) or if reforms are instituted in retirement age and other features.

The results presented here are based partly on computer simulations of present and future families covered by the Social Security system and partly on the SSA projections discussed above. The main simulation derives figures for annual income to and expenditure from the SSA's retirement (that is, OASI) trust fund over the next seventy-five years.[2]

This simulation begins with earnings records and other data concerning Social Security participants who were surveyed in 1973.[3] For subsequent years, I estimate participants' earnings based on demographic characteristics, derive benefits based on legislated benefit formulas, and determine each participant's year of death through a random process based on mortality tables published by the SSA.[4]

Cohorts born beginning in 1953 are simulated differently. In considering typical male and female wage earners born each year, I derive their expected tax and benefit futures based on mortality probabilities and the proportion that can be expected to marry. I multiply by the number born each year (plus the number born that year who later immigrate as children) who will enter covered employment, and thus derive figures for entire cohorts. To derive income and expenditure for the trust fund as a whole, I make a further adjustment for taxes paid and benefits received by adult immigrants.

The discussion is based on a version of the simulation that assumes the tax law effective at the time of the 1986 trustees' report. Results presented below use the income tax law enacted in 1986.[5]

In the main simulation, I rely on SSA projections for the proportion of Social Security benefits that are recovered for the trust fund through income taxation. These estimates are that this proportion will increase from less than 2 percent in 1986 to about 5 percent in the mid-twenty-first century. Because legislated marginal tax rates have been reduced since the SSA made its projections, I assume that from 1988 on, 20 percent less will be collected in taxes on benefits. In 1987, the transition year, I assume that 10 percent less will be collected.

This simulation is parameterized by economic, demographic, and legal assumptions. The most important economic assumption is future growth of real wages. The chief demographic assumptions are mortality probabilities by age and fertility rates. The legal assumptions are payroll tax rates and formulas for the calculation of benefits. In the scenarios below, I consider the alternative economic and demographic assumptions that the SSA itself uses for the scenarios in its annual trustees' reports,[6] and I consider fixed multiples of the payroll taxes and the benefits currently legislated.

Long-Run Financial Status of OASI under Alternative Economic and Demographic Assumptions

Table 5–1 presents the results of the main simulation using the 1986 trustees' report's intermediate assumptions about future economic and demographic

Table 5-1
Base Case: Intermediate Assumptions—Financial Flows of OASI Trust Fund
(1986 dollars in billions, discounted to 1986)

Time Period	Payroll	Taxes	Benefits	Benefit Taxes[a]	Surplus	Surplus/Payroll
1986–2010	39,584	4,366	3,997	114 (141)	483	1.22%
2011–2035	38,540	4,232	4,422	158 (198)	−31	−0.08%
2036–2060	34,460	3,784	4,925	196 (244)	−946	−2.74%
1986–2060	112,584	12,381	13,344	468 (584)	−495	−0.44%

[a] Income taxation of benefits. Figures in parentheses refer to old tax law.

trends. It shows the basic trends, well known by now, that are expected to develop in the finances of the OASI trust fund. This trust fund will accumulate a substantial surplus over the next twenty-five years while the baby boom generation is in its peak earning years. In the following twenty-five years (more precisely, in the mid-2020s), when the baby boom generation retires, benefit payments will begin to exceed payroll tax revenues. In the third twenty-five-year period, there will be a still higher proportion of retirees to workers, and annual deficits will equal one fourth of tax receipts, or one fifth of net benefits.

For the whole seventy-five-year period, I project a deficit of nearly $500 billion in 1986 dollars discounted to 1986. This is equal to about 0.44 percent of (discounted) taxable payroll.[7] Thus, a rise in the Social Security payroll tax rate of a little less than 0.44 percent effective now, or substantially more later, would be needed to close the long-run OASI trust fund deficit if the intermediate assumptions prove to be the case.

It is worth noting at this point why I present the figures in discounted terms. First, this enables me to consider the present value of potential futures of the OASI trust fund. This is especially valuable as I compare scenarios with different time paths of surpluses and deficits. Second, it obviates the need to give explicit consideration to the interest received (or paid out) by the trust fund on its calculated surplus (or deficit), if I assume that the interest and discount rates are identical. Of course, individual participants might value their benefits at more than the expected present value, as they are paid as inflation-indexed life annuities. The 1986 present value of the surplus or deficit through 2060 will equal the sum of the 1986 present values of annual surpluses and deficits until then. As a corollary, it becomes very simple to compute how taxes or benefits can or must be changed to bring the trust fund into actuarial balance.

The system finances are also presented in figure 5–2, which shows the discounted surplus both annually and on a cumulative basis. On a cumulative basis, the system starts to run a deficit (assuming the surplus accrues and real interest is 2 percent) around 2048, and on an annual basis, around 2025. I present below some hypothetical scenarios of the surplus being dissipated or alternative economic and demographic projections that alter these conclusions substantially.

The SSA's intermediate economic and demographic assumptions are perhaps as reasonable as any, but we can be sure that they will not be realized with great accuracy.[8] It is thus important to consider the impact of a range of possible futures on the Social Security system's finances.

Table 5–2 summarizes the effects of using the SSA's optimistic and pessimistic assumptions for future wage growth, future mortality (and hence, life expectancy), future fertility, and various combinations of these parameters. Wide variations exist in results for the financial solvency of the retirement trust fund. The 1986 present value of the trust fund surplus (or deficit) through

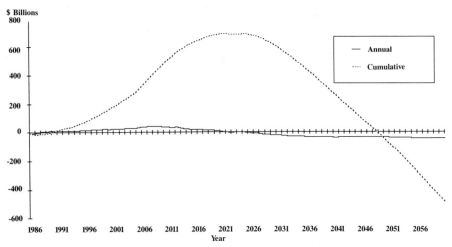

Figure 5–2. Discounted Surplus (Annual and Cumulative), Base Case

2060 ranges from + $3.4 trillion to – $2.6 trillion for the combined optimistic and pessimistic assumptions, respectively.[9] As seen in the column headed "Year Annual Deficit Begins," tax receipts exceed benefit expenditures in each year through 2060 only when the optimistic assumptions are combined; otherwise current-flow deficits begin between 2014 and 2030. The next column shows that the cumulative surplus suffices, however, to cover benefit expenditures until 2024 in the most pessimistic scenario and beyond 2060 in several of the optimistic scenarios.

The SSA's intermediate (II-B) assumption for growth in real wages, used in our base case, is that there will be an annual gain of 1.5 percent (with some fluctuation in the very short run). The optimistic assumption considers a gain of 2.5 percent annually, and the pessimistic assumption considers a gain of 1 percent.

Interestingly, higher wage growth is better both for the system's finances and for participants in the system. An increase in the trust fund's annual surplus (taxes minus benefits) proves consistent with a higher ratio of benefits received to taxes paid for the participants. The reason for this is that increases in taxes, which vary with total wages, precede the increases in benefits to which wage growth leads. The wage index is used in the formula for determining benefits, and so a faster rise in this index provides a higher rate of return for participants. What balances the books is a growth in the unfunded liabilities of the retirement trust fund. These liabilities could become quite burdensome if wage growth slows in the future.

It is clear in table 5–2 that variation in wage growth changes taxes and benefits in the same direction but that taxes change to a greater extent. High

Table 5–2
System Finances, Various Economic and Demographic Scenarios, Seventy-five Year Totals (1986–2060)
(1986 dollars in billions, discounted to 1986)

Scenarios	Taxes	Benefits	Benefit Taxes	Surplus	Variation of Surplus from Base Case	Surplus as Percentage of Taxable Payroll	Year Annual Deficit Begins	Year Cumulative Deficit Begins
Base case	$12,381	$13,344	$468	-$495	$0	-0.44	2025	2048
High wage growth	18,021	17,781	639	878	+1,373	0.54	2030	by 2090
Low wage growth	10,170	11,516	398	-948	-453	-1.03	2020	2035
High mortality	12,306	12,267	429	468	+963	0.42	2027	by 2080
Low mortality	12,522	14,743	521	-1,700	-1,205	-1.49	2018	2035
High fertility	13,095	13,365	469	199	+694	0.17	2026	by 2080
Low fertility	11,516	13,315	467	-1,332	-837	-1.27	2021	2040
Overall optimistic for trust fund	19,177	16,376	587	3,389	+3,884	1.94	a	a
Overall pessimistic for trust fund	9,644	12,653	441	-2,567	-2,072	-2.93	2014	2024

a Remains positive indefinitely

wage growth increases the long-run surplus by $1.37 trillion, which more than offsets the long-run deficit expected under the base case. Low wage growth deepens the long-run deficit by about $450 billion.

In assumptions about mortality, what is optimistic for the solvency of the retirement trust is pessimistic for participants, and vice versa. The trust fund is more solvent when people die sooner and collect less in benefits. Table 5–2 shows that under the SSA's high-mortality (low life expectancy) assumption, the trust fund is better off by $963 billion over the seventy-five-year horizon, but that under the low-mortality assumption, the system is worse off by $1.2 trillion.

Alternative assumptions about fertility matter only for those cohorts not yet born, but because Social Security participants begin paying taxes some forty years before they receive benefits, fertility rates will have a big impact on trust fund finances in the next century.[10] Indeed, today's low fertility rates are the most widely cited source of probable future problems in Social Security finance. Current fertility rates are about 1.9 children per woman over her childbearing years. The SSA's intermediate assumption is that this will increase within the next two decades to 2.0 children per woman. The optimistic and pessimistic assumptions are 2.3 and 1.6, respectively.[11] The results of the simulation, shown in table 5–2, are that high fertility would add $694 billion to the trust fund surplus, more than eliminating what is otherwise a deficit, while low fertility would add $837 billion to the deficit.

Under the combined optimistic and pessimistic assumptions for trust fund finances, the differences from the intermediate scenario for long-run surplus are + $3.88 trillion and − $2.07 trillion (see table 5–3). The present value of taxes differs between these extreme scenarios by a factor of nearly 2, while benefits vary by a factor of about 1.3.

Figure 5–3 shows how the size of the accumulated trust fund varies over the next seventy-five years for the overall optimistic, intermediate (base case), and pessimistic scenarios. Note that the continuing increase in the trust fund occurs only when all the optimistic assumptions occur simultaneously. For any one of the optimistic assumptions alone, interest on the trust fund is eventually insufficient to cover the difference between current benefits and current taxes, and the principal itself is exhausted before 2090 (see table 5–3, last column).

Financial Impact of Alternative Uses of the Potential OASDI Trust Fund Surplus

I noted in the previous section that only under the combined optimistic assumptions for wage growth, mortality, and fertility can we hope that the retirement trust fund will take in at least as much each year in taxes as it pays

Table 5-3
Various Scenarios for Trust Fund Surplus, Seventy-five-Year Totals (1986–2060)
(1986 dollars in billions, discounted to 1986)

Scenarios	Taxes	Benefits	Benefit Taxes	Surplus	Variation of Surplus from Base Case	Surplus as Percentage of Taxable Payroll	Year Annual Deficit Begins	Year Cumulative Deficit Begins
Base case	$12,381	$13,344	$468	–$495	$0	–0.44	2025	2045
Pay-as-you-go tax rates	12,868	13,344	468	–8	+487	0.00	n.a.	n.a.
Pay-as-you-go benefits	12,381	12,832	443	8	+487	0.00	n.a.	n.a.
Benefit ratchet, unfunded	12,381	16,662	591	–3,690	–3,195	–3.28	2010	2010
Benefit ratchet, funded by taxes	16,064	16,662	591	–8	+487	0.00	n.a.	n.a.
Surplus dissipated, funded by taxes	13,565	13,344	468	0[a]	+495	0.00	n.a.	n.a.
Surplus dissipated, adjusted benefits	12,381	12,112	420	0[a]	+495	0.00	n.a.	n.a.

[a] $689 billion surplus through 2025 has been dissipated.

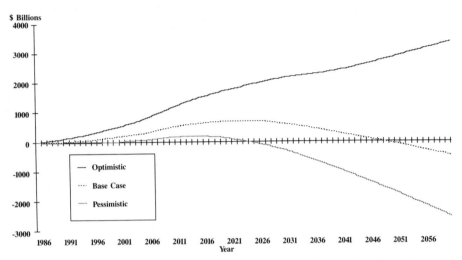

Figure 5–3. Discounted Cumulative Surplus for Alternative Scenarios

out in benefits. In all other cases, an accumulation in the trust fund is necessary to forestall the time when taxes must be raised or benefits reduced.[12] Under intermediate assumptions, for example, an annual deficit will begin in 2025, but the accumulated surplus will keep the trust fund solvent until 2048.

It has always been difficult to accumulate a large trust fund surplus. It is in the interest of each session of Congress, and each administration, to raise benefits (or perhaps to lower taxes, although that has not yet been tried) if possible. Raising benefits conveys transfers to those receiving or soon to receive benefits while imposing much of the cost of the action on future generations which do not vote yet. Similarly, lowering taxes helps a current generation of workers while requiring higher taxes from future generations than would otherwise be necessary.

The situation is now particularly acute for a major demographic reason: In less than thirty years, the baby boom generation will begin to retire. If we do not accumulate a trust fund surplus before then, future adjustments in payroll tax rates or in benefits will have to be much greater than would otherwise be necessary.

Figure 5–4 depicts the combined (employer and employee) tax rates that would be required each year to fund currently legislated benefits (given intermediate assumptions) without adding to or drawing upon an accumulated surplus. Until 2025,[13] tax rates could be lower than those currently legislated, but thereafter they would increase drastically.

Conversely, figure 5–5 shows the level of benefits that could be funded by each year's tax receipts. This level is presented in the form of a ratio to benefits as provided for under current legislation. It is apparent that benefits

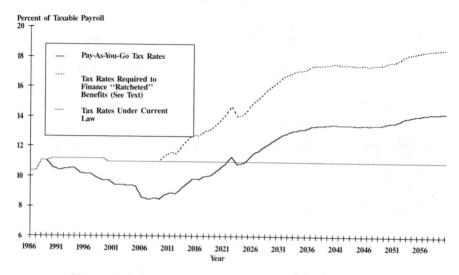

Figure 5–4. Tax Rates, Current Law and Pay-As-You-Go

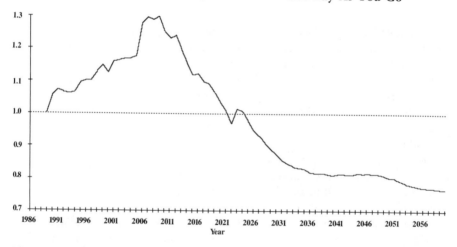

**Figure 5–5. Pay-As-You-Go Benefit Ratio, Given Taxes, to Maintain
Annual Balance**

could be raised intermittently through 2009, to a level 30 percent higher than
that now legislated, but that thereafter they must either decline or, perhaps
more plausible politically, be maintained through increases in payroll tax rates.
The tax rates required to finance these increased benefits are depicted in the
broken line of figure 5–4.

Table 5–3 summarizes the financial impact several ways of dissipating the trust fund surplus that is projected to grow over the next thirty-five to forty years. The line "Pay-as-you-go tax rates" considers the scenario in which, beginning in 1990, tax rates are set each year at a level that exactly covers that year's benefit payments. Similarly, the line "Pay-as-you-go benefits" considers the adjustment of benefit levels to match projected tax receipts. The tax rates and benefit levels of these scenarios thus follow the heavy lines depicted in figures 5–4 and 5–5, respectively.

The benefit ratchet scenarios consider the cases in which benefits rise to their pay-as-you-go peak in 2009 but do not subsequently decline. The first of these scenarios notes the enormous deficit ($3.69 trillion) generated when the higher benefit level is not funded with taxes, while the second considers the case of taxes rising, in a pay-as-you-go fashion, to fund the increased benefits.

The last two scenarios consider what will happen if the surplus that is projected to accumulate over the next forty years is dissipated, or directed to other purposes. Two very plausible possibilities for this are that the surplus could be used to cover some of the massive deficit in Social Security's HI fund that (absent a major reform) will develop within a few years,[14] or that the surplus will, in the face of federal budget deficits, be used to fund other expenditures. The first of these scenarios raises taxes in a pay-as-you-go fashion from 2025 on. Thus, these scenarios are equivalent to the earlier pay-as-you-go scenarios from 2025 on; they lack only the period in which tax or benefit levels are more favorable for participants than the levels currently legislated. The chief result for system finances (see table 5–3) under all these scenarios— except, of course, the unfunded ratcheting of benefits—is that the long-run surplus is, by construction, essentially zero.

Projections of Net National Saving and Its Components under Alternative Hypothetical Scenarios

Let's turn now to estimates of net national saving and its components under alternative hypothetical scenarios concerning the future of Social Security financing and various other factors. Before turning to the results, let me reiterate that these are meant only to be simple simulations designed to highlight some emerging national policy issues. They are not meant to be taken as a thorough analysis of the likely evolution of any of the components, let alone all of them. Nor do they exhaust the various interesting alternative scenarios. In these calculations, I use the SSA projections, which differ slightly for OASI from my own, as discussed above.

Note that net national saving, which I label total saving (TS) is the sum of private saving (PS)—that is, gross private saving, net of depreciation, the sum of personal and business saving; state and local government saving

(*SLS*)—traditionally measured by the state and local surplus, although the simultaneously accruing liabilities in the pension funds are not properly accounted for, nor is net state and local capital formation; and federal government saving (*FS*)—traditionally measured by the federal government surplus, although the simultaneously accruing future pension liabilities and federal government capital formation are not appropriately treated either.[15] Thus,

$$TS = PS + SLS + FS \tag{5.1}$$

I decompose *FS* into the federal surplus excluding Social Security (*FSXS*) and the OASDI surplus (*OASDIS*) and HI surplus (*HIS*). Thus,

$$FS = FSXS + OASDIS + HIS \tag{5.2}$$

Before turning to the basic simulation results, it is worth anticipating the discussion in the next section concerning the importance of net national saving for investment and international capital flows by recalling from the national income identity that

$$FS = I - PS - SLS + NFI \tag{5.3}$$

where *I* is domestic investment and *NFI* is net foreign investment. Holding national income constant, changes in *FS* must be matched by corresponding changes in *PS, I, SLS,* and/or *NFI*. Once I establish the likely effects on national saving in this section, I will discuss the implications for investment and net foreign investment in the next section.

Let's start out with some particular base case assumptions. For simplicity, I assume in most, but not all, of the calculations that the net private saving rate is constant at 6 percent of GNP, close to its historical average. I discuss cases in which Denison's law holds—that is, the gross private saving rate is constant. In that case, the growth of the capital consumption allowance will decrease net private saving. I also discuss a simple conservative calculation of the impact of changing demography on the saving rate through time. But in the remaining cases, the net private saving rate is assumed constant at 6 percent. The state and local surplus, according to the Commerce Department, has been abnormally high for the past several years, in part due to funding issues in their pension systems. It is presumed to run 1 percent of GNP for the next five years, then to decline for the following ten years, until it reaches a balanced budget and remains there from the turn of the century on. This leaves us with federal government saving, the non–Social Security surplus or deficit, and the OASDI and HI surplus or deficit. I consider several alternatives for the non–Social Security deficit. In the base case, I have the non–Social Security deficit evolve to keep the national debt-GNP ratio constant at current levels. Holding constant the ratio of national debt to GNP,

I ignore the distinction between the primary budget deficit and interest payments, except in one scenario in which I explicitly model a balanced primary budget.

I consider various alternative scenarios or rules with respect to the remainder of the budget, either explicitly or implicitly, via rules on the overall budget. For example, I examine net national saving under Gramm-Rudman with and without HI balanced, a balanced budget from the year 2000 on, continuing federal government deficits, the optimistic and pessimistic SSA assumptions, a zero primary deficit, pay-as-you-go OASDI, and benefits ratcheting up in the era of the OASDI surplus.

The results of the simulation are portrayed in figures 5–6 through 5–18. Net national saving and its components are plotted for the seventy-five year projection period usually employed by the SSA, in this case 1986 to 2060. A variety of interesting features emerges from these graphs. For example, consider figures 5–6 and 5–7, which estimate net national saving under Gramm-Rudman plus the remaining assumptions described above. The net national saving rate rises abruptly from its current 2 percent to about 7 percent by 1991, due largely to the substantial decrease in the federal government budget deficit. It then declines gradually to 6 percent around the turn of the century for about a decade, then declines sharply to under 4 percent after 2026. Importantly, the comparison of figures 5–6 and 5–7 reveals that by moving HI into budget balance, we would raise the net national saving rate by about 2 percentage points in the period after the turn of the century. I do not discuss here what combination of tax increase and/or benefit reduction would be used to balance HI; I assume that it occurs in a manner that does not affect the other components.

Figure 5–8 presents net national saving under a balanced federal budget for the year 2000 and thereafter. This might be thought of as simulating a strict balanced budget requirement, such as that advocated by supporters of a constitutional amendment. As can be seen, net national saving rises substantially, then gradually falls, reflecting the surplus turning to deficit in OASDI and the HI deficit. The non–Social Security part of the budget is required to be in balance.

In what might be thought of as a base case, with the debt-GNP ratio (excluding Social Security) held constant, figures 5–9 and 5–10 project net national saving with federal and OASDI deficits and, correspondingly, with the HI budget in balance. The net national saving rate falls precipitously beginning about the year 2005; in the base case, it falls to under 1 percent of GNP by the year 2030. A balanced HI budget adds the usual couple of percentage points to the net national saving rate early in the next century.

Figures 5–11 and 5–12 use the base case assumptions for *PS* and *SLS* but replace the intermediate SSA assumptions by the optimistic and pessimistic ones, respectively. They also allow the non–Social Security budget deficit to evolve based on the alternative assumptions on factors such as GNP growth.

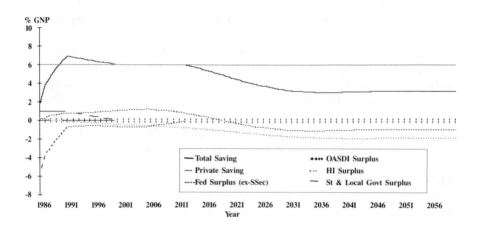

Figure 5–6. Net National Saving under Gramm-Rudman

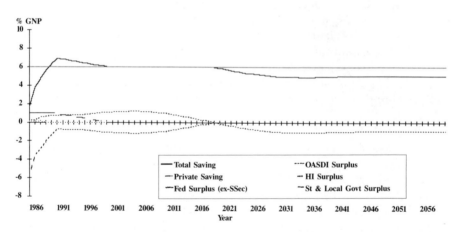

Figure 5–7. Net National Saving under Gramm-Rudman (HI Trust Fund Balance)

Net national saving is substantially higher under the optimistic Social Security assumptions, as the status of the OASDI fund and HI fund improve enormously, as does, to a lesser extent, the non–Social Security deficit. In fact, net national saving not only declines much less to slightly under 4 percent in the peak of the baby boom's retirement, but also begins to rise above 4 percent later on. Under the pessimistic assumptions, as expected, net national

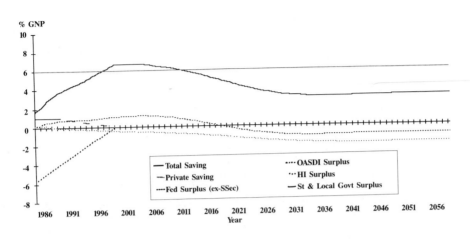

Figure 5–8. Net National Saving under Balanced Federal Budget (2000 and after)

saving takes a nosedive, turning negative about 2015. This is due to the very large deficits in HI cumulating by then and to the fact that OASDI will have turned to deficit about five years earlier, thereby offsetting all private saving.

Figure 5–13 portrays net national saving under a zero primary deficit—that is, the federal budget net of interest payments. As can be seen, net national saving falls but remains positive, if paltry, by the first quarter of the next century.

Figures 5–14 through 5–16 highlight some potential reactions to the building of the OASDI surplus. Figure 5–14 portrays net national saving and its components under pay-as-you-go OASDI, assuming that either the tax increases to finance deficits or the benefit decreases during the period of OASDI surpluses do not affect the other components of net national saving. Dissipating the early surplus, compared to the base case, lowers net national saving substantially in the first three decades of the projection. Net national saving falls to 3 percent by the turn of the century and eventually declines still further to about 2 percent of GNP. Note, however, that net national saving under pay-as-you-go OASDI, while substantially lower for the next thirty years or so, eventually is higher, partially offsetting base case projections of subsequent large OASDI surpluses.

Figure 5–15 presents net national saving under the alternative described in detail in the previous section concerning the possibility of benefits ratcheting up during the period of the OASDI surplus and remaining at those higher levels thereafter. Net national saving plummets as in the previous case for the next thirty years, then declines precipitously, becoming negative about 2016

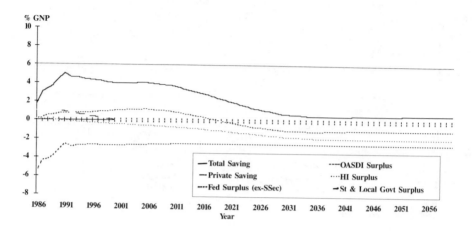

Figure 5–9. Net National Saving under Federal and OASDHI Deficits (Base Case)

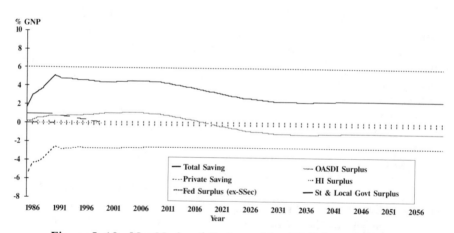

Figure 5–10. Net National Saving under HI Balanced Budget

and falling to − 5 percent of GNP by about 2030. Undoubtedly, well before such a national catastrophe occurred, various alternative policies would be adopted. This is the flip side of the $3.7 trillion deficit estimated for this case in the previous section. Note that if I were to add a tax increase and/or benefit cuts in the HI system to this case, net national saving would rise about 2 percentage points, as shown in figure 5–16.

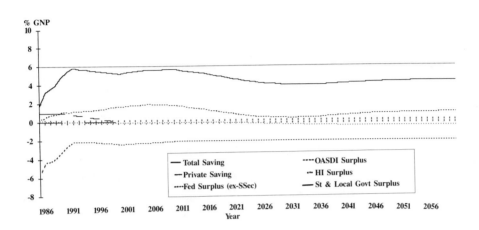

Figure 5–11. Net National Saving under Optimistic Social Security Assumptions

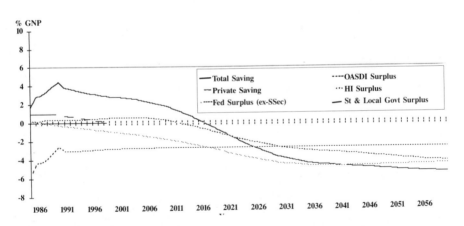

Figure 5–12. Net National Saving under Pessimistic Social Security Assumptions

Figures 5–17 and 5–18 estimate the impact of dissipation of the OASDI surplus (assuming HI is balanced) by using it to finance the general federal deficit and increase spending, respectively. The impact of the dissipation of the surplus and how the funds are used, is substantial.

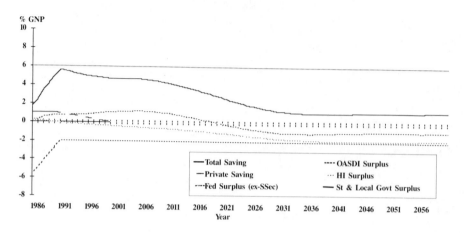

Figure 5–13. Net National Saving under Zero Primary Federal Deficit

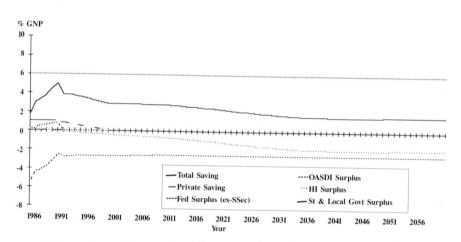

Figure 5–14. Net National Saving under Pay-As-You-Go OASDI

Finally, figures 5–19 and 5–20 present two simplistic scenarios in which the private saving rate varies; first because of changes in the age structure of the population and second because of the alleged constancy of the gross private saving rate, Denison's law. In figure 5–19, I have allowed the net private saving rate to vary with the age structure. I use SSA projections of the fractions of the population in the three age cohorts 20–44, 45–64, and 65 and over; assume that the relative income per household of the three groups remain as

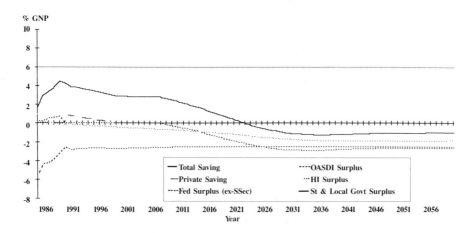

Figure 5-15. Net National Saving under OASDI Benefit Ratchet

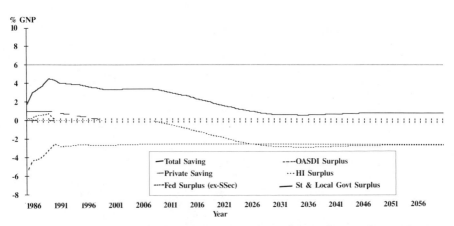

Figure 5-16. Net National Saving under OASDI Benefit Ratchet and HI Balanced Budget

estimated in 1984 (see Boskin, Kotlikoff, and Knetter 1985); and, for simplicity, assume that the saving rate of people in their peak earning years is twice that of younger workers, whereas the saving rate of the elderly is − 3 percent. The rates are calibrated so that the overall rate in 1984 is 6 percent. There is substantial controversy concerning whether the elderly save or

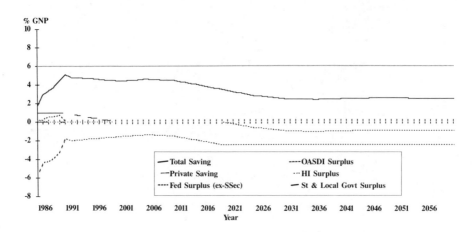

Figure 5–17. Net National Saving Assuming OASDI Surplus Finances Federal Deficit and HI Budget Balanced

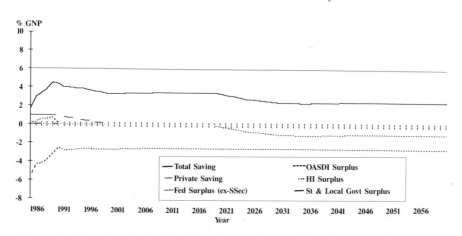

Figure 5–18. Net National Saving Assuming OASDI Is Spent and HI Budget Balanced

dissave during retirement, at what rate, and the implications this might have for a number of important aspects of saving behavior. I present this as a hypothetical situation that might result in saving rates changing. As figure 5–19 demonstrates, however, the saving rate merely varies from 5.8 to 6.2 percent.

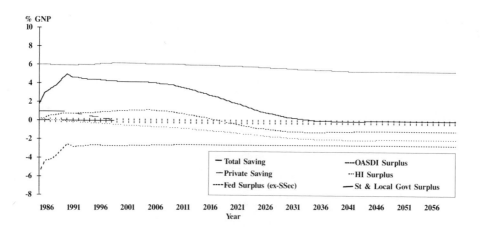

Figure 5–19. Net National Saving Assuming Private Saving Varies with Age Structure

We would need either a much more dramatic change in relative incomes or a substantially greater variation in the saving rates by age for large variations in the private saving rate to occur. Of course, this is possible if the elderly do dissave and/or if relative incomes change in a way that will dramatically change the relative income weighting underlying figure 5–19. In any event, relative to the base case, the variations are quite modest.

Not so modest are the implications of Denison's law, which asserts that the gross private saving rate is constant. Ignoring any feedback from changes in the net saving rate to the rate of investment, capital formation, and depreciation, I simulate a simple scenario in which the capital formation process in the economy results in a gradual rise in the capital consumption allowance over the next forty years. I presume that this rise is about 2 percentage points. Clearly, with the gross private saving rate constant, the net private saving rate must decline by 2 percentage points in this case.

Under the other assumptions of the base case scenario, net national saving, as depicted in figure 5–20, declines by 2 percentage points, holding all the other components constant. In this case, national saving turns negative by 2016, as it falls continuously from 1991 on, the year in which I begin the simulation of the gradual rise in the capital consumption allowance. I have chosen this form for no particular reason other than simplicity, nor would I expect the capital consumption allowance necessarily to move at this rate or to remain constant after 2020; I present these results because of some people's strong belief in Denison's law.

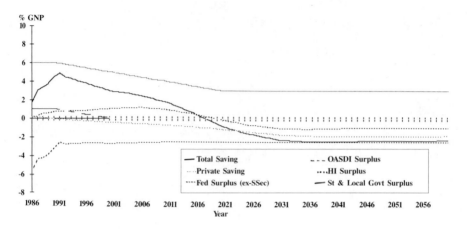

Figure 5–20. Net National Saving Assuming Denison's Law

Tables 5–4 through 5–6 highlight some of the important effects of Social Security on national saving. Table 5–4 projects net national saving and its components as a percentage of GNP for the seventy-five-year period and for each of the usual twenty-five-year subperiods for the base case, with and without HI balanced. It shows that the total national saving rate is a little over 2 percent for the entire period in the base case and 3.33 percent when HI is balanced. These seventy-five-year averages are composed of a small OASDI deficit, a federal deficit of 2.33 percent of GNP, a very small state and local surplus, a constant 6 percent private saving rate, and the HI deficit in the base case and an HI balanced budget from 1991 in the second case. The three subperiods show interesting variations. The net national saving rate is substantially higher in the first twenty-five-year period, averaging slightly over 4 percent. In the second period, the net national saving rate falls to 1.7 and 3.1 percent, respectively. In the third twenty-five-year period, the corresponding net national saving rates are 0.5 and 2.8 percent. Given the other assumptions, the primary difference revolves around the OASDI and HI surplus/deficit pattern.

Table 5–5 presents estimates of net national saving averaged over each of the three twenty-five-year periods and the entire seventy-five-year period for various alternative future financing scenarios. It reveals the substantial impact Social Security financing alternatives might have on net national saving. For example, consider the period 1986–2010. Moving from the base case with accumulation of the OASDI surplus to pay-as-you-go OASDI (that is, tax rate cuts to match outlays) reduces net national saving by 20 percent, from 4.0 percent to 3.2 percent of GNP. Still more dramatic changes occur with other financing scenarios and in the later periods.

Table 5–4
Projected Net National Saving and Its Components as a Percentage of Projected GNP [a]

	1986–2060	1986–2010	2011–2035	2036–2060
Base case				
Total	2.1	4.0	1.8	0.6
OASDI	−0.1	0.9	−0.3	−1.0
Private	6.0	6.0	6.0	6.0
HI	−1.2	−0.3	−1.3	−1.9
Federal	−2.7	−3.0	−2.5	−2.5
State/local	0.1	0.4	0.0	0.0
Base case (HI balanced)				
Total	2.5	4.3	3.1	2.5
OASDI	−0.1	0.9	−0.3	−1.0
Private	6.0	6.0	6.0	6.0
HI	0.0	0.0	0.0	0.0
Federal	−2.7	−3.0	−2.5	−2.5
State/local	0.1	0.4	0.0	0.0

[a] Data are simple averages of annual total.

Table 5–5
Projected Net National Saving as a Percentage of Projected GNP

Scenario	1986–2060	1986–2010	2011–2035	2036–2060
Gramm-Rudman	4.5	5.9	4.3	3.1
Gramm-Rudman (HI balanced)	5.5	5.9	5.5	5.0
Balanced federal budget (2000 and after)	4.2	5.3	4.3	3.1
Base case	2.1	4.0	1.8	0.6
Base case (HI balanced)	3.3	4.3	3.1	2.5
Optimistic SSA assumptions	4.6	5.1	4.5	4.3
Pessimistic SSA assumptions	−1.3	2.9	−1.7	−5.0
Zero primary federal deficit	2.7	4.5	2.3	1.1
Pay-as-you-go OASDI	2.3	3.2	2.2	1.6
OASDI benefit ratchet	0.8	3.2	0.2	−1.1
OASDI benefit ratchet (HI balanced)	1.9	3.5	1.5	0.8
OASDI surplus finances federal deficit (HI balanced)	3.3	4.3	3.1	2.5
OASDI surplus spent (HI balanced)	3.0	3.5	3.0	2.5
Private saving varies with age structure	2.0	4.1	1.7	0.1
Denison's law	−0.1	3.2	−1.0	−2.4

Table 5–6
Percentage Change in Net National Saving Due to Social Security Surplus or Deficit, by Period, for Alternative Financing Scenarios[a]

Scenario	1986–2060	1986–2010	2011–2035	2036–2060
Gramm-Rudman	– 21.4	11.3	– 27.8	– 47.6
Gramm-Rudman (HI balanced)	– 1.0	18.8	– 5.4	– 16.3
Balanced federal budget (2000 and after)	– 20.5	14.0	– 27.8	– 47.6
Base case	– 38.0	17.0	– 47.0	– 82.0
Base case (HI balanced)	– 3.7	26.8	– 9.9	– 28.1
Optimistic SSA assumptions	20.7	37.2	16.0	8.9
Pessimistic SSA assumptions	– 137.9	– 10.8	– 41.7	– 71.4
Zero primary federal deficit	– 32.7	15.0	– 151.9	– 251.0
Pay-as-you-go OASDI	– 32.4	– 5.2	– 38.1	– 53.9
OASDI benefit ratchet	– 77.5	– 6.4	– 94.6	– 131.4
OASDI benefit ratchet (HI balanced)	– 43.5	3.4	– 56.6	– 77.4
OASDI surplus finances federal deficit (HI balanced)	– 3.7	26.8	– 9.9	– 28.1
OASDI surplus spent (HI balanced)	– 12.9	3.9	– 14.5	– 28.1
Private saving varies with age structure	– 43.4	16.5	– 50.5	– 96.2
Denison's law	– 302.4	23.5	– 335.8	– 594.8

[a]Data are simple averages of annual total.

Table 5–6 presents an alternative method of viewing how quantitatively important the Social Security surplus or deficit will be as a percentage of other net national saving over the seventy-five-year period and in each of the twenty-five-year periods. For the base case, over the seventy-five-year period, the Social Security deficit, including the HI deficit, offsets 38 percent of all other net national saving. This decomposes into adding 17 percent in the first twenty-five years, offsetting almost one half in the second twenty-five years, and off-setting more than four fifths in the third twenty-five-year period. In the case where HI is balanced, by whatever combination of tax increases and benefit reductions, Social Security offsets substantially less of other net national saving. The Gramm-Rudman cases demonstrate substantially higher other net national saving and, therefore, the Social Security surplus or deficit offsets a more modest fraction of net national saving. The other cases indicate just how much might be at stake in net national saving in alternative future Social Security financing policies. For example, in the case where benefits rise during the years that otherwise would have had a surplus and then remain elevated, more than three fourths of all other net national saving will be offset by the

OASDI deficit, starting with a small offset the first twenty-five years and then offsetting all other saving. Undoubtedly in such a case, there would be some adjustment in taxes and/or the remainder of the budget to compensate.

I have outlined the results not just to present an array of potential scenarios or to present estimates of net national saving that should be viewed in any way other than hypothetically, but to highlight how important the direct effects of Social Security can be on net national saving. That effect clearly can be enormous in any year, in each of the twenty-five-year subperiods considered, as well as in the seventy-five-year projection period of the SSA. Assumptions concerning the other components of net national saving will affect the level of net national saving but still leave the situation where the status of the future financing of OASDI will have an enormous direct impact on net national saving in the United States. Of course, the direct impact might be offset or accentuated by the impact of OASDI on private saving and/or other components of government saving and borrowing.

Implications for Investment, International Capital Flows, Trade, and Productivity Growth

The results reported above were designed to highlight the potentially significant impact of alternative policy options on the net national saving rate, with respect to accumulation or dissipation of the OASDI surplus. Net national saving is important for a variety of reasons. Saving is the method by which individual households transfer resources from one part of their lifetime to another—for example, from their peak earning years to retirement. Government sector saving or borrowing is, among other things, the method by which the public sector attempts to transfer resources, at least tax burdens, intertemporally. More directly, net national saving is available to finance domestic investment or net foreign investment. A higher net national saving rate might help increase the level of domestic capital formation or decrease the need for imports of foreign capital. Simplistic analyses suggest that a high rate of capital formation will temporarily increase the rate of economic growth and lead permanently to a higher level of income by making labor more productive due to the higher capital-labor ratio. In a closed economy, a higher saving rate will be invested in the long run. In an open economy, a higher saving rate will increase U.S. capital flows abroad and/or decrease foreign capital flows into the United States. As discussed above, the United States has in recent years been a substantial importer of foreign capital. These imports have become significant enough to make the United States a net debtor, at least if the books are taken at face value (U.S. assets overseas are usually treated at historic cost). Thus, despite the short-run benefits, each year that the United States imports large amounts of foreign capital results in an annual stream of claims against that investment in the future as interest, dividends, and rents to foreigners. Ultimately, the only way to pay those returns is for the United States to export more than it imports. For example, in 1986 the United States imported $144 billion of net capital from abroad. For simplicity, if we assume a return of 10 percent, this would commit the United States to an increase of net exports of $14 billion a year.

Thus, a low net national saving rate will either be matched by a low domestic rate of capital formation or, if investment in the United States exceeds net national saving, continued foreign capital inflows into the United States.

The extent to which the United States must ultimately finance its domestic capital formation from its own saving is uncertain. While recent declines in net national saving have been offset substantially by importing foreign capital, there is no convincing example in economic history of an advanced economy financing its long-term development by continuing to rely on foreign capital to finance its investment. The success stories of external finance–assisted growth have been of less developed countries, whether recently or historically, such as the United States and Canada in the nineteenth century. Feldstein and Horioka (1980) and Summers (1986) present evidence suggesting that domestic investment, at least in the long run, must be financed by domestic saving. While the subject is far from closed, no one can be sure how long foreign investors will be willing to pour several percent of GNP into the United States annually. Eventually, foreign portfolios will become less and less diversified as the share of their assets in dollar-denominated securities grows to significant proportions. They would thus demand higher returns to compensate for this increased risk.

Even if we conclude that in the long run, domestic capital formation must be financed by national saving, the contribution of capital formation to economic growth with respect to the magnitude and time frame is a source of some controversy. Recent studies, such as those by Denison (1985) and Jorgenson, Fraumeni, and Gallop (1987), come to quite different conclusions with respect to the quantitative significance of capital formation in postwar economic growth and in the productivity slowdown of the 1970s.

While no precise quantitative estimate can be given detailing the impact of changes in the rate of net national saving upon domestic capital formation and international capital flows, and correspondingly on productivity growth and/or future trade patterns, the qualitative patterns are clear and the quantitative impact is likely to be important. Low rates of net national saving are likely to lead to low rates of domestic investment in the long run and substantial international capital flows into the United States in the short run. Thus, the policy options with respect to Social Security have substantial ramifications for the future performance of the economy well beyond the importance that they rightfully deserve in terms of the retirement income security of current and future retired persons.

Conclusion

This chapter has documented how the systematic deviation from pay-as-you-go finance of the Social Security system is planned to result in significant surpluses for the next several decades in OASDI. Subsequently, OASDI will run large deficits. HI is projected to run large and growing deficits beginning in the 1990s.

Unless offset by changes in private saving or non–Social Security budget deficits, these deviations from pay-as-you-go finance will cause substantial systematic swings in the net national saving rate. Alternative scenarios with respect to the disposition of the OASDI surplus over the next three decades lead to important changes in the net national saving rate. These swings are likely to be significant enough to cause quantitatively important changes in the level of domestic investment that can be financed internally and/or the patterns of net foreign investment. Thus, future trade patterns and productivity growth will be affected, perhaps substantially.

The chapter highlights the important role Social Security's future financing patterns will have on the course of the economy, quite independent of whether these patterns affect private saving behavior. The potential interaction of Social Security and private saving, and the potential interaction of the state of the Social Security surplus (or, perhaps more accurately, its expected state) and the federal government's deficit in the remainder of the budget will be important as well. The chapter has demonstrated the substantial reduction in the net national saving rate that will occur if the OASDI surplus of the next three decades does not accrue and is used instead to raise benefits, reduce taxes, or fund other government programs (the most likely candidate being the HI deficit). The likely response of private saving to the various alternative scenarios is a source of controversy, partly because there is a major debate concerning the methods by which the Social Security system might affect private saving, as well as concerns about the quantitative magnitudes of any impact that might have occurred historically. Changing demography, patterns of risk and risk bearing in the economy, household formation and dissolution, and perceptions of the risks involved in Social Security wealth as opposed to other types of assets also might make extrapolations from earlier studies somewhat hazardous [see Auerbach and Kotlikoff (1987) for some interesting simulation results with respect to changes in demography].

It might generally be thought, however, that if Social Security OASDI surpluses are used to raise benefits substantially, this might lead to a decrease in saving for those then in their peak earning years, who expect to receive higher benefits without subsequently having to pay higher taxes (netting out any private intrafamily intergenerational transfers offsetting this effect, assuming that they are far less than dollar for dollar). Other methods of dissipating the surplus would have analogous results, depending on the time pattern of changes in expected benefits and taxes for persons of various ages. There is also the important fact that the growth of Social Security, changing demography, and changes in financial markets, along with the deviations from pay-as-you-go finance, alter the perceived risk attached to any potential claims to future Social Security benefits. For example, current well-off prime-age earners might believe that Social Security will be means tested at an income level below their expected other resources when they reach old age in order to finance any deficits that result. One might expect these perceived risks also to affect private saving behavior.

Of course, changes in net national saving might directly affect interest rates, which might in turn affect desired private saving, contributions to defined benefit pension plans, and the valuation of existing stocks of wealth. While the short-run openness of the economy to international capital flows might be expected to mitigate any effect on interest rates, all of the advanced economies will be aging rapidly and might experience reductions in private saving and pressure on their public budgets.

Finally, there is an additional way in which private saving behavior might be altered. In response to the pressures involved in financing future Social Security benefits for the baby boom generation, it may well be that the remainder of the federal budget and/or public policy with respect to private saving, such as rules governing pension plans and the taxation of saving, might respond in an attempt to encourage private saving. Of course, the extent to which they would be successful in doing so raises a host of other questions to which only imprecise answers can be given.

In conclusion, this chapter should be viewed as highlighting the important role that Social Security's future financing pattern might play in net national saving (directly through the accumulation of a surplus and subsequent larger deficit and indirectly through the potential interaction of Social Security and private saving) and the potential interaction of the state of the Social Security system's finances and the federal government's deficit in the remainder of the budget. The numerous caveats concerning the direct calculation discussed above, as well as the issues concerning the response of private saving, should be borne in mind when interpreting the results.

Notes

1. If the report were to present the correct calculation, based on its own assumptions and methodology, the resulting figures would be more optimistic under each of the four sets of assumptions used. A comparison of Tables 10 and F2 in the 1986 report shows that taxable payroll is projected to rise at a rate slightly below the assumed interest rate (under each alternative set of assumptions). This means that the earlier positive annual balances should be given greater weight than the later negative annual balances. Thus, the long-run actuarial balance should be reported as a little higher.

2. For further information on this simulation, or rather on an earlier version of it, see Boskin, Avrin, and Cone 1983.

3. The 1975 Social Security Exact Match File merged individual records from the 1973 Current Population Survey with records of covered earnings.

4. Social Security Administration, Actuarial Study No. 92 (1984).

5. My calculation is certainly rougher than that undertaken by the actuarial staff of the SSA. As a result, my projections of aggregate taxes and benefits vary from those of the 1986 trustees' report. Between now and 2010, I derive less in annual and cumulative surpluses (due to deriving less in tax receipts) than what the trustees' report suggests is likely. My figures in the early 2010s are close to those of the trustees' report, but thereafter, until about 2040, I derive greater annual surpluses or lower deficits than those projected in the trustees' report. After 2040, I again generate higher annual deficits.

6. I do not consider alternative assumptions for unemployment, female labor force participation, immigration, or real interest rates.

7. This is slightly more than the 0.29 percent long-term actuarial deficit presented in the trustees' report. I discussed above how the latter figure is not very meaningful and how a calculation comparable to mine would yield a lower deficit. A further difference is that my calculation assumes the new, lower marginal tax rates. Under the old tax law, my simulated deficit is about 0.34 percent of taxable payroll. Finally, it should be noted that I make no effort to calculate the future deficit in disability insurance (DI). The SSA calculates this deficit as averaging 0.15 percent of taxable payroll, or half as large as the OASI deficit. Thus, SSA total projected OASDI deficit is 0.44 percent of taxable payroll. The projected deficit in HI is another 3.5 percent.

8. For an analysis of the inaccuracy of the economic and demographic assumptions used in the past, see U.S. General Accounting Office 1986.

9. Undiscounted, but still in 1986 dollars, the respective figures are + $14.7 trillion and − $11.1 trillion. Subsequent figures also are presented in discounted terms. To remove discounting, multiply by 4.33.

10. The level of immigration, especially of young people, will have an impact for the same reason. I leave this matter for future investigation.

11. In my simulation, I use the SSA figures for numbers of births each calendar year, which are derived from these fertility rates. It should be noted that the fertility rates used by the SSA refer to the "average number of children who would be born to a woman in her lifetime if she were to experience the birth rates by age observed in, or assumed for, the selected year and if she were to survive the entire child-bearing period."

12. Of course, the consumption of the economy as a whole is limited by what is produced by those still working. Thus, in some sense Social Security benefits always must be funded at the time they are paid. Still, the method of financing Social Security determines who has what claims, and this has important implications for both equity and efficiency.

13. The higher tax rate shown for 2022 is a quirk resulting from the way my simulation handles the rise in retirement age, from sixty-six to sixty-seven, which occurs around that time. I simulate the change as occurring all at once rather than being phased in over several years.

14. In practice, it is more likely that a portion of OASDI's payroll tax will be reallocated to HI. The analysis of OASI finances would then be similar to that of the pay-as-you-go tax rate scenario.

15. See Boskin, Robinson, and Huber (1988) for a discussion of federal, state, and local government saving when account is taken of capital formation, as well as of a number of other factors.

References

Auerbach, A., and L. Kotlikoff. 1987. *Dynamic Fiscal Policy.* Cambridge, England: Cambridge University Press.

Barro, R.J., and M. Feldstein. 1978. "The Impact of Social Security on Private Saving: A Debate." Monograph, American Enterprise Institute.

Boskin, M.J. 1986. *Too Many Promises: The Uncertain Future of Social Security.* Homewood, IL: Dow Jones-Irwin.

Boskin, M.J., M. Avrin, and K. Cone. 1983. "Modeling Alternative Solutions to the Long-Run Social Security Funding Problem." In *Behavioral Simulation Methods in Tax Policy Analysis,* edited by M. Feldstein. Chicago: University of Chicago Press, pp. 211–46.

Boskin, M.J., L.J. Kotlikoff, and M. Knetter. 1985. "Changes in the Age Distribution of Income in the United States 1968–1984. National Bureau of Economic Research Working Paper No. 1766.

Boskin, M.J., L.J. Kotlikoff, D.J. Puffert, and J.B. Shoven. 1987. "Social Security: A Financial Appraisal Across and Within Generations." *National Tax Journal* (March): volume XL, number 1, pp. 19–34.

Boskin, M.J., L.J. Kotlikoff, and J.B. Shoven. 1985. "Personal Security Accounts: A Proposal for Fundamental Social Security Reform." Policy Paper, Center for Economic Research, Stanford University, September.

Boskin, M.J. and D.J. Puffert. 1987. "The Financial Impact of Social Security by Cohort." Mimeo, forthcoming in *Contemporary Issues in Retirement,* edited by E. Lazear and R. Ricardo-Campbell. Stanford, CA: Hoover Institution.

Boskin, M.J., and D.J. Puffert. 1987. "Social Security and the American Family." National Bureau of Economic Research Working Paper No. 2117.

Boskin, M.J., M.S. Robinson, and A. Huber. 1988. "Government Saving, Capital Formation and Wealth in the United States, 1947–1985." Mimeo, forthcoming in *The Measurement of Saving, Investment, and Wealth,* edited by R. Lipsey and H. Stone. Chicago: The University of Chicago Press.

Denison, E. 1985. *Trends in American Economic Growth, 1929–1982.* Washington, D.C.: Brookings Institution.

Feldstein, M., and C. Horioka. 1980. "Domestic Savings and International Capital Flows." *Economic Journal* (June): volume 90, pp. 314–29.

Jorgenson, D., B. Fraumeni, and F. Gallop. 1987. *Productivity Growth in the United States.* Cambridge, MA: Harvard University Press.

Summers, L. 1986. "Issues in National Savings Policy." In *Saving and Capital Formation: The Policy Options,* edited by G. Adams and S. Wachter. Lexington, MA: D.C. Heath.

Thompson, L.H. 1983. "The Social Security Reform Debate." *Journal of Economic Literature* 21, no. 4 (December): 1425–67.

U.S. General Accounting Office. 1986. *Social Security: Past Projections and Future Financing Concerns.* Washington, D.C., March.

Comment

John B. Shoven

Before turning to Michael Boskin's chapter, I would like to make some general comments about the U.S. federal retirement system. The Social Security system must be considered a huge success. For the most part, elderly in the United States enjoy a standard of living and level of dignity that would be impossible to achieve in the absence of the program. Past successes, however, should not be an excuse for not improving the system and making it more efficient and more capable of handling the challenges of the twenty-first century. I am a coauthor of chapter 7 of this book, and after reading that chapter, you should know a great deal about how I would improve the system. I would like to emphasize that the goal set forth in that chapter is designed to improve the system, not to shrink or scrap it. Let me review a few of the advantages of this plan.

First, by linking payouts and pay-ins, workers are able to treat Social Security contributions as deferred compensation rather than taxes. In that case, Social Security taxes would not distort labor supply decisions nearly as much as they do now. Second, mailing participants annual reports of the status of their account would provide people with the information they need to allocate their lifetime resources more efficiently. A recent study by Stanford colleague Doug Bernheim (1988) found that people near retirement have large standard errors in their forecasts regarding the amount of their Social Security retirement benefits. Third, the plan proposed in chapter 7 attempts to lessen the unintended social engineering in the Social Security benefit structure, which occurs by offering people in different social circumstances very different deals. Our plan would offer everyone the same actuarial terms, with the exception of a clean, intended progressivity to aid households with low lifetime incomes.

Taken on its own terms, Michael Boskin offers some very valuable lessons about the consequences of alternative policies regarding the handling of the projected OASDI trust fund surpluses of the next twenty years or so. The reader is struck by the importance of the choices we face during the "grace period" of 1990 to 2010. The long-term financing of the system, and indeed the economic environment for the entire twenty-first century, are considerably affected by the decision either to increase benefits, to lower tax rates, or to accumulate a massive surplus to help finance the baby boom retirements in 2010 to 2050.

The conclusions of his chapter, while not all original, are very important. He shows that the system's finances are extremely sensitive to forecast assumptions and that the system is large enough to affect national saving significantly. This country's current economic woes (inadequate productivity growth, weak dollar, and so on) can largely be traced to a shortfall in national saving, and the point to be learned from Boskin's chapter is that Social Security, through its trust fund accumulation policy, will directly and greatly affect national saving. The chapter can be criticized for failing to capture possible behavioral responses in the private sector to different Social Security accumulation policies, but the magnitudes that Boskin finds are significant enough to withstand substantial modification. The author openly admits the simplicity of the underlying computations; I agree with him that they are startling and revealing.

I would like to add a number of points regarding Social Security and the U.S. retirement system. First, as Boskin shows, the system does not operate on a truly pay-as-you-go basis. Instead, it has a legislated structure of benefits and taxes and uses the taxes, if they are adequate, to pay the benefits. If the taxes are insufficient, benefits are not automatically lowered. Instead, the trust fund is depleted, and we enter one of the periodic Social Security financial crises. In the period immediately ahead, Social Security projects that the tax collections will greatly exceed the benefit payouts, with the result being a vastly expanding trust fund. Like Michael Boskin, I doubt very much that the fund will actually be allowed to accumulate. In reality, Social Security is an unfunded defined benefit pension scheme. It actually might be better if it were an explicitly pay-as-you-go plan.

Second, the financial balance of the system over the seventy-five-year period at which Boskin looks is very sensitive to assumptions. These concern not only economic forecasts, which are treacherous, but also health and mortality. I recently completed a study examining the Social Security consequences of smoking (Shoven, Sundberg, and Bunker 1987). In that work, John Bunker of the Stanford Medical School, Jeff Sundberg, and I develop separate mortality tables for smokers and nonsmokers. Of course, it is well known that male smokers have a shorter life expectancy than nonsmokers by about seven years. A male smoker earning a median income gives up (in expected value terms) about $20,000 of Social Security retirement benefits, whereas a female smoker gives up about $10,000 worth. To smokers, this is an additional cost of smoking; to the Social Security system, this is the expected surplus it gains from smokers. It is not surprising that if fewer people smoke, they will live longer, and this will have some consequences for the national retirement system. People are smoking less, and if no one at all smoked, the system's financial balance would be affected to the tune of about $500 billion. This simply illustrates how the system is affected by behavioral or medical developments that significantly affect mortality for a significant fraction of the population.

Finally, let's look at national saving. The amazing thing about personal saving is the small fraction of the population that does it. Most people arrive at retirement with almost no financial assets other than a pension. Their wealth consists of Social Security, possibly a private pension, and possibly an owner-occupied house. A corollary of this is that in recent years, all net aggregate personal saving has consisted of net contributions to private pension funds. And even that saving flow has been weak, for transparent reasons. Most workers with private pensions participate in defined benefit plans. These plans promise workers benefits based on their length of service and their wage and salary history. The plans are funded by firms based on a comparison of existing assets in the plan and the expected present value of benefits. The firm is a classic target saver. The high real interest rates and the historic stock market climb of the past four or five years have resulted in most pension funds in this country being overfunded. Therefore, new contributions are very sluggish. This might be one of the reasons why private saving has not responded positively to high real interest rates. This almost perverse reaction to high rates of return on financial assets might be diminished over the long run if the trend away from defined benefit plans, and toward defined contribution plans, continues.

Let me conclude by returning to my opening remark. Social Security has been a great success, but it would be greatly improved if it were streamlined to look more like a private annuity plan to the participant. This would mean that participants would earn a common expected rate of return and would be kept informed of the status of their account. Further, it would mean that the system would not face the tremendous uncertainties vividly illustrated by Michael Boskin.

References

Bernheim, B. Douglas. 1988. "Social Security Benefits: An Empirical Study of Expectations and Realization." In *Contemporary Issues in Retirement,* edited by E. Lazear and R. Ricardo-Campbell. Hoover Institution. Also National Bureau of Economic Research Working Paper No. 2257.

Bernheim, B. Douglas and John B. Shoven. 1958. "Pension Funding and Saving." In *Pensions in the U.S. Economy,* edited by Z. Bodie, J. Shoven, and D. Wise. National Bureau of Economic Research and University of Chicago Press, pp. 85–114.

Shoven, John B., Jeffrey O. Sundberg, and John P. Bunker. 1987. "The Social Security Cost of Smoking." National Bureau of Economic Research Working Paper No. 2234.

6

Medicare and the Health Care Costs of Retirees: Problems in Choosing the Future

Mark V. Pauly, Ph.D.

Retirement planning for the elderly ultimately concerns the availability of goods and services to the elderly household. Pensions, Social Security, private savings, life insurance benefits, and intrafamily transfers all have as their objective the maintenance of some level of real well-being. But even when the level of cash flows to the household has been established, the level of real well-being can still be disturbed, sometimes seriously, by expenses incurred in connection with illness. Some elderly households do in fact experience substantial medical expenses; for example, nursing home expenses can amount to as much as $100,000 per year (DHHS 1986). For this reason, planning how to pay for those illness-related costs, whether via insurance or some other mechanism, is an important part of the private planning for retirement, and the adequacy of that private planning is an important object of public concern.

In this chapter, I discuss possible options for paying for illness-related costs of the elderly that might represent an improvement over current practice, given the environment in the next century. I use the words *illness-related costs* rather than *medical care costs* because I wish to emphasize that much of what is of concern to the elderly is not medical in the sense of acute illness or even in the sense of doctors and hospitals viewed in isolation. Instead, my views on possible strategies for the next two decades come from considering a process of aging and reduction in functional capacity that has nonmedical as well as medical causes, uses nonmedical as well as medical resources, and requires nonmedical as well as medical insurance. This type of consideration indicates a need to integrate policy directed at illness-related costs with the overall policy of providing cash payments to retirees and with the bequests retirees might leave. My approach is frankly speculative (rather than directly policy relevant), directed at outlining the important considerations that ought to influence choice rather than offering proposals ready for enactment.

In large part the reasons for increased concerns about public and private roles in elderly health care are the same as those that motivate concern about public and private pensions and annuities. Demographic shifts and greater longevity have increased the number of elderly per worker, leading to concern about the ability and/or the willingness of workers to provide current levels of support. I have discussed this issue with regard to Medicare elsewhere (Pauly 1986); suffice it to say that, eventually, these changes can be expected to lead to diminution in the relative share of public support for elderly health care.

This earlier work, however, was primarily positive analysis. In the present chapter, I investigate the normative question of what ought to be the relative roles of public and private providers, at least in a conditional sense. Because so much of the public role ultimately depends on empirical unknowns, such as the extent of potential private market adverse selection, the desire for equity, and the extent of moral hazard (described later in the chapter), those normative conclusions are even more tentative than usual. The criteria of optimality I use is generally based on Pareto optimality or economic efficiency, but I have extended the concept to include individuals' preferences toward others' use of medical care.

In this chapter, I first discuss why there is special public concern for illness-related costs, along with a simple model of family illness-related expenses and the process of aging. Next, I briefly review existing public and private mechanisms for financing illness-related expenses for the elderly, along with projections (such as they are) for the future of those mechanisms if they remain in their current form. Then I talk about the areas in which current public and private policy is thought to be most deficient—the financing of nursing home care and catastrophic illness–related expenses. I consider an area in which severe private sector problems are expected to exist—employer-funded health insurance for retirees. Finally, I conclude with a set of options for improvements in public and private sector performance in this area.

Social and Individual Objectives

My remarks in this chapter focus on retirees over sixty-five who are not disabled when they stop working. These individuals have certain desires or demands for the amounts and types of medical care they will have available when they retire. In addition, it seems reasonable to suppose that there are some social objectives—which I will define by the desires of persons other than the direct consumer—that pertain to retirees' consumption patterns. It is necessary to define the willingness to pay for others' consumption of health care and to determine a person's optimal consumption based on others' concerns. This "externalities from consumption per se" concept (Pauly 1970) underlies my view of social preferences. One aspect of social preferences is embodied in the welfare nature of Social Security. This system transfers funds from higher-income persons to lower-income persons. The same sort of compulsory welfare transfer is embodied in the Medicare program, except that benefits are in the form of a health insurance policy, and part of the cost comes from lumpsum premiums paid by the elderly and from general tax revenues, as well as from the payroll tax.

While one can take the existence of Social Security and Medicare as evidence that there are social objectives to be pursued, one need not assume that the current form of those programs is the best way to meet these objectives. Our empirical understanding about consumption externalities is minimal; the appropriateness of a given program allocating various roles to the public and private sectors will therefore depend on assumptions made about voter/taxpayer objectives. Indeed, much of the debate about public policy toward health care represents a difference in individuals' willingness to pay for others and to impose their preferences on others.

Individual Objectives and Retirement Illness-Related Costs

Here I outline a simple model of an individual's desired pattern of illness-related costs and their financing during an exogenously given period of retirement. For simplicity, I consider only a one-person elderly household, so all bequests will go to persons outside the household. I first offer a description of the health status pattern the individual can expect to experience.

I assume that, upon retirement, the individual is in a state labeled "healthy." Health levels can be affected by acute illness during this state, but in general the individual's expected pattern of illness, use of medical care, and expenditure is much the same as that of adults under sixty-five. The other state I label "incapacity." An individual in this state is unable to perform all of his or her usual household production functions, such as cooking, shopping, cleaning, visiting friends, and so on. This person consumes somewhat more physician and acute care services, but most of the person's additional expenses are for household custodial functions. Moreover, the individual expects that his or her incapacity will worsen and will soon result in death. The probability of exiting the incapacity state for the healthy state is assumed to be zero; one empirical piece of support for this assumption is that only about a quarter of persons who stay in nursing homes for more than thirty days are ever discharged to their homes.

The timing of initiation of the incapacity state, the length of time spent in the healthy state, and the length of time spent in the incapacity state are all unknown. The individual does know, however, that when he or she enters the incapacity state, the demand for household production substitutes will increase. This might take the form either of purchased services or of labor donated by family members. It also might be reasonable to assume—although

I do not believe it is universally true—that the individual prefers to retain as much functional independence as possible, even when he or she enters the incapacity state. Even if family members donate time, however, the amount of purchased services needed to maintain a given level of well-being is higher in the incapacity state than in the healthy state.

We assume that the individual's initial wealth and earnings from work are given. One might imagine a lifetime expected utility function (beginning with the planning period at the time at which work begins) that depends on consumption of other goods, certain illness levels and use of medical care in each period, and a bequest at the end of life.

Maximizing expected utility is constrained by the requirement that expected consumption cannot exceed the initial endowment plus income from work and by the (given) probability distribution of all states. If the three relevant states (health, incapacity, and death) can be identified, and if insurance is sold at fair premiums, the person will choose to insure against the occurrence of the incapacity and death states. (If the desired bequest depends on the timing of death, there also will be a demand for death benefits.)

In this model, if full contingent claims markets were available, all consumption would be paid for by an annuity, and medical insurance would cover medical care costs. An even better solution would be to have a single insurance that paid an illness-conditioned indemnity. There is no role for direct saving or individual wealth beyond the retirement period; life insurance transfers bequests. If the optimal bequest is zero, this household will choose to be without tangible wealth, since insurance is a more efficient method of transferring consumption. Life insurance is the most efficient way of making bequests, if they are desired.

However, if the market for annuity insurance is imperfect, as seems true in reality, then savings will be used to transfer consumption between states, to protect against the risk of varying length of life, and as a way of making bequests (Kotlikoff and Spivak 1981). The optimal mix between savings and insurance depends on the cost of insurance, where *cost* is defined broadly to include loading, moral hazard, and adverse selection (defined below). In effect, health insurance protects savings, and savings substitute for insurance.

How would the level of savings or wealth vary over the lifetime and as a function of the state of health? When an acute illness strikes, the main function of insurance should be to help equalize wealth across states of health and time periods. But if the individual enters the chronic illness state, which will be followed by death, it is no longer as important to protect wealth in excess of the desired bequest. Chronic illness serves as a signal that life expectancy has been reduced. If the insurance benefits cover custodial care as well as medical care—that is, if the insurance benefits pay for all consumption as well as for medical care—there would be no reason to insure against fluctuations in wealth in excess of the desired bequest.

There is thus a difference between the function performed by health insurance in the healthy state and the function performed by insurance in the incapacitated state. In the healthy state, insurance protects the wealth the individual will need for consumption when he or she recovers. In the incapacitated state, insurance primarily protects the bequest. The expected bequest might actually rise at the onset of chronic illness, even without health insurance. Although future consumption per time period is higher in the incapacitated state, the expected number of future years of life is reduced, so current levels of assets might equal or exceed desired levels. Whether or not insurance will be purchased in either state, and how much, depends on the administrative cost and the extent of moral hazard and adverse selection.

Moral hazard refers to the propensity of insureds to have a higher average expenditure than the uninsured (or the less well insured). When moral hazard is present, insurance purchases will be positive, but the insurance coverage people purchase is often limited by deductibles and copayment. In contrast, adverse selection occurs when insureds are better able to predict their expected expenses than insurers. It too can limit insurance coverage.

Public intervention in such a market could be justified on the grounds of at least partial market failure. That market failure could arise from excessive selling costs in the private sector. It also could arise from adverse selection per se, although the most that would, strictly speaking, be required here is compulsory purchase of a specified amount of insurance coverage.

A modification of this simple model is suggested by Bernheim, Shleifer, and Summers (1985). They suggest that the promise of bequests is used in part to motivate children to continue to provide care for or attention to their parents. Especially if one parent has already died, the time period in old age when care is most desired by the parent, but most costly (in subjective terms) to the child, is when chronic illness strikes. The loss of the potential bequest through the cost of chronic care might be especially painful to the elderly person (although other people in society might not attach the same values), since loss of bequest means loss of control.

Social Concern

Incorporating social concern into the overall problem of financing medical care for the elderly might be approximated by imagining that shortfalls in use of medical care by low-income persons below the level of appropriate use (perhaps proxied by middle-class use), in ways that affect health, is of special concern. The ideal solution here need only involve a public subsidy. It need not involve either public production of medical care or public regulation.

Such a program probably would involve a subsidy directed at those thought to be especially in need. That is, a program motivated primarily by social concern would look more like a welfare program than a social insurance program.

The form of optimal coverage would ordinarily involve levels of subsidized coverage that decrease as income increases. The notion is that high out-of-pocket payments would be more likely to discourage use others would regard as appropriate if income or wealth were low than it if were high. This approach, which concentrates on subsidizing consumption of medical care, does not indicate whether premiums should be charged for this subsidized insurance, other than to say that the premium must be below the market premium for the level of coverage. The higher the premium at any income and coverage level, the greater the chance that some people will reject the subsidized coverage. About all one can say is that using health insurance premiums as a way of redistributing income within the elderly population—that is, charging some elderly a high premium in order to charge others less—is a peculiar method of income redistribution, since presumably the nonelderly rich are no less appropriately taxed to help the elderly poor than are the elderly rich. Since the House Ways and Means Committee has considered funding increases in Medicare coverage by what is in effect a progressive income tax applied to the elderly, one should not dismiss the peculiar as politically unfeasible. Perhaps the notion is that the tax on high-income elderly represents a recapturing of the subsidy embodied in Medicare, a subsidy to which the well-to-do elderly are, after all, not really entitled.

I believe that growing concerns about the Medicare program and changes in the elderly's circumstances will force a reexamination of the motivation for publicly provided insurance for the elderly. Is it intended to provide welfare benefits to the elderly poor, or is it intended as a social insurance remedy for middle-class market failure? On the one hand, increases in the relative well-being of the elderly make it more difficult to imagine a program with uniform benefits for all elderly as achieving welfare goals for a heterogeneous population. On the other hand, catastrophic insurance coverage, especially for nursing home care, is not well supplied by the private market, a prima facie case of market failure possibly justifying social insurance for all.

Current Health Insurance Patterns

The current Medicare program provides uniform and identical insurance coverage to all eligible elderly persons regardless of health. Medicaid supplements the coverage for low-income elderly, while private Medigap coverage generally covers hospital and physician payments for the nonpoor. Indeed, more than 70 percent of Medicare beneficiaries buy Medigap coverage, despite administrative cost percentages (loading fees) that, at 30 to 50 percent, are three or four times higher than for the group health insurance bought by people under sixty-five.

The Hospital Insurance (HI) part (Part A) of Medicare currently shows a positive trust fund balance but is expected to be exhausted, at current tax and projected expenditure rates, by 2002. In actuality, whether and when tax rate increases might be needed to continue to fund expenses depends primarily on what is assumed about the rate of growth in benefits. [Indeed, the date at which the trust fund will have a zero balance is continually being revised to later dates by the Health Care Financing Administration (HCFA) actuaries.] The Diagnosis Related Group's (DRG's) prospective payment system has served to slow the growth in inpatient payments, and has therefore delayed the date at which the trust fund will be exhausted. To some extent, this fall in inpatient payments has been offset by an increase in outpatient payments largely covered under Part B, which is funded by general tax revenues and monthly premium payments.

The No-Change Future of Medicare

The Part A trust fund, regardless of its level of balance, is presumably taken as a given in health care finance. The real question concerns the role it might assume in the future.

A scenario that is probably a reasonable description of the past DRG program is one in which levels of Medicare spending are adjusted, subject to political pulling and tugging, to fit the revenues generated by the earmarked payroll tax (plus adjustment of other political budgetary objectives). The DRG system makes this possible because the prospective payment rate can be adjusted to the revenues expected to be available. If quantity can be forecast, such a process can work perfectly. A voucher for annual benefits can produce even greater control.

It is probably not very useful to examine the details of forecasts for the Part A trust fund; to judge from past performance, the government's ability to forecast the expenditure portion of that program is not good. This is even more of a problem today, since the expenditure level is not really determined by exogenous losses. Instead, especially after the DRG payments are fully phased in and capital payments are added on, the hospital insurance benefit payments are largely under Medicare's control. Because the government can determine the level of DRG prices, it can, within broad limits (and given some reasonably accurate estimates of admission rates and case mix) set the price level to be consistent with the tax collections flowing into the trust fund. High accounting profits for hospitals on Medicare (with HCFA doing the accounting) make hospital threats that cutbacks or slowdowns will threaten quality appear to be empty. The real issue is not whether the trust fund will be exhausted, but rather what combinations of tax rates and access/quality/amenity we will choose to provide to the elderly.

In any case, only the hospital insurance part of Medicare is subject to DRG payments and to trust fund–earmarked taxation constraints. Real total Medicare benefits have in fact not been slowed down, and outpatient costs have grown especially rapidly. I think it reasonable to assume that even these costs will eventually be brought under control, but there probably will continue to be a skewed attention to the inpatient portion. The real question is not what demographic shifts will require—since within very broad limits Medicare benefits can be set at any level—but rather what level of real medical benefits for the elderly the political process will support. In many ways, this problem is the same as that of Social Security, the only real difference being the availability of general revenues and premium payments by the elderly for financing Medicare. My own view of the demographic trends is that, after about the year 2000, the growth in the tax price on workers for Medicare (as for Social Security) will be so large that it will offset a modest upward shift in voter age. The relevant question does not concern cutbacks in that part of Medicare supporting the nonelderly, but rather the form the new system might take.

Having stated the problem in this way, one immediately sees the difficulty. There is no objective standard of adequacy to which one can refer, especially since variations in cost probably have little effect on measurable health. Moreover, even the economic rationales for government intervention have no direct link with what the political process will support once intervention has occurred. A complete theory needs at least to take some account of political feasibility.

Public and Private Funding of Acute Illness Costs for the Elderly

Current Patterns of Coverage

Medicare covers acute care expenses above a deductible, but there are upper limits on covered hospital days, unlimited copayments on physician services, and no coverage whatever of prescription drugs (an expense now usually covered by commercial major medical policies). In addition, Medicare does not cover care in nursing homes and provides only very limited coverage in skilled nursing facilities.

In rough terms, Medicare pays for a little more than half of all elderly medical expenses, and Medicaid pays a little less than 10 percent. Of the remaining 40 percent plus, about three fifths is covered by private Medigap insurance, with the remainder paid out of pocket by the elderly or their families. Private Medigap insurance is purchased by more than 70 percent of the elderly. Fewer than 20 percent of the elderly, generally those with low (but not poverty-level) income or wealth, have only Medicare insurance to protect them.

Much of the private insurance is bought individually (at fairly high loadings and with after-tax dollars), but a sizable portion of existing elderly obtain Medigap coverage as part of their employee-funded retirement package. Unless employers should cut back on availability—and no one is sure that cutbacks are yet occurring—this fraction will surely grow, since about a third of current workers work in firms (predominantly large and high wage) that will provide them with tax-free Medigap coverage if they retire from those firms.

Faced with increasing budgetary difficulty, politicians are naturally interested in whether part of the burden of Medicare might be shifted to the private sector. One way of shifting would put more of the cost on the elderly, while an alternative would shift the cost onto employers, with an ultimate shift probably onto coworkers. This shift onto employers has already occurred to some extent, as the Medicare law has been changed to require employer coverage of the working elderly and of the first year of cost for kidney disease patients. But there is a conflict in the making if Medicare should imagine shifting any additional burden, since many employers, believing that they bear the burden of employee benefits, claim that they are already strained by existing obligations for employer-provided postretirement coverage. I consider this issue in more detail toward the end of the chapter.

Shifting Medicare Costs onto the Elderly

One solution to Medicare's cost and budgetary problem is to push more of the cost onto the elderly themselves. Since on average the elderly are no more likely to be poor than the nonelderly workers who pay payroll taxes, and since there is already a substantial intergenerational transfer built into Medicare, a modest reduction in this transfer is not obviously unfair. My earlier comments suggest, however, that shifting costs onto the elderly is an inappropriate way to fund welfare transfers to the poor elderly.

In any case, once one begins considering the shifting of Medicare costs by cutting or constraining benefits, difficulties with the social insurance format immediately arise. Regardless of how the burdens are shifted, it seems plausible that some elderly can bear them better than others, and yet a social insurance approach would imply a uniform cutback, something that is sure to involve oppressive burdens on some millions of elderly. It is simply impossible to have a homogeneous program fit a heterogeneous population.

The closest approximation to equitable treatment on the expenditures side turns out, as usual, to have potentially undesirable efficiency consequences. A strategy of limiting benefits but making private supplementation difficult or impossible imposes penalties in kind, the value of which rises with income. The DRG system imposes costs in this manner. That system pays a fixed price per inpatient admission, causing hospitals to reduce length of stay. But since early discharge surely does not mean early recovery, the cost of caring for the convalescing patient are shifted onto the family. Sometimes these costs are monetary, as when the family must hire help to care for the ill person. More frequently costs are paid in kind, as a spouse or child shoulders the burden of caring for an invalid.

There is the potential for inefficiency here, since it is virtually impossible to pay the hospital so that the patient can remain there beyond what the hospital sets as its limit. (Note that the DRG system does not require that the hospital discharge early.) The burden of early discharge (measured by willingness to pay to avoid it) presumably falls more heavily on the well-to-do. While there is no obvious reason not to reduce the subsidized coverage to the relatively well-to-do elderly, that reduction should not have been undertaken in a way that makes supplementation difficult and imposes similar reductions on lower-income elderly.

Catastrophic Acute Care Costs under Medicare

Medicare coverage for hospital bills starts to shrink after sixty days in the hospital. Moreover, the 20 percent copayment obligation under Part B (physician services) has no upper limit. While the event is quite rare, some of the elderly do suffer high out-of-pocket hospital and physician expenses, something that rarely happens with private insurance policies because of the wide prevalence of major medical coverage.

The Department of Health and Human Services (DHHS) has, therefore, proposed adding catastrophic coverage to Medicare and financing the additional benefits with a compulsory addition of about $5 per month to the Part B premium paid by the elderly person (DHHS 1986). Since the heavy general revenue subsidy to Part B means that few elderly decline it, the new plan amounts to public production of catastrophic coverage financed by a head tax on the elderly. (Interestingly, the DHHS claims that such a head tax is more equitable than an arrangement with deductibles and copayments that increase with income.)

Is the provision and production of such coverage an appropriate role for government? It is not difficult to understand why some catastrophic coverage is probably appropriate for all the elderly. Not only does the absence of coverage lead to potential underconsumption in the case of serious illness, it also leads to transfer of the cost to nonusers in a society unwilling to permit gross undertreatment. And virtually all risk-averse persons would be expected to gain from insurance coverage against wealth-threatening losses in the healthy state.

So there is a rationale for imposing mandatory catastrophic coverage financed in some fashion. The DHHS's proposal, while desirable on efficiency grounds, will surely shift some of the burden of paying for currently uncompensated acute elderly care from the nonelderly users of the hospital (or from the hospital's owners or managers) back onto the elderly.

The most critical questions are those of the form of payment and the method of production of the catastrophic insurance. The DHHS proposal gives a monopoly on production of insurance to the public sector. There is a theoretical rationale for this; Medicare can administer its insurance at an administrative cost percentage about one fifth of that of private coverage. Of course, the compulsory nature of Medicare coverage reduces selling costs, and a private firm given a monopoly in selling subsidized Part B coverage could do as well as the HCFA.

The real issue in the allocation of roles is not cost but the ability of consumers to get what they want. It is a virtual certainty that if HCFA administers catastrophic coverage, it will come to be concerned about the high cost of such coverage. There will probably be some moral hazard associated with the coverage, although the fact that private major medical coverage is reasonable in price means that costs will not run away. Moreover, medical care costs seems inexorably to increase over time, especially in the case of illnesses with high-tech treatments. While some elderly might, as payers of premiums, come to appreciate the HCFA's cost-control efforts, others might not. And yet they would have no alternative under the catastrophic insurance proposals, regardless of how heavy-handed the HCFA's cost-containment efforts proved to be.

It does not seem so difficult to provide alternatives. A simple scheme would be to provide catastrophic coverage within existing Part A and B premiums as a default option, paying for the last-dollar coverage by increasing up-front deductibles and copayments, ideally in a way related to income. People could then buy alternative coverage against these increased payments either from the HCFA or from private insurers, if they so chose. Adverse selection is unlikely to be a problem for the HCFA, and the competition such a scheme would permit should be good for all. The methods suggested for funding the acute care catastrophic coverage are apparently warped by the need to keep the accounting tax burden low. The original DHHS proposed a lump-sum premium of about $5 per month, while the Congressional proposals would combine a small flat premium with an income-related tax on the elderly. All this seems a convoluted way of raising taxes by hiding them as premiums. There is no obvious distributional principle to settle the matter. If one looks at catastrophic coverage for the average elderly person as a welfare benefit, one would wish to fund it through an income-related tax on all citizens. If, in contrast, one viewed it as correction of market failure, one might choose the fixed premium approach.

Medicare and Vouchers

A fundamental change in Medicare, which actually moves in a similar direction, is contained in the various proposals and demonstrations designed to investigate the effective form of a voucher for Medicare benefits. To date, demonstrations have looked only at Health Maintenance Organization (HMO) or employer-administered options, but there is also a possibility of vouchering out all Medicare coverage. Such an arrangement is subject to well-known pros and cons. It clearly depends on knowledgeable consumers, and some assistance in making choices is surely an acceptable role for government.

The main attraction of capitation is related to giving government a less directive role. Under a voucher arrangement, the government would limit its own risk and tailor its contribution to whatever fit current budgetary and tax policies. Moreover, government could limit Medicare vouchers to those who also could purchase private supplementary insurance to the equivalent of a cash transfer, at least to the extent that the voucher could be easily supplemented.

Other Acute Care Costs and Private Insurance

As noted above, the great majority of the elderly have some type of private insurance. That insurance covers about 12 percent of all medical care costs (using a broad definition of medical care), at a premium cost per year that averages approximately $500 per person. This private insurance currently benefits from some very important (though somewhat unintentional) public subsidies. The main question to be addressed here is the appropriateness of these subsidies, alternative arrangements, and the likely impact of Medicare limits for the future.

Most of the elderly buy their Medigap coverage on an individual basis. While it might appear surprising that such coverage is purchased so frequently despite a typical loading of 30 percent or more, there are some plausible explanations. One explanation, which refers directly to the public sector, is based on the empirical fact that both total medical expenses and Medicare benefits are substantially higher for those elderly who buy Medigap policies than for those who do not. Garfinkel and Corder (1985) estimate that 1980 average expenses for the services Medicare covers were $1,818 for those with Medigap versus $1,087 for those with Medicare only, while Medicare benefits were $988 for those with supplementary coverage and $729 for those without. While some of these differences reflect the fact that those who buy Medigap coverage tend to have a higher income than those with Medicare only, it does appear that the coverage of Medicare's deductibles and copayments in most Medigap policies induces 35 percent more Medicare benefits, an amount worth more than $250 per person.

Although Medigap coverage is associated with an extra $250 in real health care benefits, the cost of those benefits is reflected neither in the Medigap premium nor in the Medicare (Part B) premium. It is as if the $500 Medigap policy receives an extra $250 subsidy from Medicare, probably enough to offset much if not all of the loading in the Medigap policy.

Another determinant of the form of Medigap policies is that, in most instances, they provide much better front-end coverage than they do catastrophic coverage; indeed, the federal standards (under the Baucus Amendment) that certify policies require coverage of the 20 percent copayment with no more than a $200 deductible (Scheffler 1986). For this reason, and because the majority of Medigap coverage is written by tax-subsidized, nonprofit Blue-Cross–Blue Shield plans that have traditionally concentrated on first dollar coverage, it is very difficult for the elderly to buy a catastrophic-only Medigap policy. In this sense, the Bowen plan solves a problem that might be partly of the government's own making, since the heavy subsidy to front-end Medigap coverage and the standards that encourage such coverage probably have caused the neglect of truly catastrophic acute care coverage.

In addition to the subsidy to Medigap from Medicare, there is also a sizable minority of the elderly who receive their Medigap coverage as part of their retirement benefit, with the premium partially or wholly paid by the employer. Such an arrangement adds an additional tax advantage. While funds cannot easily be set aside to accumulate tax-free health benefits (in contrast to pension benefits), employer expenses are tax deductible for the employer and tax free for the retiree. Despite the current tax subsidy, problems with employer-provided retirement health benefits have led to proposals (and a little action) to make such arrangements even more tax advantaged.

Two considerations about these benefit plans are currently causing problems for the firms that provide them. One consideration is that, in the absence of any obligation to fund these benefits, firms are alleged to have failed to anticipate the increases in payments that have occurred as the number of retirees has grown (Goeppinger 1987). The firms themselves, and the unions with which they negotiated their benefits, frequently profess to be surprised by the size of the growth in payments as a function of the demographics of their work forces and to be terrified by the future (heretofore unanticipated) liability. (There is almost no consideration of the possible offsetting gains in wages or worker quality and retention from past or present workers in view of the availability of these benefits.) That this liability is variously forecast to have a present value of from $100 billion to $2 trillion neither soothes these fears nor gives them precision. (The larger amount exceeds the current asset value of the firms providing benefits.)

The second consideration is a trend in recent court decisions that makes failure to anticipate especially costly. In the past, employers presumed that they could terminate their coverage of benefits for both existing and future retirees if they wished. Recent court decisions have held that firms cannot cancel or change such benefits for existing retirees; the only ground for exemption is an explicit statement reserving the right to change. Nevertheless, what firms had formerly interpreted as beneficence is now being interpreted by the courts as a contract. In turn, the Financial Accounting Standards Board is contemplating requiring firms to estimate the size of this liability and enter it on their balance sheets, with deleterious effects. It has been proposed (and implemented, to a slight degree) that firms be given the same tax advantages if they formally fund such benefits as they currently receive for pensions. No one has, to my knowledge, proposed taxing the employer-provided health benefits (but applying the usual deductions for medical expenses) or the value of the insurance provided as income to the elderly. Should the elderly be afforded protection beyond the interpretation of current law, and should employers be helped with their problem?

Is there really a problem? If the firm anticipated the future, and regardless of whether it explicitly funded, it presumably offered such benefits only if the present value of the future benefit payments it expected to make was less than the reduction in labor costs (or improvement in labor quality and persistence) that this benefit allowed it to achieve. At most, the additional liability imposed by the court decision is the expected value of additional benefits caused by eliminating the chance of default (the probability of default times the amount of benefits to be paid), not the full cost of the benefits. And if the actuarial value of future benefits for existing workers is to be shown as a liability (for the benefit of less well informed investors), the present value of lower future wages that this promise has presumably bought should be shown as well. Of course, if benefit managers who thought they could enjoy the satisfaction of paternalism now find that such behavior is costly, someone will have to pay.

It is difficult to see an important public interest calling for further subsidization of this insurance through more favorable tax treatment, just as it is difficult to see a rationale for full tax deductibility of health benefits to current workers (Pauly 1986). In this case, what is already being subsidized is approximately $500 more of retirement income for relatively high income retirees, at least 80 percent of which goes for first-dollar insurance benefits, which stimulate use of care of probable low marginal value. One might (as an alternative to the Bowen plan) wish to preserve and even enhance tax subsidies to employer provision of truly catastrophic coverage. But such a policy runs into the usual problem that the subsidy will be large for higher-income persons and will in any case surely not produce universal major medical coverage for the elderly.

The problem of postretirement health benefits seems largely of the firms' own making. The unanticipated court decisions may have contributed to the problem, but even then there is no obvious reason why that unexpected loss should fall on the general taxpayer. Subsidizing lost Medigap benefits for well-to-do retirees who suffer a total loss of $500 per year hardly classifies as catastrophic coverage or as welfare benefits. Moreover, even retirees who lose benefits do not lose Medigap coverage; they could continue to buy it individually (as the great majority of elderly do), paying the premium with after-tax dollars, and still receive the Medicare subsidy.

There probably is a rationale for some type of regulation and/or disclosure, and perhaps some program for easing the transition between insurance plans as firms enter and exit. But beyond this, it does not seem that employment-related acute health insurance would need a major subsidy. Such coverage could be the way in which limits on Medicare spending are accommodated by the reasonably well-to-do, given the likelihood that the individual Medigap market probably suffers from adverse selection. But here again, only monitoring, not subsidy or control of such benefits, would seem to be warranted.

For Medigap as a whole, the critical question is the extent of social concern about medical expenses not currently covered by Medicare. On the one hand, one could assert that the coverage Medicare currently provides to all defines the limits of social concern. Not only should there then be no further subsidy to Medigap coverage, it should actually be taxed, to offset the subsidy Medicare provides to it. On the other hand, one might assert that there is some social concern about expenses not covered by Medicare but covered by Medigap, albeit perhaps less concern than for the expenses Medicare covers. But if this is the case, the current pattern of subsidy only to those who actually buy Medigap (rather than to all who incur the expenses), and the even larger subsidy to high-income retirees with employer benefits, seems less than rational. Indeed, the near-poor elderly, about whom society should be most concerned, are exactly the group that buys no Medigap coverage, benefits from no Medicare subsidy, gets no Medigap provided by employers, and is required to fend for itself as best it can.

The most obvious solution here would be to taper Medicaid, extending partial benefits to the near poor and then imposing a tax on Medigap coverage. From the experience of many state Medicaid programs, however, voters seem disinclined to extend Medicaid benefits. The proceeds of the Medigap tax might also, however, be used to provide welfare subsidies.

Chronic Illness and Social Welfare

While better coverage of rare catastrophic acute care expense is desirable, its addition to Medicare is generally regarded as a marginal change. A benefit with an expected value of $60 per year is not likely to make a major impact. The most important medical expense problem alleged to be facing the elderly is costs associated with chronic illness not covered by Medicare. Such coverage is provided to low-income elderly under the Medicaid program, but no assistance is furnished until a household spends down by means of medical expenditures that reduce wealth to a low level. There is no subsidized benefit to families of average wealth while they retain that wealth. A chronic illness, which I will interpret as reflecting entry into the incapacitated state, involves a number of expenses not covered by Medicare or private insurance. Some of these expenses are not really medical, but instead represent the inability of the incapacitated person to perform usual household production activities such as shopping, meal preparation, cleaning, household repairs, and laundry. Some represent medical services that Medicare does not cover, though Medigap policies often do, such as prescription drugs.

But the largest single item is nursing home care, which represents 42 percent of the out-of-pocket cost for the elderly (Rice and Gabel 1986). The cost of a year of nursing home care is estimated to be about $22,000, which is twice the consumption expense (including housing) that the average healthy elderly person would make. The likelihood of using a nursing home over one's lifetime is at least one in three; the fraction of the elderly in a nursing home at any point in time is 8 percent. Some stays are less than thirty days, as recovery after hospitalization for a person in the basically healthy state; these people represent a large fraction of nursing home admissions but a small fraction of total expense. Of those in nursing homes in 1980, about 14 percent had total health care costs below $1,000. But in the incapacitated state, if the stay exceeds thirty days, the person will very rarely leave the nursing home until death, and the annual cost will be high.

Chronic illness does, therefore, represent a rare event of fairly high costs compared to being in the healthy state. The only way to obtain public assistance with chronic illness costs is to spend down into Medicaid eligibility and to enter a nursing home. Both the forced bankruptcy involved in Medicaid and the absence of coverage for possibly less costly in-home care substitutes are often regarded as defects of current public policy. Private insurance coverage for nursing home care, though subject to much current discussion, still covers only about 1 percent of the costs (in contrast to the 46 percent provided by Medicaid) and almost never covers the cost of household help as a nursing home substitute.

While the use of nursing homes is fairly rare among the elderly, the presence of some form of dependency is not. Manton and Soldo (1985) estimated that in 1980 about 4–6 million elderly, or about 19 percent of the elderly not in nursing homes, had some limitations on activities of daily living or instrumental activities of daily living. About one quarter of this group received at least some formal care services, and about 15 percent paid something for formal care (as opposed to informal care provided by family members or friends). The aggregate expense for noninstitutional formal care was about $2 billion (of which $1.2 billion was paid out of pocket). This compares with nursing home costs of approximately $30 billion.

Interpreting Private Demand: An Initial Look

The nursing home care and insurance situation presents two puzzles. Most important, why has a private market in nursing home insurance failed to emerge? And second, for those not on Medicaid, why has a private, organized arrangement for delivery of nursing home substitute care not come into existence on a large scale? The closest the private market has come to providing either of these services is the life care community, which integrates insurance and the full package of household production services, a tie-in sale that is not preferred by most elderly. I take up this question in more detail below; here I provide some preliminary thoughts to motivate the discussion of welfare-based public intervention.

The fact that insurance and substitute care largely fail the market test is, in health care, not necessarily proof that they are inefficient or unfeasible. At various points in time, health insurance in general and private coverage for the elderly in particular were both absent, and insurers solemnly asserted that such costs were uninsurable.

There are some obvious obstacles to providing private insurance coverage for nursing home care. One obstacle is that, since employment groups are not available to the retired, such insurance would be sold on an individual basis. Even for those individual insurers for whom adverse selection should be a minor problem, such as fire or earthquake insurance, individual loadings typically average 30 percent or more, in contrast to the 10 percent or less common in group health insurance. In part this high loading simply reflects the cost of individual selling. But it also might reflect the cost of purposeful selling intended to select good risks (at any premium); it might reflect the underwriting policies of the insurer (Friedman and Manheim 1986). And even if adverse selection did not increase administrative costs, it could still account for the unwillingness of healthy elderly to buy coverage at premiums that cover costs.

The other potential impediment to insurance coverage is moral hazard. That there are multiple ways of dealing with chronic illness among the elderly is beyond doubt. In states where the availability of nursing home beds has been severely constrained by Certificate of Need rules, the elderly who cannot find a bed do cope. Whether the probability of using a nursing home responds to the lowered user price inherent in more insurance coverage is not known. For the elderly with severe activity limitations, who need constant attendance, there probably is not much of an effect of coverage on total cost. Not only is there little discretion as to provision of services, but the full set of services also will have fairly similar costs whether it is furnished inside or outside a nursing home. There is probably a greater chance of moral hazard for household help coverage unless information on the state of illness can be used to control use.

Premiums for commercially feasible nursing home insurance would average about $600 to $1,000 per year, with positive variation with age. While many of the elderly could afford such premiums (in the sense of having sufficient discretionary income), Friedman and Manheim (1986) calculate that, for reasonable values of risk aversion and individual insurance loading, the demand would be zero. From a lifetime perspective, nursing home expenses—

roughly equivalent to $12,000 net additional cost per year in the nursing home—are not inordinately high, but they can be high relative to the individual's income when the need occurs.

Social Concern and Nursing Home Coverage

At present, the problem of nursing home cost is largely a problem of financing for all the elderly, not a problem of access to health care that would improve health. One reason is that nursing home care is largely custodial, not health improving; there is rarely a recovery, even to the level of independent functioning.

A more serious reason is that in virtually all states, the quantity of beds demanded exceeds the number of beds available. State Certificate of Need programs have fixed the number of beds at a number less than needed to satisfy demand, largely as a way of controlling Medicaid use for which the states must pay. (The excess demand comes from Medicaid beneficiaries; the price for the nonpoor can be set at the market-clearing level.) This means that more generous or more widespread nursing home insurance coverage could at best reallocate beds (away from Medicaid beneficiaries) and reduce financial risk, but it would not affect health in some aggregate sense. At worst, such coverage would simply transfer rents to the bottom line of largely for-profit owners of nursing homes, as prices increased. Beds do not have to stay constrained, but the potential attractiveness to state Medicaid programs of controlling use by controlling supply probably means that they will.

Given the problem of supply-side constraints, it is clear that Medicaid does provide a form of coverage to all, but with a deductible equal to one's wealth (less some amounts that can be left to one's spouse). It is precisely this spending into bankruptcy that some find objectionable.

In the context of the model outlined earlier, it is clear that the only real effect of more generous Medicaid coverage would be to preserve bequests. In effect, chronic illness is like a confiscatory estate or inheritance tax, and loosening Medicaid eligibility or providing Medicare coverage loosens the bite of that tax. But it would not lead to more medical care, or better health, for the elderly. At most, and depending on the form such additional public coverage might take, it might increase the quality or amenities of care. It is even possible, as Gertler (1986) has shown, that if better coverage provided by the public sector increased the prospective price paid to profit-maximizing homes for public clients, the quality of nursing home care provided to public patients might decline as the quantity of such patients accepted rises.

Regardless of the impact on actual volume of care provided, should public policy (and public financing) be directed at alleviating the drain of nursing home care on the wealth of the elderly? Two cases must be distinguished.

If the elderly person has a healthy spouse, high nursing home expenses for one spouse can affect the wealth and the (largely nonmedical) consumption of the other spouse. One might argue for additional public subsidy here, as a way of maintaining the real consumption level of the healthy spouse. If there is a welfare rationale for Social Security, the notion would be to increase Social Security payments to permit the healthy spouse to maintain consumption. If the family also receives other income, such as pensions or housing consumption, the welfare-based public interest is less clear.

The other (and more common) case is the situation in which the elderly person is in a one-person household, in which case the only rationale for preventing bankruptcy is to protect bequests to children or other nonelderly. In the model outlined earlier, the reduction in the well-being of the elderly person comes from the reduction in expected bequests. (That model does not allow for a stigma attached to bankruptcy itself.)

An alternative view is that the object of social concern is simply the burden of out-of-pocket costs. Rice and Gabel (1986), for example, show that more costly nursing home stays in particular display increasingly large fractions of out-of-pocket costs, and they conclude that "our results support the notion that additional coverage is needed by some of the elderly," (p. 17) because nursing home costs can consume the savings of a lifetime. As noted, there would probably be a utility gain to the family from insuring this cost; at least risk-averse heirs should want to insure their bequest. But, again, it is not obvious that this is a matter of public concern.

While there can be a substantial utility gain from reduction in risk—a risk that is borne by heirs as well as by the elderly household—it is less obvious that there is a welfare dimension to this transfer. Introspection is our only guide here, but my introspection tells me that I have little concern about my elderly neighbor's (usually grown) children, over and above what is already embodied in social schemes for dependents. One might have concern for the real income of a surviving spouse, though here again Social Security and annuities permit income to continue, and Medicaid permits an owner-occupied dwelling to be retained.

What would seem to be required is not provision of larger transfers to the elderly with chronic illness than the transfer embodied in Medicaid, but rather a removal of the stigma associated with a drawing down of wealth. Perhaps all that is needed is a change in terminology, some less emotional word than bankruptcy or impoverishment.

If the lifetime is near its end, the same arguments that justify an estate tax would suggest that there is little social interest in protecting that saving. Instead, what is needed is a humane and dignified method of caring for the individual while he or she is alive, while not protecting excess wealth. One simple approach would be to establish a deductible related to wealth at the time the person enters the nursing home and indicate that the elderly person would become eligible for Medicaid coverage once this deductible is covered. The deductible would, however, be reduced if the individual recovered functioning. Providing benefits after thirty days and collecting only a wealth-related deductible after death would be one practical solution.

More fundamentally, we must determine whether there is a social interest in preserving the elderly's peace of mind, an interest so strong that the Bowen proposal's tax expenditures for nursing home insurance would be justified. Can we justify taxing nonelderly to preserve bequests to nonpoor children? There might be a lifetime utility maximization model that would justify such a policy, but it would, at a minimum, require careful attention to distributional considerations.

Given the limit on nursing home beds, the primary benefit to the elderly from better coverage of chronic care would be in the form of coverage for noninstitutional formal assistance to the chronically ill or feeble elderly. For those elderly who need continuous assistance (for example, five limitations in the Activities of Daily Living [ADL] score), coverage of such care could probably be provided without much danger of moral hazard, since there really are few alternatives but to render care to a patient who needs help with eating and movement and is incontinent. Paradoxically, however, the cost of such care rendered outside of a nursing home also is high, so that any incentives with regard to location probably would not affect total cost much. The main consequence of broadening coverage for such severely incapacitated persons to include noninstitutional formal care would be to avoid the nursing home beds limitation.

For those with fewer limits on activities, there could potentially be a type of moral hazard associated with coverage of formal care (institutional or noninstitutional). While there is as yet little evidence on the subject, and some reason to believe that, when the patient's care is carefully supervised, there is little substitution, there is nevertheless a possibility that insurance coverage will induce substitution of formal care for care provided by family members and friends. When care delivered by others is covered, families would be expected to try to lighten their burden.

The effect of this moral hazard is likely to be primarily distributional (and there might even be social preferences for a more equal distribution of the burden of care). The allocative effects that usually characterize moral hazard might be small, since the real resources needed to provide care (primarily labor time) must be sacrificed whether the care is provided by the family or others. Indeed, if one compares nursing home care with care provided by the family at home, the only real saving is in the structural capital (assuming there is excess square footage in the family's house); because one attendant can care for several patients in a nursing home, while there is only one patient in a family setting, the labor consumed per patient is probably less at the nursing home. It is primarily the conversion of household production to market production, and the consequent monetarization of the transaction, that makes formal care look more costly.

Private Long-Term Care Insurance: Is There Market Failure?

While the welfare-related social concern for nursing home and chronic care insurance might not be high, there is a serious question about the failure of markets in such insurance to emerge for the nonpoor. If the current inability of such insurance to satisfy the market test is permanent, there are implications for public intervention (in the form of social insurance) as a remedy for market failure.

One real possibility, however, is that the market will devise ways to furnish such insurance. The history of health insurance is, after all, a saga of health insurers discovering that expenses they were sure were uninsurable could in fact be insured, and at a profit. Below I offer some thoughts on the form such feasible insurance might take, but both the design of potentially profitable market insurance and the analysis of public intervention must consider the possible reasons for the current failure of markets to exist.

Private health insurance or health insurance–type arrangements currently cover only about 1 to 2 percent of nursing home costs. The life care community, as a form of implicit insurance, also does not cover more than a tiny fraction of the elderly. There has been an upsurge of interest by insurers in testing the waters of long-term care insurance, although typical policies pay only limited indemnity benefits. One insurer has just introduced coverage for noninstitutional care. Those insurers marketing long-term care insurance profess optimism, but the most ambitious attempt to sell coverage to a large set of customers, a group insurance marketed through the American Association of Retired People, has not yet generated large sales.

Surveys designed to ascertain whether the nonpoor elderly can afford long-term care insurance (in the sense of having sufficient discretionary income to cover a premium for partial coverage) generally do indicate the potential for a large market. But surveys asking the elderly what they would be willing to pay for such coverage generally come up $300 to $500 short of the premium for full coverage. A paper by Friedman and Manheim (1986) simulates the demand for long-term care coverage, given conventional empirical estimates of risk aversion, and finds that the demand is virtually zero at loadings of 30 percent (not unusual for an individual policy), while demand would be high if the insurance could be made available at group loading percentages of 10 percent of premiums. They conclude that the key to making markets in long-term care insurance work is getting the loading down, and they advocate a brokerage role for government as an attempt to arrange for group purchasing advantages.

Friedman and Manheim attribute the high loading on long-term care insurance to the costs insurers incur to avoid adverse selection (underwriting costs). While this might be true, it is instructive to note that other individual insurances where adverse selection should be less of a problem (such as fire insurance) also sell at loading nearly as high as for individual health insurance.

More generally, if there is a problem of adverse selection in long-term care insurance, does that imply a market failure that government can correct? The first point to note is that it is possible that zero insurance is both an equilibrium and a Pareto optimal point, even if almost all consumers would buy positive amounts of insurance at fair premiums. The main reason is that there might be a set of truly high risks with probabilities of entering a nursing home near unity, who would therefore optimally choose zero coverage at a market loading. For instance, if the loading is 10 percent but a person's probability of use is 0.95, he or she would be better off with no insurance than with paying $1.045 for the first $1 worth of benefits, since he or she could be paying more for the insurance than the actual benefit received. Yet at the same loading, with the same utility function, a person whose probability was 0.1 might well be eager to buy the first dollar of coverage at a price of $0.11. But then any policy with a premium less than actual benefits will attract the high risks, even if the insurer (or the government) can observe the total amount of insurance purchased. Adding the high risks to the set of purchasers might so increase the price of even the first dollar of coverage that the lower risks would choose to buy no coverage at all.

Such a situation is Pareto optimal, since no feasible alternative insurance arrangement can be offered to the lower risks and still make them better off. [Some situations with insurance might also be Pareto optimal, but these alternatives cannot be reached in a Pareto optimal fashion from the "no one buys insurance" situation.] Thus, adverse selection, in addition to explaining why nursing home insurance does not exist, also could mean that there is no mutually beneficial alternative other than trying to devise better ways to identify risk levels.

Another possible reason why a moderately well-to-do elderly person might not buy nursing home insurance, even in the absence of serious adverse selection, is that the marginal utility of wealth might fall once one enters the incapacitated state. Since death or loss of ability to enjoy consumption is imminent, there might no longer be any reason to preserve wealth in excess of that needed for the nursing home stay. Indeed, if the individual's marginal utility of consumption in the incapacitated state is low, this would imply that there should optimally be little coverage on welfare grounds as well.

Of course, one might still wish to preserve the bequest potential as a method of inducing one's children to be attentive, with a strategic bequest as the tool. In this case, one might want to overinsure the incapacitated state so as to have a larger bequest to manipulate. Nevertheless, and not surprisingly, theory alone does not allow us to judge whether the failure of nursing home or chronic care insurance to emerge necessarily represents a private market failure correctable by government.

Are there ways in which the private market might be able to offer long-term care insurance, ways that the public sector might at least try to encourage with moral support (and research)? The most obvious way of funding insurance for chronic care among the elderly is to pay for it during one's working (and healthy) years. The vehicle could either be annuity insurance or life insurance. The only difference is that benefit payment would be conditional on occurrence of chronic illness. Instead of providing tax and Medicare subsidies to Medigap coverage provided by employers to retirees, a sensible strategy would be to offer tax-free status only to chronic care benefits provided to the elderly. Taxing the actuarial value of employer-provided Medigap benefits and taxing Medigap coverage to offset the Medicare subsidy might well raise more than enough funds to pay for publicly provided chronic care insurance. Given the eagerness of employers to do something about the coverage they furnish to retirees, this might be an ideal opportunity to redirect that coverage. For persons nearing retirement, existing group life or pension insurance could be modified. For example, whole life insurance represents a savings fund that could be triggered when chronic illness strikes. The public sector role here is to provide the research needed to develop a reliable and nonmanipulable measure of the presence of such illness. In many ways, the problem is similar to that with disability insurance.

Conclusion: Optimal Public and Private Medical Insurances for Retirees for the Year 2000

It is important to distinguish between acute care insurance for the great majority of the elderly who are basically healthy and chronic care insurance for those who have entered the incapacitated state that usually results in death. For acute illnesses, three important normative principles ought to be implemented over the next two decades, given the likely background of diminishing support from nonelderly taxpayers.

One principle is that the insurance coverage for the elderly (whether public or private) ought at least to be brought from the sixties into the eighties. Medicare currently duplicates the Blue Cross–Blue Shield policies of the mid-sixties. Optimal Medicare coverage should look like the modern comprehensive policies now being purchased by the nonelderly. These policies have nontrivial deductibles and copayments (sometimes related to income), upper limits on out-of-pocket expenses, and coverage of all medical care expenses (including drugs) once the deductible is satisfied. The proposals to update Medicare by adding catastrophic coverage are fully consistent with this view, but attempts to limit front-end cost sharing (or even reduce it) are not.

The second principle is that tax-financed subsidies to the elderly for health care ought to be related to the income and wealth of the elderly household. Given the large redistributive component already inherent in Medicare, maintenance of the social insurance form leads both to insufficient coverage for the near-poor elderly (largely because of the nontapered, all-or-nothing nature of Medicaid) and incentives for excessive use for moderately well-to-do retirees. Additional tax breaks for employer-provided Medigap coverage is counterproductive, in this view.

The third principle is that any publicly subsidized insurance should be easy to supplement privately. Otherwise, there can be inefficiency associated with limiting the quantity or quality/amenity of care below the level that moderately well-to-do elderly would be willing to buy. Of course, to the extent that the publicly provided expenditure is supplemented, it has no differential alternative effect (compared to an income transfer of equivalent cost). Nevertheless, this principle suggests that awarding a monopoly on determination of price to a public insurer, as is now being done in the DRG system and is contemplated in the Bowen catastrophic acute coverage, will be inefficient and engender conflicts between an economizing bureaucracy and a set of non-poor elderly willing and eager to buy better.

In the case of chronic care insurance, the critical element is a careful consideration of objectives. Is there public interest in maintaining the ability of the elderly to pass on the bequests they desire? Are the nonelderly, nonrich willing to tax themselves for the benefit of the heirs of the moderately well-to-do elderly? If the answer to these questions is negative, then the optimal public arrangement is to require the elderly person's wealth to be drawn down before a public subsidy is triggered. Here again, there is a role for using Medicaid to subsidize insurance coverage in a continuous fashion in order to offset current incentives Medicaid offers to avoid buying coverage. For the chronically ill elderly person with a healthy spouse, the wealth or income of the survivor should continue to be maintained at adequate levels (for example, the level paid by Social Security). Even here, there is no obvious reason for public subsidy of the well-to-do.

In the private sector, there should be research directed at determining whether there is correctable market failure in chronic care insurance. The most promising scheme appears to be provision of retirement health insurance for chronic care as a fringe benefit earned during the working years. Conversion of existing pensions or life insurance into chronic care benefits as individuals retire, or before chronic illness strikes, might be a way of providing such coverage to many of today's elderly.

References

Bernheim, B. Douglas, Andrei Shleifer, and Lawrence Summers. 1985. "The Strategic Bequest Motive." *Journal of Political Economy* 93, no. 6 (December): 1045–76.

Davis, Karen, and Diane Rowland. 1986. *Medicare Policy.* Baltimore: Johns Hopkins Press.

Department of Health and Human Services (DHHS). 1986. "Statement by Otis R. Bowen, MD," November 20.

Friedman, Bernard, and Larry Manheim. 1986. "Should Medicare Provide Expanded Coverage for Long Term Care?" Paper presented at the Conference on Twenty Years of Medicare, University of Pennsylvania, October.

Garfinkel, Stephen, and Larry Corder. 1985. "Supplemental Health Insurance Coverage among Aged Medicare Beneficiaries." NMCUES Descriptive Report 5, DHHS Publication 85-2025, August.

Gertler, Paul J. "Regulated Price Discrimination and Quality: The Implications of Medicaid Reimbursement Policy for the Nursing Home Industry." Research Paper No. 267, Department of Economics, State University of New York at Stony Brook, May, 1985.

Goeppinger, Kathleen. 1987. "Postretirement Welfare Benefit Plans: An Emerging Priority of the 80s." *Employee Benefits Journal.* (March): 32–36.

Kotlikoff, Laurence, and Avia Spivak. 1981. "The Family as an Incomplete Annuities Market." *Journal of Political Economy* 89 (April): 372–91.

Manton, Kenneth, and Beth Soldo. 1985. "Dynamics of Change in the Oldest Old." *Milbank Memorial Fund Quarterly* 63 (Spring): 206–28.

Pauly, Mark. 1970. *Medical Care at Public Expense.* New York: Praeger Publishers.

Pauly, Mark. 1986. "The Positive Political Economy of Medicare, Past and Future." Paper presented at the Conference on Twenty Years of Medicare, University of Pennsylvania, October.

Rice, Thomas, and Jon Gabel. 1986. "Protecting the Elderly Against High Health Costs." *Health Affairs* 5 (Fall): 5–21.

Scheffler, Richard. 1986. "Medigap Enrollment: Current Status and Future Directions." Paper presented at the Conference on Twenty Years of Medicare, University of Pennsylvania, October.

Comment

Robert P. Inman

Pauly's discussion of health care insurance for the elderly, particularly the role of Medicare, focuses on the details of many important policy issues now confronting Medicare. Since I have little with which to quarrel in Pauly's specific recommendations, it is most productive for me to center my comments on how his analysis fits within the wider agenda of the provision of income for the elderly.

It does not take much stretching to see the important connections between old age health insurance and old age income protection. Indeed, once an annuity has been provided—the task of ERISA protections and Social Security—there are only two major threats to the flow of consumption that the annuity will provide. The first is inflation, and the second is prolonged and major illness. The elderly face important risks with regard to their health status. Some will have long and productive retirements and then die without prolonged disabilities. Others pass away suddenly, only shortly after retirement. For these elderly, the primary effects of illness are on the elderly's length of life. For others, however, illness might not only shorten life, but also impose significant economic hardship because of prolonged periods of disability. Professor Pauly sees this economic burden of chronic care for the elderly—correctly, I believe—as the central issue in the design of Medicare policy. Simply put, Medicare, like Social Security, is primarily an income-protection policy for the elderly in which the risks are those associated with the contraction of a major long-term illness. The risks are high (the likelihood of using a nursing home over one's lifetime is 1 in 8), and the added costs if in a nursing home can be as much as $12,000 per year. For a typical elderly person whose wealth in retirement is limited to a modest home and some savings, this is a sizable loss indeed.

Professor Pauly identifies three alternatives for insuring against these large risks of chronic illness in old age. The first option is to self-insure by precautionary savings in preretirement and postretirement or by relying on an extended family network in which the children agree to take care of the financial needs of their elderly parents (perhaps for a price, called a bequest). While we do observe self-insurance, there are no doubt significant advantages to being able to pool the risks of chronic illness in old age. If so, we should observe the emergence of a second option, called market insurance, bought either individually or through groups via employee retirement plans. Private markets might, however, be limited in their ability to cover all risks. Because of the difficulty of identifying individual risks of chronic illness, full separation of high-risk groups from low-risk groups might not be possible. If so, only pooled-risk plans are feasible. But such plans might not be economically viable. The high-risk elderly might drive the premium upward so as to discourage the participation of the low-risk elderly, but plans with only high-risk households cannot be sustained in the private marketplace. This is the problem of adverse selection—that is, high risks drive the low risks from the market—and it might limit the extent of private insurance coverage for chronic illness. We are left, then, with the third option, a possible need for public insurance for this risk.

There are two strategies for the design of such public insurance. The first is to consider poverty induced by chronic illness to be no different from poverty caused by other unfortunate events and to simply combine all such assistance into a single, means-tested income guarantee that is indexed by the recipient's health state. Sicker individuals—defined as those with increased disabilities—will receive higher income guarantees so as to insure them a minimum bundle of non–health-care-related goods and services. The second strategy is to target federal government assistance specifically to the encouragement of health insurance for chronic illnesses. The federal government can either provide that insurance directly, or it can offer subsidies for the purchase of privately provided insurance. Professor Pauly prefers the second strategy.

Down both these routes to reform lurks an important problem, however. How do we define and identify those who qualify for benefits? Without a clear and effective measure of disability, there will emerge a strong set of incentives to abuse the provision of insurance, whether provided indirectly as an income grant or directly as reimbursement for increased health care costs. A major effort to cover the costs associated with long-term illness, for the elderly or for the population in general, raises the real possibility of a cost crisis in nursing home care, perhaps not unlike the one we have experienced in acute care services. But we can learn from those experiences. Who are the primary parties who will make the decision to use, or not to use, a nursing home facility? Who will decide the length of stay? What are the incentives of each of the responsible agents to use, or not to use, the nursing home? What is the present supply of nursing home beds, how elastic is that supply, and what are the viable alternatives to nursing home care for the chronically ill? We should have asked—and answered—all these questions of the acute care industry before we passed Medicare and Medicaid in 1965. We have the chance to ask these questions now of the nursing home industry before we decide just how to extend public insurance into the coverage of care for the chronically ill. I can think of no one more capable of providing us with careful answers than Professor Pauly himself.

7

Personal Security Accounts: A Proposal for Fundamental Social Security Reform

Michael J. Boskin
Laurence J. Kotlikoff
John B. Shoven

After Defense Department spending, Social Security is the largest program in the federal budget. For more than half the working-age households in the United States, Social Security taxes exceed personal income taxes. Further, for most elderly households, the future payments they will receive from Social Security constitute their most valuable asset, with the possible exception of their house. Social Security is not only large; it is also effective. It has provided substantial income security to the elderly, kept many elderly out of extreme poverty, and transferred hundreds of billions of dollars from younger, wealthier generations to older, poorer generations. For cohorts of elderly in the 1950s, 1960s, 1970s, and even 1980s, it has offered a relatively high, if declining, rate of return on tax contributions.

The success of Social Security has diverted attention from a number of significant shortcomings in its design. These problems fall into four categories:

1. Financial solvency
2. Equity
3. Efficiency
4. Uncertainty and lack of information

It is well known that the Social Security system is not funded; its financial assets at any point in time amount to only a trivial fraction of the future payment obligations of the system. The true funding source to meet these future obligations is the taxes or contributions of future workers. The system is in perpetual bankruptcy if these future tax receipts are ignored. But Social Security

We thank Martin Feldstein, James Tobin, and Social Security's Office of the Actuary for helpful comments. Douglas Puffert provided excellent research assistance.

is not strictly a pay-as-you-go plan. Such a plan would simply pay to beneficiaries the money that was collected each period from payroll taxes. Social Security does not have the inherent flexibility of such a plan. Instead, it more closely resembles an unfunded defined benefit pension plan, where the benefit formula is not explicitly adjusted to changes in the cash flow of the system. A major problem with an unfunded defined benefit plan is that it is very susceptible to financial crises. If the benefits are slightly more generous than the taxes collected for a period of time, the system quickly runs into a liquidity problem. The financial position of Social Security depends to a much greater extent on short-run business cycles and on long-run productivity changes and demographic developments than would a true pay-as-you-go system. This, along with the difficulty in forecasting both demographic and economic developments, explains the repetitive financial crises of Social Security.[1]

The Social Security system is not equitable in that it offers very different rates of return to households in similar circumstances. Some of the distinctions seem quite arbitrary and yet can cause benefits to differ by tens of thousands of dollars. For example, a divorced woman who did not work while married is not entitled to any benefits based on her former husband's Social Security if the marriage lasted less than ten years. If, however, the couple was married for more than ten years, the divorced woman might be entitled to benefits worth $100,000 or more. To us, this seems inequitable, inappropriate, and probably unintentional social engineering. There are other examples of such inequity. Two-earner married couples often receive a much lower rate of return on contributions than one-earner families, and single people, on average, do worse than both. Large families benefit from certain aspects of the insurance programs without paying more than smaller families. Those covered participants with short working careers or short careers in jobs covered by Social Security earn a higher rate of return than those with longer careers. In general, the system seems highly inequitable and capricious in its treatment of a vast number of households.

The uneven treatment and the complicated procedures involved in accurately determining or even roughly assessing one's future benefits leads to the third problem, economic inefficiency. The link between contributions and payouts is sufficiently weak that most workers may view their benefits as unrelated at the margin to their tax contributions. This means that the nearly 15 percent contribution rate for Social Security (including the hospital part of Medicare) must be added to the marginal tax rate of the personal income tax in order to compute the total marginal tax rate on earnings. Given that the economic waste due to distortionary taxation rises with the square of the marginal tax rate, it is easy to see that the Social Security payroll tax could be doubling the distortionary costs of the tax system. These extra distortions are unnecessary. If taxes and benefits were linked more closely, from the individual's perspective, Social Security contributions would be viewed not as taxes, but primarily as a form of deferred compensation similar to pension contributions, albeit yielding a potentially lower than market return. Social Security contributions would, to a very large extent, be a use of income rather than a tax and would not have the sizable disincentive effects of the latter.

The complicated benefit formulas just mentioned bring us to our final category of problems with Social Security: uncertainty and lack of information. The typical worker is given no concrete information regarding insurance coverage by Social Security. It takes an extreme effort to determine what a survivor's benefits would be in case of death of a spouse or what would be a reasonable expectation of one's future retirement annuity. Even at the time of retirement, there are numerous stories of different offices of Social Security coming up with different benefit amounts for the same individual. There is a similar lack of information regarding the disability insurance part of the Social Security program. Most workers have no idea about whether they qualify for disability insurance, let alone how much they would receive should they become disabled. The point is that people face a situation of great uncertainty and lack of information and therefore make uninformed and probably inefficient decisions regarding private insurance coverage and savings.

The revisions of the Social Security system, such as those that occurred in 1983, have been prompted by the system's recurring financial crises. The outcomes have been to change the contribution rates or the benefit formulas or to tax part of the benefits, but the fundamental design of the system has been neither changed nor studied. It is our believe that what is needed to address the four problem areas we have identified is structural reform of the system rather than tampering with tax or benefit schedules.

The Personal Security Accounts (PSA) proposal incorporates many reform ideas that have been previously advanced by members of Congress and government commissions. Chief among these is *earning sharing,* which was recommended by the 1979 Social Security Advisory Council and by the five members of the National Commission on Social Security Reform (Greenspan Commission) selected by the Democratic leadership. In addition, there are several features of the PSA plan that reflect principles of and practices in private saving and insurance markets. These include actuarial benefit calculations, a tight and clear link between contributions made to and benefits received from Social Security, the individual ownership and portability of PSAs, and annual PSA reports.

Our goal in proposing a reform in the structure of Social Security is not to alter the goals of the system, but rather to meet those goals more effectively and efficiently. In our PSA proposal, we recognize the need for mandatory public provision of social insurance. Private insurance markets are hampered by severe problems of adverse selection, making their pricing far from actuarially fair, and they fail to offer inflation-protected life annuities. We, therefore, retain the five insurance functions of Social Security (old age, disability, spousal survivor, child survivor, and old age hospital insurance). We also recognize the desirability of a progressive social security system. The existing Social Security system is redistributive in that it offers a better rate of return to low-income participants than to high-income ones. This kind of redistribution, which is clearly intentional, could not be accomplished by private insurers. Our proposed reform retains redistribution from high- to low-income households. In fact, it makes it much more explicit and also eliminates the capricious redistribution from low- to high-income households that now occurs.

A discussion of Social Security reform must include the extent to which past policy constrains current options. We have had an unfunded system for nearly fifty years and have accumulated an unfunded liability of several trillion dollars. While the merits of having a funded system can be discussed in theory, switching to a funded system at this point would cause an enormous intergenerational transfer. One generation would be asked to pay for two retirements, their own and that of the retired elderly at the time of the switch. Since this is undesirable from our perspective and likely to be politically infeasible, we accept the continuing nature of the plan. We also believe that the system cannot be changed for the currently retired or for those who are near retirement. Therefore, we propose that at the initiation of the PSA reform, only those under forty-five be enrolled in the new plan; those forty-five and older at the plan's initiation would remain under the current Social Security system.

The basic idea of our reform is to tighten the link between contributions and benefits and to offer households an insurance package more customized to their needs. Despite the continued unfunded nature of the plan and its progressivity, the new system would mimic private insurance in many more respects than does the current system. Each individual would have a PSA. Contributions credited to these accounts would be spent (in an accounting sense) for the five types of insurance policies mentioned above in proportions that would depend on the age structure of the family. The progressivity of the PSA system results from grossing up credited contributions for those with low incomes and grossing down credited contributions for those with high incomes. The rate of return implicit in the annual purchase (in an accounting sense) of additional insurance policies will vary from year to year according to the overall financial circumstances of the system. In this way, the system will have the increased flexibility necessary to avoid periodic financial crises. However, previous rates of return used in calculating benefits received for previous contributions are fixed and guaranteed. The system will be more equitable in that rates of return would not systematically differ for one- and two-earner couples and for single individuals and married couples. The efficiency advantage of our plan stems directly from the tighter link between pay-ins and insurance coverage; thus, calling the payments contributions rather than taxes becomes more appropriate. Finally, the uncertainty regarding one's coverage and accrued benefits will be eliminated by sending each participant an annual statement detailing taxes paid, credits received, and insurance benefits purchased with the credits.

In the next section, we describe the proposal in detail. We then analyze problems of inequity and inefficiency under the current system, pointing out how these problems would be resolved with PSAs. Finally, we summarize the advantages of the PSA alternative.

The PSA System

The PSA proposal changes Social Security's determination of Old Age, Survivors and Disability Insurance (OASDI) benefits. It also modifies OASDI taxation. The proposal does not deal with the Hospital Insurance (HI) component of Social Security, although reforms similar to those proposed for OASDI seem feasible. The PSA system is designed to adjust the generosity of Social Security automatically to changes in financial projections, but these adjustments are made at the margin—that is, they affect the accumulation of additional Social Security benefits but do not alter benefits that were accumulated in the past. These features, as well as the provisions for the transition to PSAs, are discussed here.

The main issue with respect to the transition is the establishment of initial PSA accounts for those under age forty-five; those forty-five and older at the initiation of PSAs will not become PSA participants but will continue receiving benefits under the current Social Security system.[2] While we attempt to be as specific as possible in laying out the PSA plan, it should be clear that we are describing a generic alternative to the current structure of Social Security, so many of the specifics of this scheme could be modified somewhat without altering the basic advantages of PSAs. Our description of PSAs begins with an illustration of the determination of PSA credits and benefits.

Benefit Determination under PSAs: An Illustration

The provision of benefits under PSAs can be easily understood by considering the example of John and Sally Doe, who are ages forty-one and thirty-five in the year 1999. John and Sally have a daughter, Josey. All dollar figures in the example are in 1986 dollars and are purely hypothetical in the sense that they might be substantially greater or smaller than those that would actually arise under the PSA plan. In the year 1999, John pays $2,000 and Sally pays $1,000 in Social Security taxes. Their combined tax payment of $3,000 is less than the average tax payment for married couples, so they receive thirty-six hundred PSA credits.[3] This illustrates that:

> The PSA system maintains progressivity under Social Security by providing poorer (richer) families with PSA credits that are larger (smaller) than actual family tax contributions.

The thirty-six hundred PSA credits are divided equally between John and Sally, each of whom receives eighteen hundred credits worth of insurance benefits. Hence:

> The PSA system involves complete earnings sharing in its determination of benefits.

The Social Security system spends John's eighteen hundred credits on the following four insurance policies. These policies are additions to those purchased for John in previous years based on previous accumulations of PSA credits. The four policies are:

1. An additional old age annuity
2. An additional disability annuity
3. An additional old age spousal survivor annuity payable to Sally if John dies
4. An additional child survivor annuity payable to Josey if John dies.

Four corresponding additional insurance policies are purchased for Sally with her eighteen hundred credits. If John and Sally were childless, Social Security would spend none of their credits on child survivor annuities. If John were single with no children, all his PSA credits would be spent on an additional old age annuity and an additional disability annuity. In sum:

> Each of OASDI's four major types of insurance are provided by PSAs. Social Security tailors its purchase of these policies to the specific needs of each family.

The allocation of John's eighteen hundred credits to the four additional insurance policies is determined exclusively by Social Security in light of John's family composition; that is:

> Like the current Social Security system, the PSA system entails forced saving and forced purchase of disability, survivor, and old age health insurance.

John's eighteen hundred PSA credits are spent by Social Security in the following way: twelve hundred credits are spent on an additional old age annuity, two hundred seventy credits are spent on an additional disability annuity, two hundred are spent on an additional spousal survivor annuity, and one hundred thirty are spent on an additional child survivor annuity. This allocation is purely hypothetical. The Social Security Administration (SSA) would establish a simple formula for allocating credits among the insurance policies that would take into account the composition of the family and the age of the participant. Thus, Social Security would allocate relatively more credits to the purchase of disability insurance for younger participants than for older participants, since the need for disability insurance is obviously much greater for a worker age thirty than for one age sixty.

Actuarial Benefit Calculations

The amount of each annuity purchased with the PSA credits is based on an actuarial calculation that equates the present expected value of each annuity's payments to the amount of credits spent on that annuity. The rate of return used by Social Security in 1999 in these actuarial calculations is identical for all policies and all PSA participants. Thus, apart from the explicitly progressive provision of PSA credits,

All PSA participants receive identical rates of return on their PSA credited contributions.[4]

Old Age Annuity. This annuity is available starting at age sixty-two independent of the recipient's labor earnings. For a participant age a in year t, the additional old age annuity, $A(a,t)$, purchased with PSA age a, year t credits, $C(a,t)$, is determined by the following:

$$C(a, t) = A(a, t) \sum_{i = 62}^{100} \frac{P_{i,a}}{(1 + r_t)^{(i - a)}} \qquad (7.1)$$

where $P_{i,a}$ is the probability that the PSA participant will survive to age i given that he or she is currently age a. In equation 7.1, $A(a,t)$ and $C(a,t)$ are both measured in dollars of constant purchasing power; that is:

PSA annuities are fully indexed for inflation.

The term r_t is the guaranteed real rate of return paid on all PSA credits in year t. We describe below Social Security's annual determination of this rate of return. The total indexed old age annuity received by PSA participants starting at age fifty-two is the sum of the annuities, $A(a,t)$'s, purchased at each age.

Spousal Survivor Annuity. Surviving spouses age sixty-two and over are eligible to receive the sum of all spousal survivor annuities purchased in any year by any deceased spouse. The actuarial formula determining the purchase of additional spousal survivor annuities in exchange for additional PSA credits is presented in Appendix 7A.

Child Survivor Annuity. This annuity is the sum of all child survivor annuities that are still in effect and that were purchased by any deceased parents on behalf of the child. The annuity is paid to surviving children prior to the child's attaining age eighteen. Unlike the spousal survivor annuity, the child survivor annuities are five-year term insurance policies providing an annuity to a surviving child based on the natural parent's death within five years of the time PSA credits are spent on this form of insurance. The five-year term policy ensures an adequate level of child survivor protection in the case a parent dies when the child is quite young. They also assure continued insurance protection (for five years) in case a parent or parents become unemployed and suffer a drop in their accumulation of PSA credits. The actuarial formula determining these five-year term child survivor annuities is presented in the appendix.

Disability Annuity. Like the child survivor annuity, PSA disability annuities are designed as five-year term policies, providing benefits in exchange for PSA credits if the insured participant becomes disabled within five years of the purchase of the policy and is under age sixty-two at the time of the onset of the disability. Each year's expenditure of PSA credits on disability insurance will provide additional five-year term disability annuities to the participant. In the event of disability, the disabled participant will collect the sum of the annuities purchased in the current year and the preceding four years. PSA disability insurance will provide annual payments to disabled workers prior to their reaching age sixty-two. In addition, this insurance policy will have a PSA credit surrender value at age sixty-two that will be spent on an additional old age annuity. This feature will ensure that workers who become disabled when quite young will receive adequate old age income after age sixty-two despite their having accumulated a relatively small old age annuity prior to age sixty-two. Since the age sixty-two cash surrender value is designed to protect the young disabled, its size relative to the disability annuity will be a decreasing function of the participant's age. The actuarial formula determining this annuity is presented in the appendix.

Annual Reports

Tables 7 – 1 and 7 – 2 present a hypothetical PSA report for John Doe in 1999 with the dollar amounts expressed in 1986 dollars (the actual 1999 report would have dollar amounts expressed in 1999 dollars). Table 7 – 1 indicates John Doe's past and current tax payments and accumulation of total PSA credits, as well as the allocation of these credits to the four insurance policies. Table 7 – 2 shows the annuities that are purchased with John Doe's PSA credits and indicates the extent to which these purchased annuities are payable; recall that child survivor and disability annuities purchased more than five-year term policies.

Consider table 7 – 1. Since John does not marry Sally until he is age thirty-six and Josey is born when John is thirty-eight, no credits are allocated to spousal survivor insurance and to child survivor insurance until John reaches ages thirty-six and thirty-eight, respectively. In the first year that John begins working (at age twenty-one), Social Security allocates a disproportionately large share of his credits to the purchase of an initial disability annuity. This adjusts for the fact that if John becomes disabled after one year, he will receive only the disability annuity purchased at age twenty-one, while if he becomes disabled at, for example, age thirty, John will receive the sum of the five disability annuities purchased at ages twenty-five, twenty-six, twenty-seven, twenty-eight, and twenty-nine. A similarly disproportionately large share of PSA credits is allocated to the purchase of child survivor benefits in the first year that Josey appears, since the child survivor policies also are five-year term policies.

The annuities indicated in table 7 – 2 are purely hypothetical; they do not reflect an actual actuarial calculation based on the PSA credits of table 7 – 1. The point of the table is to illustrate PSA reporting. As mentioned, the age sixty-five disability credit surrender amounts finance additional old age annuities for those who become disabled prior to age sixty-five.

Individual Ownership and Portability of PSAs

Like John, Sally owns her own PSA account. If John and Sally become divorced, they keep their PSA accounts and, assuming they or subsequent spouses pay Social Security taxes, they continue to accumulate PSA credits and PSA insurance annuities. For example, in the case of old age annuities, the additional annuities purchased when young simply add to those purchased when divorced in determining the total old age annuity. While a divorced person spends none of his or her additionally accumulated PSA credits on survivor insurance for his or her former spouse, the former spouse is still eligible to collect an old age survivor annuity based on purchases of such annuities by the former spouse during their years of marriage. If the

Table 7–1
Sample Personal Security Account: PSA Credits and Tax Payments

JOHN DOE
1999 PERSONAL SECURITY ACCOUNT
Social Security #123–45–6789 Current Age 41
Spouse Sally Doe   #1 Child Josey Doe

PSA Credits

Age	Total	Old Age	Disability	Spousal Survivor	#1 Child Survivor
21	$500	$250	$250	0	0
22	550	440	110	.	.
23	600	480	120	.	.
.	.	.	.	.	.
35	1,000	800	200	.	.
36	800	500	180	$1.0	.
37	900	575	200	125	.
38	900	300	180	115	$3.5
39	1,500	870	300	180	150
40	1,800	1,200	270	200	130

Tax Payments

Age	Amount Paid by John Doe	Amount Paid by John Doe's Spouse
21	$480	0
22	535	0
.		
40	1,200	$600

Table 7–2
Sample Personal Security Account: PSA Annuities

1999 PERSONAL SECURITY ACCOUNT
JOHN DOE Social Security #123–45–6789

	Disability Annuities			Spousal Survivor		Child Survivor	
Age	Old Age	Purchased Payable	Credit Surrender Value	Spousal Survivor	Purchased	Payable	Purchased
21	$230	$3,500					
22	256	1,200					
23	241	1,250					
.	.	.					
.	.	.					
35	290	1,575	$1,350	$15,000	$300		
36	263	1,350	1,400	20,000	325		
37	275	1,400	1,200	24,000	310		
38	187	1,200	2,000	35,000	450	$3,700	$3,700
39	362	2,000	1,850	33,500	500	1,800	1,800
40	450	1,850				1,500	1,500

Total old age annuity $10,145
Total payable disability annuity 7,823
Total age 62 disability credit surrender value 127,000
Total spousal survivor annuity 1,885
Total payable child survivor annuity 7,742

divorced couple have children from their marriage, each former spouse is required to buy child survivor benefits for each of their children. Hence:

> PSA accounts are individually owned and are completely portable, but the PSA system requires divorced parents to continue to purchase survivor insurance for children of previous marriages.

Taxation and Accrual of PSA Credits

Social Security tax collection would be changed slightly from current practice by taxing combined earnings of spouses at scheduled rates rather than taxing each spouse separately. For married couples under age sixty-two, the proposal establishes a covered earnings ceiling on the couple's combined earnings and collects taxes on earnings up to this ceiling. For single heads of households, a 30 percent lower earnings ceiling is established. These changes are appropriate because single individuals typically have smaller insurance needs than married couples. Relative to the current system, only high-income, single-earner couples will experience tax increases. The proposal leaves unchanged the time path of scheduled Social Security tax rates.

Under the fully phased-in PSA system, Social Security taxation and the accrual of PSA credits and benefits ceases once a participant reaches age sixty-two. In the case of married couples, younger spouses are taxed as single individuals once the older spouse reaches age sixty-two. Assuming these younger spouses are still working, they will continue to accrue PSA credits and purchase benefits that enter into their own PSAs. The earnings of spouses over age sixty-two will be taken into account in the progressive provision of PSA credits in exchange for Social Security taxes.

Social Security Financing and Choice of Annual Guaranteed Rates of Return

The PSA proposal involves no significant change in the time path of aggregate Social Security taxes or aggregate benefits. Under PSAs, Social Security would continue to be self-financing, with benefits paid to older retired generations financed by taxes on young and middle-age workers. Unlike the current system, however, the PSA system has provisions that would avoid short-term funding crises such as those of 1977 and 1983 and that would automatically eliminate long-run deficits.

The choice of the term r_t, the guaranteed rate of return to be used in calculating each year's purchase of additional annuities, which appears in equation 7.1 and the equations in the appendix, will be chosen each year by an independent board of actuaries to ensure long-run balance between benefits and taxes and the preservation through time of a significant trust fund equal to at least three years of benefit payments. The significant trust fund will insulate the system from short-run fluctuations in tax receipts due to recessions, and the annual rate of return will be automatically adjusted to maintain balance in present value between tax receipts and benefit payments over the succeeding seventy-five years. Hence, as demographic or economic projections change, the annual rate of return will be adjusted downward in the case of projected seventy-five-year deficits and upward in the case of projected seventy-five-year surpluses. Since the government will guarantee the payment of all purchased annuities, the board of actuaries will use conservative projections in determining the annual rate of return. It is important to note that changes in the annual rate of return affect only the purchase of additional benefits and leave unchanged PSA policies purchased in the past. Thus,

> The choice of each year's rate of return will affect only the calculation of the purchase of retirement, survivor, and disability annuities in that year; annuities purchased in previous years based on previous rates of return will never be altered.

The Transition to PSAs

To minimize disruptions for those retired, those soon to retire, and those who are disabled.

> All Americans forty-five years and older and those currently receiving Social Security disability payments are exempt from the PSA system and will continue to pay taxes and receive benefits as mandated under current law.

For Americans under age forty-five at the time of the introduction of PSAs, benefits will be determined based on their PSA credits.

Determination of Initial PSA Credits. At the start-up of the PSA system, all PSA participants will receive an initial allocation of PSA annuities. These annuities will be calculated by treating each initial PSA participant (those under age forty-five) as if he or she had always been enrolled in the PSA system. Thus, Social Security will use information on past tax contributions, past marital status, and past birth of children to determine the PSA credits that would have been earned and the PSA annuities that would have been purchased in each year in the participant's past.

While we realize that this counterfactual historical simulation will require somewhat more information than is currently available to Social Security, particularly marital and birth of children histories, we feel such information could easily be obtained from PSA participants. Random auditing of this information plus penalties for fraudulent statements should minimize problems of cheating. In simulating PSA histories, we propose that the board of actuaries use a 3 percent real rate of return for each past year's annual PSA rate of return.[5]

During the transition to complete PSA participation, there will be couples in which one spouse participates in PSA and the other does not—that is, one spouse is younger than forty-five and one spouse is forty-five or older at the time of the initiation of PSAs (this includes participants and nonparticipants who subsequently marry). In these cases, Social Security will calculate PSA credits and annuities for the participant, pretending that his or her spouse is also a participant. For the nonparticipant, Social Security will calculate Social Security benefits based on current law, pretending, where relevant, that the PSA participant is a nonparticipant.

Taxation during the Transition. At the initiation of PSAs, all couples, including nonparticipants, will be taxed based on the PSA method of taxation, which has a higher taxable earnings ceiling for couples. For high-earning PSA nonparticipants who are single, this will mean a small reduction in taxes relative to the current system, and for certain high-earning couples, this might mean a small increase in taxes. But, as described below, such a change would reduce some of the current system's more egregious inequities.

Other Features of PSAs

Initial Age of PSA Participation. The initial age of participation is eighteen. Participants married to nonparticipants under age eighteen will receive PSA credits and annuities in the same manner as described above for the case of older participant-nonparticipant couples.

Universal Coverage. All Americans under age forty-five at the initiation of PSAs will be enrolled in the program. The method of allocating initial PSA annuities described above avoids the problem of giving excessively large returns to many new enrollees. Such a problem would arise if the current Social Security system immediately instituted universal coverage.

Eliminating Earnings Testing and Income Taxation of PSA Benefits. Under the PSA system, benefits would not be subject to an earnings test, nor would benefits be subject to income taxation.

Problems of Inequity and Inefficiency under the Current System and Their Resolution under PSA

Equity Issues

Under the current Social Security system, a variety of benefits beyond the worker's basic retirement annuity are available to qualifying dependents, with no requirement that the worker contribute additional amounts to pay for these benefits. These marginally free benefits include dependent benefits for current and former spouses, survivor benefits for current and former spouses, and survivor benefits for children. Since these marginally free extra benefits are not earnings tested, many of the recipients of these transfers are quite well-to-do middle- and upper-income households. Those who pay for these transfers are single workers with no dependents and low-, middle-, and upper-income two-earner couples that qualify for either no or quite small dependent benefits. These workers are taxed the same as those with qualifying dependents, but their families receive little or none of the system's marginally free benefits.

The amount of lifetime marginally free benefits can be sizable relative to the worker's lifetime tax payments. Table 7–3 presents projections of lifetime Old Age and Survivors Insurance (OASI) benefits and taxes for different middle-income households under current law.[6] The households are married couples in three cohorts in which the husband's share of total household labor earnings ranges from 50 to 100 percent. The calculations take 1985 total household labor earnings of $25,000 as a benchmark. The three cohorts are the cohort born in 1930, the cohort born in 1960, and the cohort that will be born in 2005. In the calculations, total household labor earnings prior to 1985 equal $25,000 deflated by a wage growth factor reflecting growth in average wages between the year in question and 1985. Total household earnings in future years equal $25,000 times a growth rate factor reflecting the growth in real wages projected by the Social Security actuaries in their intermediate 1985 projection and the projected age profile of earnings. Lifetime benefits and taxes, including income taxation of Social Security benefits, are calculated as present expected values as of age twenty-five using male and female mortality probabilities. Lifetime benefits include retirement and spousal survivor benefits but do not include child survivor benefits, disability benefits, or health insurance benefits. Lifetime Social Security taxes exclude disability and health insurance taxes. All dollar figures are expressed in 1985 dollars. A 3 percent real interest rate is used in forming present values.

The table points out two well-known types of redistribution in the current system. First, there is an intergenerational redistribution. Earlier cohorts

Table 7–3
Intergenerational and Intragenerational Inequity:
Middle-Income Households with $25,000 of Earnings in 1985

	Husband's Share of Total Earnings		
	100%	67%	50%
1930 Cohort (age 25 in 1955)			
PV benefits	$50,231	$44,779	$41,591
PV taxes	42,509	48,817	48,570
PV transfer	7,722	– 4,038	– 6,979
1960 Cohort (age 25 in 1985)			
PV benefits	78,257	65,906	60,770
PV taxes	103,157	101,699	100,978
PV transfer	– 24,899	– 35,792	– 40,208
2005 Cohort (age 25 in 2030)			
PV benefits	149,971	126,414	116,915
PV taxes	198,009	195,102	193,666
PV transfer	– 48,036	– 68,688	– 76,751

[a]All figures are present expected values measured in 1985 dollars discounted to the year each cohort was age twenty-five. A 3 percent real interest rate was assumed in forming these present values. Earnings prior to and after 1985 equal, respectively, $25,000 times a year-specific factor reflecting historic and projected growth in real wages.

are projected to fare much better under Social Security than later cohorts. Thus, for the 1930 one-earner couple, the present expected value of benefits exceeds the present expected value of taxes by $7,722; this difference is – $48,036 for the middle-income, one-earner couple born in 2005. These intergenerational transfers are associated with the unfunded financing of Social Security, as well as projected changes in the age structure of the population. Most observers believe, as do we, that this intergenerational redistribution, while probably not fully intended, cannot and should not be changed radically or rapidly for political and other reasons.

The second type of redistribution, intragenerational redistribution, is another story. As mentioned, redistribution between one- and two-earner couples arises because dependent and survivor benefits are available to nonworking spouses, with no additional tax contributions required from the working spouse. The redistribution between such couples is substantial, and it is projected to continue indefinitely.

Compare for the 1960 cohort the current system's treatment of one-earner couples and two-earner couples in which both spouses are equal earners. The difference, in expected present value, of lifetime benefits less lifetime taxes for these two couples is $15,309 [– 24,899 – (– 40,208)], which represents more than three fifths of the couple's 1985 earnings. This redistribution occurs for older cohorts and is projected to continue into the indefinite future; for the 2005 cohort, this difference in treatment of one- and two-earner couples represents $28,713.

Measured as a fraction of age twenty-five annual earnings, the redistribution from two-earner to one-earner couples is even larger for lower-income and higher-income households (see table 7–4). For couples born in 1960 with $15,000 in earnings in 1985, the difference in treatment between one-earner and two-(equal)earner couples is almost a year's earnings. For couples with $50,000 in 1985 earnings, the difference in treatment is more than a year's earnings. The progressivity of the benefit schedule provides larger dependent as well as retirement benefits per dollar contributed for lower-income couples; hence, the inequality between one- and two-earner couples measured as a fraction of earnings is greater for lower-income than for middle-income households. In the case of higher-income households, the ceiling on taxable earnings limits the amount of taxes that a single high-earner couple pays, although, over a range, it does not limit the amount of taxes paid by the high-income, two-earner couple. Thus, a single-earner couple with $50,000 of 1985 earnings is projected to pay $138,302 in present value in Social Security taxes, while a two-earner couple in which each spouse earns $25,000 is projected to pay $201,956 in present value in taxes.

An issue not addressed in tables 7–3 and 7–4 is the redistribution between two-earner couples in which both spouses always work and two-earner couples in which one spouse works sporadically. The tables are also deficient in that they take account neither of child survivor benefits nor of disability benefits and taxes.

Table 7–4 also demonstrates the unequal treatment between single individuals and one-earner married couples, as well as between single individuals and married couples in which one spouse accounts for most of the household's total earnings. Take the case of a two-earner couple with $15,000 of earnings, $10,000 of which is earned by the husband. The present value transfer is − $6,565 per spouse. For a single male earning $7,500, the present value transfer is − $11,565, or $5,000 less than the per spouse transfer of − $6,565. Another element of redistribution from single persons to married couples not included in these calculations is the provision of survivor benefits to children.

In addition to transfers from single individuals and two-earner couples to one-earner or close-to-one-earner couples, the Social Security system also systematically transfers from men to women. In table 7–4, the $25,000 male earner who never marries is projected to lose $25,845 from participating in Social Security. The corresponding female who never marries loses only $14,604. This difference is due to the greater longevity of females.

Equity and PSAs

The PSA proposal eliminates the redistribution from single individuals and two-earner couples to one-earner or primarily one-earner couples. It does so while still maintaining progressivity in Social Security. Under a PSA system, benefits are tightly tied to tax payments. Households do not receive addi-

Table 7–4
Intragenerational Inequity: Present Value Transfer for 1960 Cohort (Age 25 in 1985)

Total 1985 Earnings	Couple			Single		
	Husband's Share of Total Earnings			1985 Earnings	Male	Female
	100%	67%	50%			
$10,000	$5,283	$-1,203	$-2,762	$5,000	$-4,331	$-2,756
$15,000	-13,129	-15,812	7,500	-11,565	-3,140	
25,000	-24,899	-35,792	-40,208	12,500	-25,815	-14,604
50,000	-61,459	-115,877	-120,263	25,000	-66,090	-47,385
80,000	-64,779	-159,607	-192,073	40,000	-99,694	-86,112

tional benefits unless they receive additional PSA credits, and households making identical tax payments (per spouse in the case of couples) receive identical credits (per spouse). Thus, the progressive formula relating taxes to credits would be based on taxes paid in the case of single individuals and on taxes paid per spouse in the case of couples.

Since it appears politically infeasible to use gender-specific mortality probabilities in calculating PSA insurance policies, the PSA plan, like the current system, would systematically redistribute from men to women. This redistribution would not, however, be connected to the choice of labor supply of married women; that is, wives in one-earner couples and wives in two-earner couples, where each couple has identical total earnings, would receive identical PSA credits.

The earnings-sharing feature of PSAs ensures that nonworking spouses who become divorced receive, during their marriage, PSA credits equal to those received by their working spouses. Hence, divorced persons leave their marriage with Social Security benefits, regardless of the length of marriage.

Abstracting from changes with time in the PSA discount rate, the actuarial discounting feature of PSAs ensures that workers who start contributing earlier in life, non–college graduates, receive as good a return on the PSA credits they earn when young as they do on credits they earn when old. This means that those who start working at an early age are not penalized relative to those who start work at a later age, as is true under the current system.

Another equalizing feature of PSAs is that the system eliminates those work disincentives facing spouses who will collect as dependents under the current system. At present wives and husbands with low earning potential who can collect dependent benefits on their spouse's account receive nothing in return for their own tax payments to Social Security. Hence, they face a greater work disincentive due to Social Security than do their working spouses. By basing the determination of PSA credits on total taxes paid, no matter which spouse paid these taxes, an additional dollar of taxes paid by either spouse provides the same additional benefits to the household.

In addition to discouraging the labor supply of second-earner spouses, the current system might be needlessly discouraging the labor effort of primary earners. The next section addresses the strong possibility that Social Security taxpayers do not understand the connection between their tax payments and future Social Security benefits and view Social Security taxes as providing no additional benefits at the margin.

Social Security and Economic Efficiency:
The Issue of Labor Supply Disincentives

The combined employer-employee Social Security payroll tax rate is currently more than 14 percent.[7] Recent estimates suggest that the average marginal income tax rate is roughly 27 percent (Barro and Sahasakul 1983). If marginal OASDI and HI payroll taxes provided no marginal Social Security benefits or were incorrectly perceived to provide no marginal benefits, the effective marginal federal government taxation of labor supply would average roughly 41 percent. Since the efficiency costs of distortionary taxation increase as roughly the square of the tax rate, the Social Security payroll tax might be more than doubling the deadweight loss of labor income taxation.

Auerbach and Kotlikoff (1985) use a simulation model to study the efficiency costs of running an unlinked rather than a linked Social Security system. In an unlinked system, benefits are unrelated (at the margin) to tax contributions, while in a linked system every dollar of taxes paid increases benefits at the margin by less than a dollar, a dollar, or more than a dollar depending on the design of the benefit schedule.

Calculations based on Auerbach and Kotlikoff's model suggest very sizable potential efficiency gains from having a linked rather than an unlinked Social Security system. Their results are illustrative and should not be viewed as providing concrete estimates for the United States. If, however, American workers systematically underestimate actual marginal linkage, the results suggest that the efficiency of the U.S. fiscal structure could be greatly enhanced, at a minimum, by providing better information to workers about the marginal return on their payroll tax dollars and, at a maximum, by substantially increasing the extent of the marginal linkage. Assuming workers incorrectly believe that they receive nothing at the margin in return for Social Security taxes, the model suggests that the efficiency gains from annual reporting of marginal benefit accrual could be as large as 1 percent of the gross national product (GNP) on an annual basis. That means that the possible efficiency gain is equivalent to a 1 percent larger level of GNP this year and every year in the future. This potential efficiency gain is quite substantial relative to other potential efficiency improvements that have been reported in the literature (see, for example, Ballard, Fullerton, Shoven, and Walley 1985; Auerbach and Kotlikoff 1983).

Actual marginal benefit-tax linkage under the current system can be quite significant for certain workers (Blinder, Gordon, and Wise 1980), but it appears doubtful that many Americans accurately understand the linkage. Indeed, casual conversation among the authors of this proposal and colleagues who are not students of Social Security suggest that most American economists have no understanding of the extent of marginal linkage.

Efficiency and PSAs

An important objective of the PSA plan is making perfectly clear the extent of benefit-tax linkage. The PSA proposal includes annual reports that detail exactly what additional benefits workers receive in exchange for their additional taxes. For certain workers, such as spouses who would collect as dependents under the current system and, therefore, receive nothing in exchange for their Social Security tax contributions, the PSA proposal significantly lowers the tax on labor effort. Under the PSA plan, additional Social Security tax contributions imply additional PSA credits regardless of which spouse pays the taxes. For other workers, who now mistakenly believe that they receive no marginal benefits in exchange for marginal taxes, the PSA reports would indicate precisely the additional benefits purchased with their additional tax contributions. Finally, for older workers the elimination of the earnings test under the PSA system will eliminate the significant work disincentive confronting the aged under the current system.

Summary

The PSA proposal addresses certain long-standing inequities, inefficiencies, and informational problems within Social Security. While it calls for a major restructuring of Social Security for younger and future generations, the proposal preserves the most important feature of the present system; it strengthens rather than weakens the government's role and responsibility in running Social Security, and it retains Social Security's four major types of benefits: old age annuities, spousal survivor annuities, child survivor annuities, and disability annuities. The proposal also maintains the progressive nature of Social Security and leaves unchanged Social Security's pay-as-you-go financing.

While firm in our basic support of Social Security, we believe that the current Social Security system has serious flaws that cannot be redressed with minor modifications. These design defects appear to generate major inequities, significant work disincentives, and considerable uncertainty about the receipt of benefits. If Social Security were a minor feature in U.S. economic life, modernizing Social Security's design would be of small importance. Such is not the case.

Our scheme for modernizing Social Security involves the following:

1. Providing, on a progressive basis, credits for taxes
2. Sharing credits equally between spouses
3. Appropriately allocating credits to the purchase of the PSA plan's four insurance policies
4. Using actuarial formulas to determine the size of policies purchased with PSA credits
5. Providing annual PSA reports detailing taxes paid and benefits received

By sharing earnings, PSAs eliminate redistribution from single individuals and two-earner couples to one-earner or primarily one-earner couples. By allocating credits to specific needs, the PSA plan improves Social Security's provision of social insurance. By sending annual reports, PSAs reduce potential work disincentives of workers by clarifying exactly the additional benefits they can expect in return for their additional taxes. And by guaranteeing PSA benefits, the government restores security to the country's major source of retirement finances.

Notes

1. See Boskin (1986) for a detailed discussion of Social Security's long-term finances.
2. While we prefer age forty-five as the critical age for initial PSA eligibility, the PSA plan could certainly be implemented with a younger or older initial eligibility age.
3. In determining the relationship between Social Security taxes and PSA credits, Social Security could clearly be either more or less progressive than is currently the case and would also be adapted to any desired change in program size.
4. Rates of return would differ by sex and race if unisex and unirace mortality probabilities were used in the actuarial calculations.
5. A 3 percent real return appears to represent a much higher after-tax real rate of return than the average annual risk-free real return received by investors in the postwar period.
6. These calculations are similar to those of Pellechio and Goodfellow (1983).
7. This includes 2.9 percent for HI.

References

Auerbach, Alan J., and Laurence J. Kotlikoff, "The Efficiency Gain from Dynamic Tax Return," *The International Economic Review,* 1983.

Auerbach, Alan J., and Laurence J. Kotlikoff. 1984. "Social Security and the Economics of the Demographic Transition." In *Retirement and Economic Behavior,* edited by Henry J. Aaron and Gary Burtless. Washington, DC: Brookings Institution.

Auerbach, Alan J., and Laurence J. Kotlikoff. 1985. "Simulating Alternative Social Security Responses to the Demographic Transition." *National Tax Journal* (June).

Auerbach, Alan J., and Laurence J. Kotlikoff. 1985. "The Efficiency Gains from Social Security Benefit-Tax Linkage." National Bureau of Economic Research Working Paper No. 1645.

Auerbach, Alan J., and Laurence J. Kotlikoff. 1986. "Life Insurance of the Elderly: Adequacy and Determinants." Edited by Gary Burtless. Washington, DC: Brookings Institution.

Ballard, Charles L., Don Fullerton, John B. Shoven, and John Whalley. 1985. *A General Equilibrium Model for Tax Policy Evaluation.* NBER vol., Chicago: University of Chicago Press.

Barro, R.J., and Chaipat Sahasakul. 1983. "Measuring the Average Marginal Tax Rate from the Individual Income Tax." *Journal of Business* 56, no. 4:419–52.

Blinder, Alan S., Roger H. Gordon, and Donald E. Wise. 1980. "Reconsidering the Work Disincentive Effects of Social Security." *National Tax Journal* 33, no. 4 (December).

Boskin, Michael, Laurence J. Kotlikoff, and John B. Shoven. 1982. "Personal Securities Accounts: A Proposal for Fundamental Social Security Reform." Paper presented to the National Commission on Social Security Reform, August 20.

Burkhauser, Richard. 1982. "Earnings Sharing: Incremental and Fundamental Reform." In *A Challenge to Social Security,* edited by Richard Burkhauser and Karen Holden. New York: Academic Press.

Gordon, Roger H. 1982. "Social Security and Labor Supply Incentives." National Bureau of Economic Research Working Paper No. 989.

Gordon, Roger H., and Alan S. Blinder. 1980. "Market Wages, Reservation Wages, and Retirement Decisions." *Journal of Public Economics* 14, no. 2 (October): 277–308.

Holden, Karen. 1982. "Supplemental OASI Benefits to Homemakers." In *A Challenge to Social Security.*

Johnson, Jon, Richard Wertheimer, and Sheila Zedlewski. 1983. "The Dynamic Simulation of Income Model." Vol. 1, Urban Institute Working Paper, November.

Kotlikoff, Laurence J. 1978. "Social Security, Time for Reform." *Federal Tax Reform: Myth of Reality.* San Francisco: Institute for Contemporary Studies.

Kotlikoff, Laurence J. 1980. "The Social Security and Welfare System—What We Have, Want, and Can Afford." In *The U.S. Economy in the 1980s.* San Francisco: Institute for Contemporary Studies.

Kotlikoff, Laurence J. 1984. "Reforming Social Security for the Young—A Framework for Consensus." In *Controlling the Cost of Social Security,* edited by Colin D. Campbell. Washington, DC: American Enterprise Institute.

Kotlikoff, Laurence J., Avia Spivak, and Lawrence H. Summers. 1982. "The Adequacy of Savings." *The American Economic Review* (December): Vol. 72, No. 5.

Munnell, Alicia, and L. Stiglin. 1982. "Women and a Two-Tier Social Security System." In *A Challenge to Social Security.*

Pellechio, Anthony J., and Gordon P. Goodfellow. 1983. "Individual Gains and Losses from Social Security Before and After the 1983 Social Security Amendments." Mimeo, June.

President's Commission on Pension Policy. 1981. *Coming of Age: Toward a National Retirement Income Policy.* Washington, DC: U.S. Government Printing Office.

1983. *Report of the National Commission on Social Security Reform.* Washington, DC: U.S. Government Printing Office.

1979. *Social Security Financing and Benefits: Reports of the 1979 Advisory Council on Social Security.* Washington, DC: U.S. Government Printing Office.

U.S. Congress. 1975. Senate Special Committee on Aging. *Women and Social Security: Adapting to a New Era.* Washington, DC: U.S. Government Printing Office.

U.S. Department of Health, Education, and Welfare. 1979. *Social Security and the Changing Roles of Men and Women.* Washington, DC: U.S. Government Printing Office.

Appendix 7A
Description and Determination
of PSA Insurance Benefits

Old Age Benefits

This benefit, paid in the form of an annuity, will be available starting at age sixty-two independent of the recipient's labor earnings. The size of the annuity will be determined actuarially based on the PSA credits allocated to the purchase of this benefit. For participants covered by the PSA system, each year's expenditure of PSA credits on the old age annuity adds to the old age benefit available starting at age sixty-two. For a participant currently age a in year t, the additional old age annuity, $A(a,t)$, purchased with additional PSA credits, $C(a,t)$, is determined by equation 7A.1.

$$A(a,t) \sum_{i=62}^{100} \frac{P_i^{s/a}}{(1 + r_t)^{i-a}} = C(a,t) \qquad (7A.1)$$

In equation 7A.1, $A(a,t)$ and $C(a,t)$ are both measured in dollars of constant purchasing power, and r_t is the real guaranteed rate of return on all PSA credits in year t. $P_i^{s/a}$ is the probability the beneficiary will survive to age i given he or she is currently age a.

The total constant dollar old age benefit available to PSA participants starting at age sixty-two is the sum of the $A(a,t)$s acquired at each age a, including the initial annuity acquired at the initiation of the PSA system. The sum of the $A(a,t)$s will be converted to current dollars using the consumer price index.

Spousal Survivor Benefits

Surviving spouses age sixty-two and over are eligible to receive benefits reflecting those PSA credits spent to purchase this insurance while the deceased spouse was alive. Like the old age benefit, survivor benefits are paid in the form of an annuity. Equation 7A.2 indicates the additional annuity, $Aw(aw,t)$, potentially available to a surviving wife who is currently age aw

in year t based on additional PSA credits, $Ch(ah,t)$ spent in year t on this insurance when the wife is age aw and the husband is age ah. This equation holds for wives who are younger than their husbands. Equation 7A.2' shows the annuity that $Ch(ah,t)$ will purchase if the wife is older than the husband. The husband's survivor annuities are determined by equivalent formulas by simply switching the husband and wife's ages.

$$Aw(aw,t) \left[\sum_{i=ah}^{62+x} P_i^{dh/ah} \sum_{j=62}^{100} \frac{P_j^{sw/aw}}{(1+r_t)^{j-aw}} + \sum_{i=62+x}^{100} P_i^{dh/ah} \sum_{j=i=x}^{100} \frac{P_j^{sw/aw}}{(1+r_t)^{j-aw}} \right] = Ch(ah,t) \quad (7A.2)$$

In equation 7A.2, ah is the husband's age and x equals $ah - aw$. $P_i^{dh/ah}$ is the probability that the husband will die at age i given he is age ah. The first term in the brackets in equation 7A.2 deals with the possibility of the husband dying prior to the wife attaining age sixty-two; the second deals with the husband's possible death after the wife reaches sixty-two.

$$Aw(aw,t) \left[\sum_{i=ah}^{62+x} P_i^{dh/ah} \sum_{j=62}^{100} \frac{P_j^{sw/aw}}{(1+r_t)^{j-aw}} + \sum_{i=62+x}^{100} P_i^{dh/ah} \sum_{j=i=x}^{100} \frac{P_j^{sw/aw}}{(1+r_t)^{j-aw}} \right] = Ch(ah,t) \quad (7A.2')$$

In equation 7A.2', the first term in the brackets considers the probability of the husband's death prior to the wife attaining age sixty-two; the second term deals with the probability that the younger husband dies after the wife reaches age sixty-two.

For surviving wives age sixty-two and older, the total annual real spousal survivor benefit is the sum of the $Aw(aw,t)$s acquired at each age aw of the wife when her husband is alive. For surviving husbands, total annual (constant dollar) survivor benefits are determined symmetrically. All constant dollar spousal survivor benefits are converted to current dollars using the consumer price index.

Child Survivor Benefits

These benefits are paid in the form of an annuity to surviving children prior to the child's attaining age eighteen. In each year that children are under age eighteen, a portion of the family's total PSA credits will be spent to acquire this insurance. In the case of children living with both their natural parents, PSA credits will be spent to purchase two child survivor benefits, one of which is paid to the child in the event of the mother's death and the other paid in the event of the father's death. In the event both parents die prior to the child's attaining age eighteen, the child will receive both annuities.

In the case of children whose natural parents are divorced, PSA credits will be allocated from each natural parent's total family PSA credits and spent to purchase insurance protection for that child in the event of the natural parent's early demise.

Unlike either the old age or spousal survivor benefits that provide at least some insurance protection in the future regardless of future PSA contributions, the child survivor benefits are five-year term insurance policies providing payments to a surviving child based on the natural parent's death within five years of the time PSA credits have been spent on this form of insurance. The five-year term policy was chosen both to ensure an adequate level of child survivor benefits in the case parents die quite young, as well as to provide child survivor protection in the case of an extended lapse in the natural parent's accumulation of PSA credits, due, for example, to prolonged unemployment.

Equation 7A.3 determines the additional constant dollar annual child survivor benefit, $Ac(ac,t)$, purchased in year t with PSA credits of $Cp(ap,t)$. In this expression, ac is the age of the child in year t, and ap is the age of the natural parent. The benefit $Ac(ac,t)$ is provided to the child until the child reaches age eighteen, provided the natural parent dies within five years of the purchase of this benefit. In the event of the death of a natural parent prior to the child attaining age eighteen, the total annual constant dollar benefit available to a child currently age ac is

$$Ac(ac,t) + Ac(ac - 1, t - 1) + Ac(ac - 2, t - 2) + Ac(ac - 3, t - 3)$$
$$+ AC(ac - 4, t - 4).$$

This total constant dollar child survivor benefit is converted to current dollars using the consumer price index.

$$Ac(ac,t) \sum_{i = ap}^{ap + 4} \left[P_i^{dp/ap} \sum_{j = ac + i - ap}^{18} \frac{P_j^{sc/ac}}{(1 + r_t)^{j - ac}} \right] = Cp(ap,t) \qquad (7A.3)$$

In equation 7A.3, $P_i^{dp/ap}$ is the probability that the parent, who is currently age *ap*, will die at age *i*. $P_j^{sc/ac}$ is the probability that an age *ac* child will survive to age *j*.

Disability Annuities

Like child survivor annuities, PSA disability annuities are designed as five-year term policies, providing benefits in exchange for PSA credits if the insured participant becomes disabled within five years of the purchase of the policy and is under age sixty-two at the time of disability. Each year's expenditure of PSA credits on disability insurance will provide additional five-year term policies to the insured worker. In the event of disability, the disabled participant will collect the sum of benefits from all disability policies purchased in the current year and the preceding four years. PSA disability insurance will provide annual payments to disabled workers prior to their attaining age sixty-two. In addition, this insurance policy will have a cash surrender value at age sixty-two that will be converted into additional old age annuity benefit payments from age sixty-two onward. This feature will ensure that workers who become disabled when young will receive old age benefits after age sixty-two despite their having purchased relatively small amounts of old age benefits prior to age sixty-two.

In equation 7A.4, *Cdis*(*a,t*) equals the PSA credits spent on disability benefits at age *a*. *Adis*(*a,t*) is the disability annuity payable until the worker reaches age sixty-two. *Sdis*(*a,t*) is the age sixty-two cash surrender value of the policy that purchases additional old age benefits for the disabled worker. The size of *Sdis*(*a,t*) is chosen to provide additional old age benefits to disabled workers equal to *Adis*(*a,t*).

$$Adis(a,t) \sum_{i=a}^{62} \frac{P_i^{dis/a}}{(1+r_t)^{i-a}} + \frac{Sdis(a,t)P_{62}^{dis/a}}{(1+r_t)^{62-a}} = Cdis(a,t) \quad (7A.4)$$

In equation 7A.4, $P_i^{dis/a}$ is the probability that a worker currently age *a* is disabled in year *i*, given that disability initially occurred between ages *a* and *a* + 4. $P_i^{dis/a}$ depends, of course, on age-specific mortality and disability probabilities.

Comment

Alicia H. Munnell

This work was first brought to my attention in 1982, and it has found its way back to my desk numerous times since then. Boskin, Kotlikoff, and Shoven seem determined to find some support for their proposal to reform the Social Security system, but the simple, hard truth is that their idea did not float when they first presented it to the National Commission on Social Security Reform in 1982, and it continues to founder today. The reason nearly everyone in the field finds this paper so misguided is that the authors propose drastic changes in a huge, ongoing program that affects almost every American without ever considering whether the existing structure can be modified to address current deficiencies.

Boskin, Kotlikoff, and Shoven point to five shortcomings in the Social Security system in justifying its replacement with Personal Security Accounts (PSAs). First, the current program unfairly provides greater benefits per dollar of taxes to large families and couples than to small families and single people. Second, it treats one-earner couples in a more generous fashion than two-earner couples. Third, it handles divorce in an inequitable manner. Fourth, the program is susceptible to financial crisis because workers are provided a much too rigidly guaranteed benefit. Fifth, because workers are unsure of the linkage between benefits accrued and taxes paid, Social Security produces an excess burden.

The first problem is the natural outcome of a system that is progressive, a quality of which the authors seem to approve. Given the same level of earnings, it follows that the larger the family, the poorer it will be. Therefore, it is inconsistent to say, as the authors do, that equity requires rates of return to fall with earnings but that rates of return should be equivalent, regardless of family size, for people with equivalent earnings.

The second and third problems, regarding the treatment of two-earner couples and divorced persons, have been studied extensively, and many solutions have been suggested. Several recent studies by the Social Security Administration (SSA) have found that reforms could be implemented within the current system. But earnings-sharing schemes present two basic problems that the Boskin, Kotlikoff, and Shoven proposal would do nothing to alleviate. First, certain categories of people who are supposed to be among the beneficiaries of this reform, such as divorced widows, would actually end up with lower benefits. Second, implementing any earnings-sharing provision would reduce benefits for men unless revenues were increased through higher payroll taxes.

The fourth problem mentioned by the authors is the sensitivity of the current system to economic conditions, particularly the relationship between the rate of price increase and the rate of age growth. Tax revenues vary with the growth of wages; benefits rise with increases in the consumer price index. Historically this has not been a problem because wages have grown faster than prices, but when reserves are small, recessions characterized by slow wage growth and rapid inflation can cause a short-term financing crisis. On this issue, however, three points should be made. First, the Boskin, Kotlikoff, and Shoven proposal would not alleviate this type of crisis because, in the event of slowing productivity, their plan for PSAs would result only in smaller future retirement benefits and would have no impact on the short-run situation. Second, this problem involves an equity judgment: Should the risk of a weak economy be borne by workers or by retirees? Finally, this financing problem could easily be solved, if desired, within the framework of the existing system by adjusting benefits by wage growth minus 1.5 percent, where the 1.5 percent is the long-run real wage differential assumption in cost estimates. Such a solution would eliminate the risk of financial crisis, but beneficiaries, rather than the trust fund, would feel the consequences of poor economic performance.

Regarding the fifth problem, the perception of linkages between Social Security taxes and benefits, the authors propose sending out annual statements to workers showing accumulated retirement benefits. This is a worthwhile suggestion and, indeed, represents the highlight of their work. However, such statements can certainly be issued under the current Social Security system. Efforts to do so have been hampered by inadequate computer resources within the SSA and difficulties in obtaining the addresses of people who are not yet beneficiaries. The Boskin, Kotlikoff, and Shoven proposal would do nothing to solve these practical difficulties.

To conclude, it really is time that the PSA proposal be put away. While it might be an interesting intellectual exercise, this plan does nothing either to further the policy debate concerning Social Security or to resolve any of the technical issues associated with the program.

8
Altering the Public/Private Mix of of Retirement Incomes

Lawrence H. Thompson

The debate over the respective roles of public and private retirement institutions is as old as the Social Security system and is likely to continue for as long as there is a retirement income system—which most of us hope will be a long time. For example, the version of the Social Security Act President Franklin Roosevelt proposed to Congress created both a mandatory old age insurance program and a program of voluntary, supplemental annuities. The voluntary plan would have offered citizens the option of making deposits with the U.S. Treasury. These deposits would earn interest at the Treasury rate and be returned in the form of a retirement annuity. The version that passed the Senate in 1935 allowed employers to contract out of Social Security by providing minimum pension coverage on their own. Neither provision made it into the final law. It was decided that the former gave too substantial a role to public sector provision and that the latter gave too substantial a role to private sector provision.

I mention this to illustrate how long this debate has been going on. It also illustrates, however, how few ideas are really new. In 1986 Congress created a retirement thrift plan for federal employees, a plan that in many of its particulars looks very much like the arrangement rejected in 1935. And today, many continue to advocate some form of contracting out as a way of increasing the relative role of private sector institutions.

Although the current debate has roots that are at least half a century old, it also has its own unique emphases. My sense is that much of the debate in the past involved whether to expand either the private or the public role in order to provide greater retirement options and achieve more adequate retirement incomes. The current debate tends to assume that, at least for the majority of U.S. citizens, both retirement options and retirement incomes are now adequate; some might even argue that, at least for some citizens, they are approaching being overly generous. Also, whether because of dispassionate

The views presented in this chapter are those of the author and not necessarily those of his employer, the U.S. General Accounting Office.

analyses or the current political climate, I sense little interest in a broad expansion of cash benefits under the Social Security program. Instead, the debate today seems primarily to be about the potential advantages associated with a greater reliance on private retirement income — and a correspondingly reduced reliance on government sources — in achieving adequate retirement options and incomes.

I want to pause for a moment to underscore the importance of that observation. Not so long ago, one could treat being old as a reasonable proxy for being poor. It is no longer a reasonable proxy. Some groups of the elderly, notably older single persons and especially older single women, still have poverty rates substantially higher than those of the population as a whole. But most analysts conclude that, on average, living standards of aged couples are roughly consistent with those of the nonaged.[1] It is far easier, however, to generate interest in a discussion of what is wrong with the system than what is right. There may well be a number of ways in which the current system can be improved, and it is commendable that so many people are willing to devote so much time and attention to looking for those improvements. But in our desire to improve what we now have, let us not forget how much we have achieved or underestimate the cost of giving up some of that achievement.

I believe that the primary motivation for the current concern about the retirement income system is the projection that the cost of that system will increase in future years. To be more precise, the cost of one element of that system — Social Security — is projected to rise substantially. As far as I know, we do not have any reliable projections of the future costs of the private portion of the system. This is unfortunate because I suspect that a careful analysis would show that the forces that are likely to increase Social Security's cost are likely to cause the private retirement system's costs to increase also. And I suspect that if we all began the debate with the assumption that the size of the future cost increase might not be all that sensitive to changes in the mix between the private and public sectors, we would have a very different — and probably more productive — debate.

A second motivation is a concern about the effect that the public/private mix might have on our rate of capital formation and, in turn, on the growth rate of the economy.

I suspect that a third motivation on the part of some is a desire to alter the distribution of the costs of the retirement income system. The Social Security system redistributes, substantially if also imperfectly, from those with relatively high lifetime earnings to those with relatively low lifetime earnings. In contrast, the net effect of the rather significant tax expenditures associated with the private system and of the various Social Security offset features it contains undoubtedly is to redistribute toward higher-income individuals. Absent offsetting changes in the structure of the Social Security program and the tax code, greater reliance on private sector retirement income devices is likely to make the entire retirement income system more regressive.

Finally, some participants in the debate might be motivated by a concern over labor supply effects of the system. I must confess that I do not know how to reconcile the kind of labor supply concerns commonly expressed with the kind of public/private alterations currently being discussed. In principle, the retirement income system could be encouraging retirement to a socially undesirable extent by providing retirement incomes that are either too large, are available too early in one's career, or are given on terms that require too significant a withdrawal from labor force activity in order to qualify. If the system is guilty of any of these, its costs are greater than is desirable.

It is not clear, however, why greater reliance on private sector retirement programs should lead to an increase in labor supply among the aged. Most proponents of greater reliance on the private sector do not say that they intend to reduce the aggregate amount of retirement benefits available. Most private sector retirement income sources are already available at an earlier age than is Social Security. In the past, one could have argued that Social Security provided a greater work disincentive than some private sector arrangements for those aged sixty-five and over, but the changes made to Social Security in 1983 should all but eliminate this differential.[2] Thus, the policy changes being proposed do not seem to address the concerns identified. If one is concerned about encouraging people to work longer, it seems to me that simply altering the mix between Social Security and private retirement devices would not be a very promising prescription. Indeed, it may well be counterproductive.

To summarize, then, we have a debate that I believe is motivated by some combination of four concerns:

1. Future cost of the system
2. Impact of the system on the rate of investment
3. Distribution of the costs and benefits of the system
4. Effect of the system on retirement behavior

To examine the relationship between the private/public mix and these concerns, I will explore three topics:

1. How can we alter the cost of providing an equally adequate level of retirement income to the retirees of the future?
2. Assuming that increases in our rate of capital formation or changes in the retirement system's cost are possible and desirable, how can public policy be altered to encourage either goal?
3. What are some of the implications of a change in the public/private mix of retirement income sources for the structure of both Social Security and private retirement income institutions?

Costs of the Retirement Income System

The 1987 Social Security long-range cost projections suggest, under the central assumption set, an increase in the ratio of annual costs to annual taxable payroll on the order of 50 percent by the year 2035; in 2035 costs will be just over 16 percent of taxable payroll. Under the pessimistic assumption set, costs expressed as a percent of payroll will more than double.

Aficionados of the Social Security cost estimates know that the figures I have just given overstate both the economic burden of the program and the magnitude of the projected increase in that burden. When expressed as a percent of gross national product (GNP), under the central set of assumptions total costs for the Social Security cash benefit program fall from 4.7 percent in 1987 to 4.25 percent in 2005, rise to 6.5 percent in 2035, and then decline to 6.1 percent in 2060.[3]

These cost projections have two important implications for this discussion. First, if the program were to be financed on a current cost basis, the cumulative tax increases necessary in the thirty years between about 2010 and about 2035 would total 2.25 percent of GNP. By comparison, the federal deficit this year is likely to be just over 4 percent of GNP.[4] Thus, under the central set of assumptions, the additional revenues (or benefit changes) needed to cover the twenty-first century cost growth in Social Security amount to about one half of the additional revenues (or outlay reductions) needed to balance the current federal budget. Under the pessimistic assumption set, cost as a percent of GNP will rise by 4.5 percentage points between 1987 and 2060, making the additional revenues needed in Social Security over the next seventy-five years about the same amount as is needed currently to eliminate the current federal deficit.[5] I find this comparison telling, but I have not decided whether it is more effective in telling us how serious the current federal deficit is or in telling us how manageable the future cost growth in Social Security might be.

Second, the next century's cost growth is primarily the result of a permanent shift in the projected age distribution of the population. It is not a temporary phenomenon associated with the retirement of the baby boom generation. The projections suggest that the cost growth will be temporarily dampened in the next century by the fact that the retirees at that time will come from the unusually small cohorts born between 1930 and 1945. Cost growth will then occur very rapidly as these cohorts give way to the retirement cohorts born during the baby boom. But the decline in costs occurring after the baby boom cohorts pass through the system is quite modest, amounting to less than one fifth of the cost growth occurring between 2005 and 2035. In other words, we could mislead ourselves if we define the problem to be financing the retirement benefits of the baby boom generation rather than to be financing retirement benefits in a world that has a permanently increased aged dependency ratio.

By eyeballing the numbers in the 1987 trustees' report, I conclude that under the central assumption set, one third or more of the growth in costs as a percent of payroll can be traced to the effect of one assumption—that by the year 2060, mortality rates will have fallen by 38 percent.[6] (They are assumed to fall by 58 percent in the pessimistic assumptions, which is one of the reasons that costs are higher under these assumptions.) I highlight this because it is not difficult to comprehend that the impact of longer life expectancies on Social Security costs will be no different from their impact on the costs of other elements of the retirement income system. They will also increase the employer contributions needed to finance a given defined benefit pension plan and increase the preretirement asset accumulation necessary in an individual retirement account (IRA) or a defined contribution pension plan in order to finance a given retirement annuity.

To discuss retirement system costs more generally requires us to focus on aggregate income and production flows and to avoid the temptation of generalizing to the economy as a whole from a set of concepts that are useful only for looking at cost/benefit relationships over the lifetime of a single individual. The tendency to generalize from the individual to the economy is one of the major shortcomings of much of the debate over retirement costs because it often results in what economists call the *fallacy of composition.* The fallacy goes something like this: When one farmer increases his total production, total revenues from his farm operation will increase. Given the nature of the demand for agricultural products, however, when all farmers increase their production, market prices tend to fall by more than output has increased, and total farm revenues tend to fall. Similarly, just because one individual can find a way to obtain higher return on his retirement savings does not mean that society as a whole has found a way to reduce the aggregate burden of supporting the aged population.

For all intents and purposes, our economy is organized so that no one can utilize a portion of any year's current production without having a claim of equal size on one of the current income flows generated in the production process. For the working age population, the major income claim used to support consumption is the income derived from supplying their own labor. By definition, the retired population does not have such a claim. Thus, in order to be able to consume the goods and services currently being produced, the population currently retired needs to have claims on alternative current income flows. The basic purpose of the retirement income system is to create and enforce just such a set of claims on alternative current income flows.

I will describe briefly how the retirement income system achieves this objective, but before doing so, I would like to explain the basic economic principles at work. First, ignoring for the moment the possibilities introduced by a large trade deficit, the retired can consume from current production only if they possess claims on the income generated by current production. Second, in the year the consumption occurs, the amount of income from current production that must be used to support the retired population is equal to the amount the retired will consume. This amount is equal to the amount of investment and consumption by the nonretired that must be forgone in order to allow the retired to consume. This is the true measure of the cost of supporting the retired and can be expressed either as a fraction of the total income generated that year or as an absolute amount.

A variety of mechanisms can be employed to generate the requisite claims on future income. Businesses and consumers frequently are willing to trade a claim on their future profits and labor earnings in order to consume more than they earn today. They do this through devices such as issuing stocks and bonds, taking out mortgage loans, or running up balances on their credit cards. Retirement savers enter into agreements with such businesses or consumers under which the retirement saver acquires a claim in the business's or consumer's future income.

In principle, a business could plan on financing promised retirement benefits through claims on its own future earnings or through deductions from what it would otherwise pay its own future workers. Such arrangements suffer from the risk that the firm in question will not survive as long as its current workers, however, rendering both the claim on its future income and the promised retirement benefit worthless. In recognition of this, we impose certain restrictions on most pension plans. To be specific, we require them to acquire claims on other people's future income instead. We call a plan *funded* if it relies on claims on the future income of others and *unfunded* if it relies on claims on the future income of the plan's sponsor or on that of its future workers.

Through Social Security Supplemental Security Income (SSI), and other programs, the federal government also makes retirement income promises. The federal government differs from all other economic actors in one important respect, however: It already has a claim on everyone's future income, which is called the power to tax. The government could, if it wished, acquire in the financial markets claims on future private incomes in the same way that private pensions do. By so doing, it could fully fund both Social Security and SSI.

Note, however, that while it is clearly possible to fund these government programs fully, it is not so clear what purpose is being served by such a policy. Advance funding of private sector plans is desirable because it enhances the security of the future retirement income promise. Advance funding will do little to enhance the security of a promise from the federal government, however. Claims obtained in the private market are no more effective in ensuring access to future income than is the power to tax, and they can be more difficult to enforce.

If in the process of advance funding either a private or a public plan, current consumption is reduced, advance funding can have the side effect of increasing the funds available for investment, thereby enhancing capital formation. Nothing in current public policy guarantees that this will occur, however. Consider the result if two corporations each decide to advance fund their pension plans through cash raised by issuing debentures, and each ends up investing its pension plan assets in the debentures of the other. Both plans are fully funded, but they have been funded through a series of financial transactions that have no effect on aggregate saving or investment. Similarly, the government could advance fund Social Security by investing in private sector stocks and bonds. But if in the process a deficit of equal size is produced in the general fund and this results in an increase of equal size in aggregate federal debt held by the public, the net result is simply a rearrangement of the ownership of a series of financial instruments with no effect on aggregate saving and investment.

The debate over whether to rely on funded private mechanisms or unfunded public mechanisms is frequently confused by a tendency to compare observed or implicit rates of return on the different mechanisms. It is this practice that often introduces the fallacy of composition into the analysis.

Later I discuss the effect that changes in the rate of capital formation or international capital flows can have on the future cost of a retirement income system. For the moment, however, let's assume that neither is affected by that system's structure so that we can better understand how one can be misled by focusing solely on differences in rates of return.

A generally accepted theorem holds that, in a steady state, the rate of return under a current cost financed social security program is equal to the sum of the rate of increase in the population and the rate of increase in average earnings.[7] A plausible estimate of the current magnitudes of each would suggest a nominal rate of return for a whole cohort in the neighborhood of 5 percent. Since Social Security redistributes from higher-wage persons to lower-wage persons, it is not hard to believe that the rate of return it can offer the higher-wage individuals is close to zero, whereas the rate of return it offers the lower-wage individuals might easily be 10 percent or more.

Clearly, the higher-wage individual can obtain a higher rate of return in the private market by escaping from the redistributive Social Security program. It is also quite likely that the private market offers a return higher than the implicit return earned by the cohort as a whole under Social Security. This is possible because a sufficient number of businesses and consumers are willing to trade more than $105 next year in return for $100 today. Let's assume for the purposes of this discussion that people are willing to trade $110 next year for $100 today. What does this mean about the tax revenue required to finance a social security system that is going to pay out $100 next year? It means that if the system is current cost financed from a payroll tax, the government must levy a tax of $100 next year, whereas if it were advance funded, the government could levy a tax of $90.90 this year ($90.90 being the amount that produces $100 next year at a 10 percent interest rate).

Does this mean that the social costs of the advance funded system are less? No, the cost is $100 — the amount of retirement consumption to be supported — and it is incurred next year — the year in which the other participants in the economy must reduce their consumption in order to allow the retiree to consume a portion of current output. To see how this result can be obscured by focusing on market rates of return, we need only trace through how the various transactions might work.

Assume that we adopt the advance funding approach under which wage earners are forced to come up with $90.90 this year instead of $100 next year. Where do the wage earners get the $90.90? Suppose they borrow it from a bank by taking out a home equity line of credit at 10 percent, which costs them $100 to pay off next year. Where does the bank get the money to lend? It issues a certificate of deposit (CD) to the social security fund, which just happens to have $90.90 it wishes to invest. What difference does it make whether the system is current cost financed or advance funded? In this example, the difference is one of appearance, not substance: The income claim needed next year to allow the retiree to consume $100 comes through a series of private sector transactions if the system is advance funded and from taxes if it is current cost financed. This difference might have more political significance than economic significance. Under the current cost financed scheme, next year the wage earner will complain about the cost of the social security program and vent his anger at the government, whereas in the advance funded scheme, next year the wage earner will complain about the burden of repaying his home equity loan and vent his anger on the bank that gave it to him.

If you extend my simple example to a retirement income program that continues on year after year, you should find that so long as the financing mechanism does not affect the aggregate size of retirement benefits, international trade flows, or the size of the capital stock, it has no bearing on the total social cost of the program. What advance funding can do, however, is to hide some of the costs of the retirement system in the private capital markets and change its distribution among the members of a cohort of workers. Under an advance funded program, in every year after the start-up period, the payroll tax will be lower than it would have been under the current cost financed program, but the burden on consumers for financing their consumer debt will be correspondingly higher. If consumers ignore the burden of financing their consumer debt, they will perceive a higher return on their payroll taxes under advance funding. If they include the burden of their higher consumer debt, the return will be the same under either system.

I can extend my example in any number of ways without altering its basic result. I could assume under the advance funded scheme that the reserve is invested in newly issued junk bonds from the Safeway Corporation and that instead of part of the cost of the retirement system being hidden in consumer debt, it is hidden in higher food prices. I could have assumed that the worker did not borrow $90.90 to support his consumption, but instead reduced his consumption by the amount of the tax. To replace the aggregate demand lost by the worker's reduction in consumption, the government could then run a deficit in its general fund of $90.90, selling its bonds to the bank, which in turn borrows from the social security fund. The worker then pays the $100 in the second year to the general fund so that it can retire its maturing bond. I could have assumed that the prevailing interest rate was 20 percent rather than 10 percent, making the gap between the return on the advance funded investment and the implicit return under a current cost financed social security system even greater. None of this would have changed the basic result, however. Next year the program will pay $100 in benefits, and somebody somewhere is going to have to pony up $100 out of his current income to finance them.

I also could have focused on the fact that the implicit return under social security is lower for high-wage earners. I could have allowed high-income people to opt out of social security, reducing program income by an amount greater than the program's benefits are reduced. If I am unwilling to change the structure of social security for the remaining participants, however, I will have to make up for the net revenue loss by subsidizing social security from general revenues. If I assume that I can create a tax that applies only to those who opted out, I can restore the previous distribution of burdens. If I assume that I cannot create such a tax, those who opted out will have shifted a portion of the burden onto those who did not. The incidence of the costs of the retirement income system might have changed, but the magnitude of the total cost will not have.

My analysis thus far has assumed that the structure of the retirement system does not affect the rate of growth of the economy. I explained earlier how either a private or a public plan can be advance funded without producing any net increase in resources available for investment, but I will later admit that the evidence suggests that advance funding has had some effect on aggregate saving. Therefore, let me now deal explicitly with the impact that higher growth could have on future retirement system costs.

Suppose for the purposes of this discussion that the current retirement income system could be restructured in such a way that domestic consumption were reduced, savings and investment were increased, and the increased investment caused the trend rate of GNP growth to rise by 0.5 percentage points. After fifty years, in roughly the year 2035, this change would have increased GNP by something like 28 percent over the level that would otherwise have prevailed. Some of the increase in GNP will have to be allocated to the cost of maintaining a larger capital stock if the capital stock continues to grow at the higher rate. So let's assume for the purpose of this discussion that national income is increased by only 25 percent.

The question is: What happens to the cost of the retirement income system? The answer depends on what one thinks faster growth will do to three ratios: (1) the ratio of labor income to total income (labor's share of national income), (2) the ratio of average retirement benefits to average wages, and (3) the ratio of retirees to workers. If none of these ratios changes, the absolute cost of the retirement system will increase by 25 percent, because we will have the same number of retirees and they will be receiving benefits that are 25 percent higher. If the cost of the system rises by 25 percent, its cost as a percent of GNP might fall slightly, but the fraction of national income that will have to be used to support the retired population will not change at all.

I can think of three reasons why faster growth might alter one of the critical ratios, and I am sure others could think of additional possibilities. First, although both Social Security and most private sector defined benefit plans establish initial retirement benefit levels with reference to prevailing wages at the time of retirement, neither updates benefits in retirement to reflect real wage growth. Real wage growth occurring after a person retires thus reduces somewhat the relative cost of supporting the retiree, and faster growth reduces the cost by more than does slower growth. Second, although I have not worked this through myself, I would not be surprised if a detailed analysis showed that those who rely for their retirement income on IRAs or other defined contribution plans are likely to find that their retirement incomes do not necessarily keep pace with the accelerated growth in wage levels. Thus, relative retirement incomes, and the burden of supporting them, might be lower for those relying on defined contribution arrangements. Finally, one must assume that a 25 percent increase in average real earnings will have some effect on worker preferences about retirement. Except in the unlikely event that the desire to retire is not affected by changes in real income (in economic jargon, the income elasticity of demand is zero), higher real incomes should lead to earlier retirement, increasing the relative cost of the retirement income system.

In summary, I have come up with three ways in which faster growth could affect the relative burden of the system, and it is quite possible that these effects will offset each other. As a first approximation, I think we ought to operate on the assumption that the relative burden would not be altered all that much. Reducing our consumption level today to produce a higher standard of living than would otherwise prevail in the future might be a highly desirable policy. But let's debate that policy on its merits and not pretend that it is likely to reduce the burden of supporting tomorrow's retirees.

Let's now turn to the possibilities of using international capital flows to alter the burden of the retirement income system. The economic effect of a permanent increase in our rate of foreign investment is essentially the same as the effect of a permanent increase in our rate of domestic investment except that we assume the additional risks of expropriation of our foreign investment or of adverse movements in exchange rates. To invest abroad, domestic consumption must be reduced so that we can run a trade surplus. In return, the total income available to our society in a future year will be increased. The basic difference is that in the later year, we can increase our consumption of imported goods if we invested abroad, whereas we will increase our consumption of goods produced domestically if we invest at home.

In principle, our society could use the international capital markets to advance fund the temporary extra cost of supporting the baby boom generation in retirement. We would be a net lender on the international capital markets during the working years of the baby boom cohort and then liquidate our foreign investment during that cohort's retirement years. This would be achieved by running a trade surplus over the next quarter century and then running a trade deficit in the period 2020 to 2040.[8]

As a society, we can lower the future cost of the retirement system if we are willing to make that system less generous so that in a future year, either the ratio of retirement benefits to future wages or the ratio of retirees to workers is reduced. We also might be able to deal with the temporary bulge associated with the retirement of the baby boom generation by lending abroad and subsequently liquidating our foreign investment, but the temporary bulge associated with the baby boom generation's retirement is hardly the most important problem we face. Increasing our rate of capital formation may well raise the standard of living for all members of our society in some future year, but I doubt that it will substantially reduce the relative cost of the retirement system, and I am confident that it will increase that system's absolute cost. Reducing the emphasis on public programs while increasing the emphasis on private programs will have little, if any, effect on the future cost of the system unless it also affects the generosity of the system, but it might make the system appear less costly by shifting some of the costs from current period taxes to less visible private financial market transactions.

Altering the Future Cost of the System

What can I say, then, about possible government policies to reduce future costs? If costs must be reduced, the most effective approach would appear to be to make the retirement income system less generous either by reducing the future monthly benefits of those people for whom the system is currently most generous or by encouraging workers to delay retirement without giving them an offsetting increase in their monthly benefits. In either case, I suspect that the most promising policy changes would be those designed to change private sector retirement programs. The people who now do not have private pensions and rely almost exclusively on Social Security for their retirement incomes are not, by and large, the ones with the highest standards of living in retirement. If something has to be cut back, it would seem more equitable to cut back on the various supplements to Social Security, perhaps through either repealing or reducing the favorable tax provisions that retirement saving continues to enjoy.

Alternatively, if we wish to reverse the trend toward earlier retirement as a way of cutting costs, the most promising approach would appear to be to adopt policies that raise the age at which private benefits become available, perhaps to make them consistent with Social Security. For example, we could mandate that no qualified pension plan can pay early retirement benefits before age sixty-two, the age at which Social Security benefits are first available, and that all private sector plans incorporate actuarial reductions at least as large as those in Social Security for persons retiring before age sixty-seven, the age for full benefits under Social Security in the next century. In addition, we might want to prohibit withdrawals from individual tax-deferred retirement savings plans prior to age sixty-seven.

While I have argued that increasing the rate of capital formation is unlikely to have a significant effect on the relative burden of future retirees, I also have said that it might be desirable on other grounds. If we are willing to assume that increases in the savings rate will be translated into increases in investment, policies that increase savings should accelerate growth.

In my earlier discussion of the relative costs of funded and unfunded programs, I assumed that savings rates were not affected by switching from one type of program to the other. But there is evidence that substituting a funded program for a current cost financed program might increase saving, and I am willing to assume for this discussion that increased saving will translate into faster growth. Economists have argued for at least a decade about the effect of Social Security on saving and have yet to reach a consensus that it has had a measurable impact.[9] The current consensus seems to be that about one third of the increase in private pension assets represents net additions to savings.[10] Therefore, policies that lead to a reduced reliance on a current cost financed social security program and an increased reliance on advance funded private retirement sources have the potential for increasing our savings rate. Whether any particular policy would be expected to increase saving depends on how that policy works. For example, I suspect that whatever merits might be for achieving other objectives, the use of greater tax incentives to encourage greater reliance on private retirement sources is likely to be an ineffective way of increasing our savings rate.

Over the past decade, aggregate pension plan assets have grown at an average annual rate of about 14 percent, which implies annual asset growth of about $250 billion per year.[11] If one third of this accumulation represents net additions to savings, the annual increment to savings is just over $80 billion. Unfortunately, associated with this growth in private pension assets are tax expenditures for employer pension plans, which the U.S. Treasury estimates amounted to $72 billion in fiscal year 1986.[12] In other words, tax expenditures are currently adding to the federal deficit (which is a drain on our savings) an amount almost as large as my estimate of the additional savings associated with pension plan asset accumulation.[13] If we added the tax expenditures associated with IRA and Keogh plans, estimated to be another $26 billion in fiscal year 1986, we would find that the favorable tax treatment of retirement plans totaled just under $100 billion, a sum equal to almost one half of the fiscal year 1986 federal deficit. And we could well conclude that, whatever its other merits, the policy of encouraging private provision for retirement through the tax system was achieving very little, if anything, in the way of net additions to savings.

If we want higher investment, altering our retirement system might be not only very ineffective but also unnecessary. The most obvious and direct way to increase the funds available for investment in this country is to reduce the federal budget deficit. My estimate of additional savings from pension asset accumulation suggests that the budget deficit is currently eating up more than twice as much savings as the private pension system is generating. This means that we would have to increase the size of the private pension system substantially, perhaps more than doubling it, to have the same impact on funds available for investment as we could have by eliminating the federal budget deficit.

Once the United States has balanced its budget, if we want further increases in the funds available for investment, we ought to consider adopting fiscal policies that ensure that the Social Security surpluses of the next several decades are used to free up resources for investment rather than as loans to cover general fund expenses. This means not just balancing the budget, but balancing the non–Social Security portion of the budget. The total budget would be in surplus by the amount that the Social Security fund was in surplus so that the Social Security surplus would be used to retire outstanding federal debt. Adopting this policy would have roughly the same effect on funds available for investment during the 1990s as would a policy that cost the U.S. Treasury nothing and produced a doubling of the current additional savings generated by the private pension system.

I do not wish to get into a discussion of how we might alter our trade flows to allow us to use the international capital markets to smooth out the cost of the baby boom generation's retirement. Suffice it to say that an increase in the amount of savings that we have available for investment, as a result of reducing the federal budget deficit, for example, should move us in the right direction. And I suspect that whatever additional policy changes would be necessary would have little to do with the mix of private and public retirement programs.

The Effect on Program Structure

At present just over one half of the gainfully employed persons in this country are covered by pension plans, a percentage that has not changed materially in the past five years. If Social Security were reduced substantially across the board, we might expect that pension plan coverage would expand somewhat, but we should not expect that it would come anywhere close to 100 percent. As a practical matter, therefore, increasing the reliance on private sector retirement sources without seriously undermining the retirement security of millions of current workers probably means one of two things: changing the structure of Social Security benefits or mandating universal adoption of private retirement instruments.

One could change the structure of Social Security benefits by reducing the benefits paid to higher-paid workers while keeping the benefits paid to lower-paid workers at their current level. The assumption would be that the higher-paid workers are the ones who already have pensions or could be expected to take advantage of private sector retirement programs, and that having been informed in advance of the reduction in their future Social Security benefit, they or their employers would take the steps necessary to ensure that their total retirement income did not decline. To the extent that one contemplates an expansion of defined contribution arrangements, the policy would have to be phased in over thirty or forty years to allow workers time to adjust the size of their private retirement programs.

Recognize, however, that adopting such a policy amounts to making the Social Security program more progressive. It further reduces the returns that high-wage individuals will receive from that program. Such a reduction might erode popular support for Social Security among middle- and upper-income individuals, lead eventually to an across-the-board reduction in Social Security, and harm those whose retirement incomes are currently subsidized by the Social Security system. If you care about the adequacy of the retirement incomes of the people in the lower half of the income distribution, you should be concerned about the possibility of such a chain of events.

On the other hand, if you want to reduce the role of Social Security across the board but you do not want retirement incomes to be less adequate, you will probably have to mandate a universal private pension or individual saving program. In addition, you will have to figure out a way to subsidize the retirement incomes of lower-paid workers. No doubt such proposals can be designed, but we should ask what we will achieve if to replace the current Social Security program we have to jettison the voluntary features of our current private retirement income system and introduce an elaborate system of taxes and subsidies to redistribute income within that system.

Conclusion

Here, then, is a summary of the points I have made:

1. The current retirement income system was created to ensure adequate retirement incomes and options to all U.S. citizens. For the most part, it has succeeded in achieving this objective. Although improvements are clearly possible and some are clearly needed, let's be careful that any changes we make do not inadvertently undermine what is one of our most successful domestic social policies.

2. The cost of the retirement system in any year is appropriately measured by focusing on the retiree consumption it is supporting. The relative cost of the system is determined primarily by the ratio of the average consumption level of retirees to the average consumption level of the working-age population and by the ratio of retirees to workers. To change the cost probably requires changing one of these ratios, and neither of them is likely to be directly affected by changes in the method chosen to finance retirement benefits.

3. The major cost growth currently projected in this trustees' report comes from a more or less permanent change in the age structure of the population. It first materializes at the time the baby boom generation reaches retirement age, but it is not a temporary problem associated only with the baby boom's retirement.

4. Advance funding enhances the security of private sector retirement promises but in and of itself does not alter the cost of the retirement system.

5. Greater reliance on advance funded, private sector retirement income institutions can enhance capital formation, but reducing the federal budget deficit is a far more direct and probably a far more effective way of enhancing capital formation.

6. Increasing the rate of capital formation will lower total consumption in the immediate future but can increase consumption in subsequent years. As a first approximation, however, increasing the rate of capital formation will not reduce the cost of the retirement income system.

7. The surest way to reduce the future costs of the retirement income system is to reduce the generosity of the system, either through lower monthly benefits or higher retirement ages. If one wishes to reduce monthly benefits, it is probably more equitable to adopt policies that discourage the growth of private retirement incomes, perhaps by reducing the tax advantages they now enjoy. If one wishes to encourage delayed retire-

ment, it is probably more effective to mandate increases in retirement ages under private plans than to change Social Security.

8. We might be able to advance fund the temporary increase in costs associated with the retirement of the baby boom generation by investing abroad during that generation's working years and liquidating that investment during its retirement years. The strategy probably implies nothing, however, about the desirable mix of public and private retirement income sources.

9. Social Security redistributes in favor of lower-wage earners, whereas private retirement income devices tend to redistribute toward higher-income persons. Unless explicit adjustments are made in the tax code and in the structure of the Social Security program, the most significant result of shifting the burden of supplying retirement income from Social Security to the private sector might be that the whole system becomes more regressive. We should not allow people to urge such changes without admitting their effect.

10. Finally, if we do not wish to cause a major change in the size or distribution of retirement incomes but do want to reduce the relative role of Social Security, we would appear to have two choices. We must either make the smaller Social Security program far more redistributive than the current one or mandate universal adoption of private sector arrangements and figure out a way to redistribute retirement income in the context of the new system.

Minimization of costs is not the only motivation for altering the retirement income system, but to the extent that we are concerned about costs, we must think carefully about how effective a change in the public/private mix can be expected to be and what other objectives of the system might be sacrificed if such a change were to occur.

Notes

1. See, for example, the summary in Aaron 1982, chapter 6.

2. Thompson (1983) contains a more extensive discussion of the possible effects on labor force behavior of the Social Security system and of the changes made to that system in 1983.

3. Figures quoted in the preceding two paragraphs are from U.S. Congress. House Committee on Ways and Means. 1987.

4. Author's estimate assuming the fiscal 1987 deficit is approximately $180 billion.

5. U.S. Office of Management and Budget 1987a.

6. My analysis is based on data in Table B4 of U.S. Department of Health and Human Services (1987).

7. See, for example, Aaron 1966.

8. As Japanese investors have recently learned, exchange rate movements can wipe out a good deal of the apparent financial profit that might otherwise be expected from investments abroad. The risk of adverse future movements in exchange rates can be eliminated, however, if we invest in the countries from which we subsequently wish to import.

9. The debate is summarized in Aaron 1982. See especially Feldstein 1974; Leimer and Lesnoy 1982.

10. See, for example, Munnell 1982, 1987; Avery, Elliehausen, and Gustafson 1986.

11. Employee Benefit Research Institute (1987).

12. U.S. Office of Management and Budget 1987b.

13. A recent study by the Congressional Budget Office observed that the aggregate of the tax advantages given to qualified pension plans is large enough by itself to explain the higher retiree after-tax incomes as a consequence of participation in private pensions. Thus, the growth of pension plan assets does not necessarily indicate higher saving by the participants. See U.S. Congress, Congressional Budget Office 1987.

References

Aaron, Henry J. 1966. "The Social Insurance Paradox." *Canadian Journal of Economics and Political Science* 32, no. 3 (August):371–74.

Aaron, Henry J. 1982. *Economic Effects of Social Security.* Washington, DC: Brookings Institution.

Andrews, Emily S. 1985. *The Changing Profile of Pensions in America.* Washington, DC: Employee Benefit Research Institute.

Avery, Robert B., Gregory E. Elliehausen, and Thomas A. Gustafson. 1986. "Pension and Social Security in Household Portfolios: Evidence from the Survey of Consumer Finances." In *Savings and Capital Formation: Policy Options,* edited by F. Gerard Adams and Susan Wachter. Lexington, MA: Lexington Books.

Employee Benefit Research Institute. 1986. *EBRI Quarterly Pension Investment Report.* Washington, DC. 1987.

Feldstein, Martin S. 1974. "Social Security, Induced Retirement and Aggregate Capital Accumulation." *Journal of Political Economy* 82, no. 5 (September/October):905–26.

Leimer, Dean R., and Selig D. Lesnoy. 1982. "Social Security and Private Saving: New Time-Series Evidence." *Journal of Political Economy* 90, no. 3 (June): 606–29.

Munnell, Alicia H. 1982. *The Economics of Private Pensions.* Washington, DC: Brookings Institution.

Munnell, Alicia H. 1987. "The Impact of Public and Private Pension Schemes on Saving and Capital Formation." In *Conjugating Public and Private: The Case of Pensions*. Studies and Research No. 24. Geneva: International Social Security Association, 219–36.

Thompson, Lawrence H. 1983. "The Social Security Reform Debate." *Journal of Economic Literature,* 21, no. 4 (December):1425–67.

U.S. Congress. Congressional Budget Office. 1987. *Tax Policy for Pensions and Other Retirement Saving.* Washington, DC: Government Printing Office.

U.S. Congress. House Committee on Ways and Means. 1987. *1987 Annual Report of the Board of Trustees of the Federal Old-Age and Survivors Insurance and Disability Insurance Trust Funds.* H. Doc. 100–55. 100th Cong., 1st sess.

U.S. Office of Management and Budget. 1987a. *Budget of the United States Government, Fiscal Year 1988.* Washington, DC: Government Printing Office.

U.S. Office of Management and Budget. 1987b. *Special Analysis of the Budget of the United States Government, Fiscal Year 1988.* Washington, DC: Government Printing Office.

Comment

Michael J. Boskin

As usual, Larry Thompson has provided us with a thoughtful, provocative, yet concise analysis of the most important issues involved in altering the public/private mix of retirement incomes. Thompson names numerous points with which I agree, although I sometimes interpret them differently. The cost of providing retirement income, whether public or private, is likely to rise substantially early in the next century. Thompson notes that the estimated 1.8 percentage point rise in Social Security costs from 4.7 percent of GNP in 1987 to 6.5 percent in 2035 is less than half the size of the current budget deficit. Another way to state the problem is that the costs are estimated to rise by about 40 percent and for a much longer period than the large budget deficits are expected to persist.

These numbers do not include the substantial estimated rise in Medicare costs, especially those related to the Hospital Insurance (HI) part of Social Security. While there are reasons to present both the Old Age, Survivors and Disability Insurance (OASDI) and HI numbers rather than just combining them, I believe it can be misleading to discuss only the cash benefit payments. Financing HI involves substantial resource flows, and the probability of large medical expenditures undoubtedly affects saving and retirement behavior.

Importantly, Thompson and I agree that viewing the problem as a temporary one of financing the baby boom generation's retirement can be quite misleading. We are changing into a society with a higher aged-dependency ratio, due in part to substantial gains in life expectancy, and not just experiencing the effects of historical variations in birthrates.

Thompson argues that financing the retirement consumption of the elderly must come from a reduction in the amount of income in that year's production equal to the amount of forgone investment and consumption by the nonretired. Further, since the retired have no continued earnings, they can consume only if they have claims on the income generated by current production. These claims could be through the public sector, taxing the wages or incomes of the working population, or through the private claims on returns to assets used in the production of income.

I applaud Thompson's careful analysis of advance versus current funding. Indeed, it is important to close the analysis by indicating, for example, what effect partial or complete advance funding of Social Security has on the deficit in the general fund and, therefore, on aggregate national saving. Chapter 5 in this book addresses this issue.

Thompson's examples are based primarily on the assumption that saving rates are not affected by switching from funded to unfunded programs. My own reading of the evidence is that a substantial, if less than dollar-for-dollar, increase in saving would occur. Thompson pays little attention to the possibility that this will affect real interest rates and, therefore, the level and composition of saving. Thompson agrees that a higher saving rate will likely lead (after a temporary adjustment in our current account deficit) to greater investment and increased labor productivity. After a temporary rise in the rate of growth, we will settle to a new steady state with a higher level of income. Thompson argues that this will affect the cost of the retirement income support for the elderly only if (ignoring changes in labor's share of national income and the ratio of retirees to workers) the ratio of average retirement benefits to average wages changes. While this is correct mathematically, it is by no means clear that the appropriate way to think about the optimal level and growth path of Social Security benefits is in terms of the ratio of average retirement benefits to average wages of the subsequent working population. It may well be that the retirement benefits ought to be compared to incomes of the retired during their working years, perhaps their career average earnings (see Boskin and Shoven 1987). This will give quite a different future cost of financing retirement benefits, as well as alternative notions of what is thought of as a generous, adequate, or burdensome replacement rate.

Thompson appears to believe that it makes little difference whether a Social Security surplus is invested abroad or domestically. He argues, properly, that when the foreign investment and the returns on it are repatriated, the same greater resources will be available to finance retirement consumption (assuming rates of return are equalized across national boundaries). One important difference, however, is that if saving finances domestic investment, the productivity of U.S. workers rises, U.S. real incomes rise, and the same amount of dollars financing retirement incomes in the future will be doing so relative to a larger earnings base, above and beyond the capital income generated by either foreign investment or domestic investment.

Finally, I believe that Thompson has not emphasized strongly enough the tremendous differences in burden of Social Security costs by age cohorts or generations, depending on the time pattern of Social Security taxes and benefits. Advance versus current cost funding may well result in the redistribution of trillions of dollars across generations. Consider, for example, what happens if we do not accrue the OASDI surplus currently in prospect for the next thirty years, but rather reduce taxes now and raise them more later to pay for the baby boom generation's retirement. Unless completely offset by private intrafamily intergenerational transfers or, alternatively, by an exactly compensating transaction in the remainder of the federal budget, such a policy will have a real impact on the cost of financing the time stream of Social Security benefits in the future.

Before turning to my conclusion, I believe it is necessary to examine Thompson's discussion of so-called tax expenditures for employer pension plans. The U.S. Treasury estimates that these "tax expenditures" amounted to $72 billion in fiscal year 1986. Thompson correctly compares the reduction in federal revenues, and hence the increase in deficits, with the estimated increase in saving due to private pensions. Unfortunately, the tax expenditure estimate is highly misleading. First, it presumes that a desirable tax base is a comprehensive measure of income. This has never been the tax base adopted in the United States, and attempts to analyze the appropriate tax base derived from more basic principles usually lead to consumption rather than income as the desirable tax base. If this is the case, then the tax expenditures are zero, and any taxation of tax-deferred pensions would be double taxation of saving. Thompson's point that the deficit is $72 billion larger is, however, correct if the estimated number is correct.

In addition to the usual problems in estimating such types of "tax expenditures" it is important to recognize one simple fact: The taxes are not forgiven; they are only postponed. While the advantage of deferral may be substantial, it is necessary to account for the present-value of taxes that will be paid when the funds are withdrawn from the pension system. How large an offset this deferred tax liability represents—whether it is ten or twenty cents on the dollar or forty or fifty cents—is not currently known. It obviously reflects issues such as the expected rate of return on assets in private plans compared to the government borrowing rate, the length of time between contribution and withdrawal, the effective tax rates at the time of contribution and withdrawal, and the distribution of alternative uses of the funds and their taxability in the absence of tax deferral granted contributions to private pensions. It also, obviously, reflects the weighted average contribution by age. My own preliminary analysis indicates that a substantial fraction of the currently lost revenue will be recouped.

I have focused primarily on issues about which Larry Thompson and I disagree. That is a small subset of the issues he raises and the conclusions he reaches. I would like to conclude by reiterating something Thompson mentioned in his opening remarks. In the quest to improve public retirement income systems—a venture in which I have participated and plan to participate in the future—it is important not to forget how much we have achieved with the current system. It has provided adequate income support to millions of Americans who would otherwise be indigent and has reduced the incidence of poverty among the elderly from extremely high to below that of the general population. As I have argued elsewhere, and my comments above imply, Social Security faces major problems that can and should be dealt with in the years ahead. But I agree with Thompson that it has been a source of enormous achievements and that these achievements must be recognized and maintained in any sensible reform proposals.

Reference

Boskin, M.J., and J.B. Shoven. 1987. "Concepts and Measures of Earnings Replacement During Retirement," in *Issues in Pension Economics,* edited by Zvi Bodie, John B. Shoven, and David A. Wise. Chicago: University of Chicago Press, pp. 113–141.

Contributors

Andrew B. Abel
Department of Finance
University of Pennsylvania
Philadelphia, PA 19104-6367

Emily S. Andrews
Employee Benefit Research
  Institute
2121 K Street NW
Washington, DC 20037

Robert M. Ball
Center for the Study of Social
  Policy
236 Massachusetts Avenue NE
Washington, DC 20002

Alan S. Blinder
Department of Economics
Princeton University
Princeton, NJ 08544

Michael J. Boskin
National Bureau of Economic
  Research
204 Junipero Serra Blvd.
Stanford, CA 94305

Deborah J. Chollet
Employee Benefit Research
  Institute
2121 K Street NW
Washington, DC 20037

Jerry R. Green
Department of Economics
Harvard University
Cambridge, MA 02138

Michael D. Hurd
Department of Economics
SUNY, Stony Brook
Stony Brook, NY 11794

Robert P. Inman
Department of Finance
University of Pennsylvania
Philadelphia, PA 19104-6367

Richard A. Ippolito
Pension Benefit Guarantee
  Corporation
2020 K Street NW
Washington, DC 20006

Laurence J. Kotlikoff
Department of Economics
Boston University
Boston, MA 02215

Alicia H. Munnell
Federal Reserve Bank of Boston
600 Atlantic Avenue
Boston, MA 02106

Robert D. Paul
Martin E. Segal Company
730 Fifth Avenue
New York, NY 10019

Mark V. Pauly
Leonard Davis Institute
University of Pennsylvania
Philadelphia, PA 19104-6218

John B. Shoven
National Bureau of Economic
  Research
204 Junipero Serra Blvd.
Stanford, CA 94305

Lawrence H. Thompson
General Accounting Office
441 G Street NW
Washington, DC 20548

About the Editor

Susan M. Wachter is an associate professor of finance at the Wharton School of the University of Pennsylvania and University Ombudsman. Dr. Wachter is a consultant to private industry and U.S. government agencies, such as the Federal Trade Commission, the Federal Home Loan Bank Board, the Department of Housing and Urban Development, the General Accounting Office, and the World Bank. At the University of Pennsylvania's Wharton School, Professor Wachter has received the Lindback Award for Distinguished Teaching and the Anvil Award for Teaching Excellence. In addition to journal articles, she is the author of two books and editor or coeditor of four volumes. Professor Wachter is a member of the Board of Directors of Beneficial Corporation, a New York Stock Exchange-listed financial-services firm, and is president of the American Real Estate and Urban Economics Association.